# 4th International Workshop for Computational Linguistics of Uralic Languages (IWCLUL 2018)

Helsinki, Finland
8 - 9 January 2018

ISBN: 978-1-5108-8131-0

IWCLUL 2018

**The 4th International Workshop on
Computational Linguistics for Uralic Languages**

**by ACL SIG for Uralic Languages**

**Proceedings of the Workshop**

January 8–9, 2018
Helsinki, Finland

# Preface

iii

The 4th International Workshop on Computational Linguistics for the Uralic Languages (IWCLUL) continues the annual meetings ACL SIGUR (Association of computational linguistics' special interest group for Uralic languages) after St. Petersburg (2017), Szeged (2016), and Tromsø (2015). It took place in Helsinki from 8th to 9th January, 2018 and was organized in collaboration with the NLP Research Group at the University of Helsinki.should repeat the complete info in order to let this page of the proceedings explain itself (people might not look through the other pages)

This year we received a total of 20 submissions of which we accepted 15 (one of which was withdrawn by the authors) giving total of 14 high-quality papers in the final proceedings and an acceptance rate of 75 %. The accepted papers represent a variety of languages and growing resources in the Uralic landscape: Finnish, Komi-Zyrian, Udmurt, Erzya, Northern Sámi, Pite Sámi, Nganasan and Estonian; topics covered treebanks, parsing, code-switching, language generation, automatic speech recognition, morphology, and typological treatment across all Uralic languages, among others.

During this year's annual meeting we also had the first election of the ACL SIGUR board after the establishment of the new SIG in Szeged in 2016. The current board was re-elected by the ACL SIGUR membership for two further years.

We thank the programming committee, local organisers and participants for making annual meetings of ACL SIG for Uralic languages possible.

— Helsinki, 10th of January 2018, The organisers

**Organizers:**

Tommi A. Pirinen, Universität Hamburg
Michael Rießler, Universität Bielefeld
Jack Rueter, Helsingin yliopisto
Trond Trosterud, UiT Norgga árktalaš universitehta
Francis M. Tyers, Higher School of Economics


**Program Committee:**

Timofey Arkhangelskiy, national research university, Higher school of Economics (Russia) / Alexander von Humboldt Foundation (Germany)
Csilla Horvath, Research Institute for Linguistics, Hungarian Academy of Sciences (Hungary)
Mans Hulden, University of Colorado Boulder (USA)
Heiki-Jaan Kaalep, University of Tartu (Estonia)
Tommi A. Pirinen, Universität Hamburg (Germany)
Michael Rießler, Universität Bielefeld (Germany)
Miikka Silfverberg, University of Colorado Boulder (USA)
Eszter Simon, Magyar tudományos akadémia (Hungary)
Trond Trosterud, UiT Norgga árktalaš universitehta (Norway)
Francis M. Tyers, Higher School of Economics (Russia)
Veronika Vincze, Szegedi tudományegyetem (Hungary)


**Invited Speaker:**

Veronika Laippala, University of Turku

# Table of Contents

# Conference Program

**Monday, January 8, 2018**

**9:00–9:30**      *Registration*

9:30–10:30      *Invited Talk by Veronika Laippala "How we built the Finnish dependency treebank and all the many things we did with it"*

**10:30–12:00**      **Poster presentations**

10:30–10:35      *Dependency Parsing of Code-Switching Data with Cross-Lingual Feature Representations*
Niko Partanen, Kyungtae Lim, Michael Rießler and Thierry Poibeau

10:35–10:40      *Building a Finnish SOM-based ontology concept tagger and harvester*
Seppo Nyrkkö

10:40–10:45      *Sound-aligned corpus of Udmurt dialectal texts*
Timofey Arkhangelskiy and Ekaterina Georgieva

10:45–10:50      *Automatic Generation of Wiktionary Entries for Finno-Ugric Minority Languages*
Zsanett Ferenczi, Iván Mittelholcz and Eszter Simon

10:50–10:55      *Development of an Open Source Natural Language Generation Tool for Finnish*
Mika Hämäläinen and Jack Rueter

10:55–11:00      *Guessing lexicon entries using finite-state methods*
Kimmo Koskenniemi

**11:00–12:00**      *Posters and coffee*

**Monday, January 8, 2018 (continued)**

**Presentations 1**

12:00–12:30    *Tracking Typological Traits of Uralic Languages in Distributed Language Representations*
Johannes Bjerva and Isabelle Augenstein

12:30–13:00    *New Baseline in Automatic Speech Recognition for Northern Sámi*
Juho Leinonen, Peter Smit, Sami Virpioja and Mikko Kurimo

13:00–13:30    *Initial Experiments in Data-Driven Morphological Analysis for Finnish*
Miikka Silfverberg and Mans Hulden

13:30–14:00    *Towards an open-source universal-dependency treebank for Erzya*
Jack Rueter and Francis Tyers

**14:00–15:00**    **Lunch**

**Presentations 2**

15:00–15:30    *Utilization of Nganasan digital resources: a statistical approach to vowel harmony*
László Fejes

15:30–16:00    *Parallel Forms in Estonian Finite State Morphology*
Heiki-Jaan Kaalep

16:00–16:30    *Extracting inflectional class assignment in Pite Saami: Nouns, verbs and those pesky adjectives*
Joshua Wilbur

16:30–17:00    *Analysing Finnish with word lists: the DDI approach to morphology revisited*
Atro Voutilainen and Maria Palolahti

**17:00–17:30**    **Posters and coffee**

**17:30–18:30**    **SIGUR general meeting**

**Tuesday, January 9, 2018**

**10:00–16:00    Tutorials and discussions**

# Dependency Parsing of Code-Switching Data
# with Cross-Lingual Feature Representations


Niko Partanen
LATTICE
CNRS & ENS / PSL & Université Sorbonne nouvelle / USPC
nikotapiopartanen@gmail.com

KyungTae Lim
LATTICE
CNRS & ENS / PSL & Université Sorbonne nouvelle / USPC
kyungtae.lim@ens.fr

Michael Rießler
Faculty for Linguistics and Literary Sciences
University of Bielefeld
michael.riessler@uni-bielefeld.de

Thierry Poibeau
LATTICE
CNRS & ENS / PSL & Université Sorbonne nouvelle / USPC
thierry.poibeau@ens.fr



## Abstract

This paper describes the test of a dependency parsing method which is based on bidirectional LSTM feature representations and multilingual word embedding, and evaluates the results on mono- and multilingual data. The results are similar in all cases, with a slightly better results achieved using multilingual data. The languages under investigation are Komi-Zyrian and Russian. Examination of the results by relation type shows that some language specific constructions are correctly recognized even when they appear in naturally occurring code-switching data.



## Tiivistelmä

Tutkimus arvioi dependenssianalyysin menetelmää, joka perustuu kaksisuuntaiseen LSTM-piirrerepresentaatioon ja monikieliseen 'word embedding' -malliin, sekä arvioi tuloksia yksi- ja monikielisissä aineistoissa. Tulokset ovat samantapaisia, mutta hieman korkeampia moni- kuin yksikielisissä aineistoissa. Tutkitut kielet ovat komisyrjääni ja venäjä. Tulosten yksityiskohtaisempi analyysi riippuvuuksien mukaan osoittaa, että tietyt kielikohtaiset suhteet on tunnistettu oikein jopa niiden esiintyessä luonnollisissa koodinvaihtoa sisältävissä lauseissa.







*Proceedings of the 4th International Workshop for Computational Linguistics for Uralic Languages (IWCLUL 2018)*, pages 1–17,
Helsinki, Finland, January 8–9, 2018. ©2018 Association for Computational Linguistics

# 1 Introduction

Spontaneous speech data of small, endangered languages most commonly contain code-switching, ad-hoc borrowings and other kinds of language contact phenomena originating from the non-target contact language(s). Consequently, spoken corpora originating from such data contain numerous utterances in which linguistic elements from at least two languages co-occur. The most usual occurrences are combinations of target-language utterances including lexical and morphological elements from the contacting majority language. Corpus data of this type represents a particular challenge for morphological analysis and especially for dependency parsing. Although the basic morphological properties can usually be analyzed on the basis of individual languages and parsers can be targeted towards those, the syntactic dependencies are inevitably interspersed individual tokens from different languages, and thereby cannot be easily approached with tools that are able to target only monolingual data.

The present paper looks at an approach that has been introduced as The Multilingual BIST-Parser by Lim and Poibeau (2017). The tool was developed in order to perform dependency parsing on considerably low-resource languages, and the work was originally carried out within the CONLL-U Shared Task for 2017. Lim and Poibeau (2017) have shown that multilingual word embeddings can be used to train a model that combines data from multiple languages, and these seem to be particularly useful in low-resource scenarios where one of the languages has only a small amount of available training data.

The target language in the present paper is Komi-Zyrian (henceforth Komi), which belongs to the Permic branch of the Uralic language family. The language is spoken predominantly in the Komi Republic of the Russian Federation by approximately 160,000 speakers. Computational linguistic research on Komi is so far only in a development stage. However, an FST morphological analyzer and a (rudimentary) syntactic parser based on Constraint Grammar are available at *Giellatekno/Divvun – Saami Language Technology* at UiT The Arctic University of Norway[1] and work on a complete Constraint Grammar description to be implemented into a rule-based syntactic parser is currently carried out in collaboration by Giellatekno, the Izhva Komi Documentation Project Gerstenberger et al. (2016, 2017) and FU-Lab[2], which has also created a written Komi National corpus (with over 30M words), free electronic dictionaries and a Hunspell checker (including morpheme lists).

Our own initial dependency parsing tests were conducted by testing various different language pairs with Komi as parts of multilingual word-embedding models, in order to find out which combinations can reach the best performance. In our earlier tests, the best results were achieved when the majority of the training data were from a genealogically related language, in this case Finnish. This went against our hypothesis that the genealogically unrelated contemporary contact languages would have been particularly useful from a NLP perspective due to prolonged language contact and resulting convergence in Komi grammar and lexicon. Although it is possible to build truly multilingual models, such as a parser that combines Finnish, Russian and Komi word embeddings and training corpora in order to operate on Komi, we found that a bilingual Finnish-Komi model performed best in our tests for monolingual Komi data. However, especially if the results were analyzed more in detail beyond the LAS

---

[1] `http://giellatekno.uit.no`; for the technical documentation of the research on Komi, see `http://giellatekno.uit.no/doc/lang/kom/`; Jack Rueter (Helsinki) has been the main developer

[2] The Finno-Ugric Laboratory for Support of the Electronic Representation of Regional Languages"; `http://fu-lab.ru`

and UAS scores (for explanation of these evaluation metrics, see Kübler et al., 2009, 79), the different language pairs will likely show different benefits and drawbacks in distinct areas of analysis, and testing the parsing method on data that naturally contains materials from both languages used in training is used here as one method to tease apart language specific changes in parser's behavior.

The next part of the paper describes this problem in further detail with examples from spoken language corpora.

## 2   Problem Description

The first example 1 is taken from the spoken Iźva (dialectal) Komi corpus Blokland et al. (2009–2017) (henceforth called IKDP) and represents naturally occurring spoken language mixed with Russian elements (Russian marked in boldface).

(1)    **До** школьн-ого возраста ветл-i **родитель**-яс-кед тундра-ын.
      until school-GEN age-GEN go-1SG.PST parents-PL-COMIT tundra-INES

      'Until the school age I went to the tundra together with my parents.'

The example starts with a Russian prepositional phrase meaning 'until the school age', but it is followed by a direct shift to Komi. The word for 'parents' is also Russian, but it is inflected according to Komi morphological rules and in the same manner as native Komi words would be inflected. Such morphologically integrated nouns are often described as Russian loanwords in Komi, but as will be argued in Section 6 below, this approach may not be very applicable in the context of Uralic languages spoken in Russia. We are therefore referring to it as a "mixed" form. In order to compare the sentences, two bilingual Komi-Russian native speakers[3] have translated the example into both languages. It must be noted that because both Komi and Russian have rather flexible word orders, this aspect is not taken into account in the present analysis, although there is clear variation in both languages with respect to the semantic nuances of different orderings.

Note also that the purely Komi variant of the example sentence would still include two lexical items of Russian origin, namely *school* and *tundra*. Although the basic sentence structure may look similar, Komi and Russian have rather different syntactic structures overall. For instance, Komi uses cases extensively along with postpositions, whereas Russian uses predominantly prepositions.

(2)    Школа-ö пыр-тöдз ветл-i бать-мам-кöд тундра-ын.
      school-ILL enter-GER.DUR go-1SG.PST parents-PL-COMIT tundra-INES

      'Until the school (age) I went to the tundra together with my parents.'

For the sake of thoroughness, it is also worth looking into one possible way to express the utterance entirely in Russian.

(3)    *До* школьн-ого возраста езди-л с родител-ями в тундр-у.
      until school-GEN age-GEN go-PST with parents-PL.INSTR to tundra-LOC

      'Until the school age I went to the tundra together with my parents.'

---

[3]Thanks to Vasili Chuprov and Sergei Gabov.

Based on different Universal Dependency (UD) corpora, the dependency structure of the Komi variant should be analyzed as in 4.

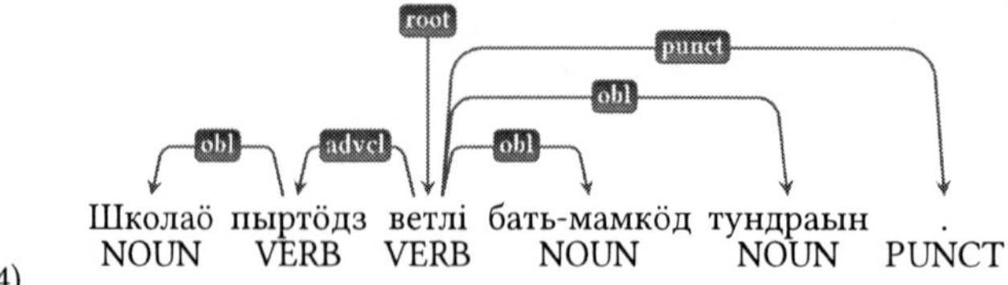

(4)

The Russian tree, on the other hand, is 5.

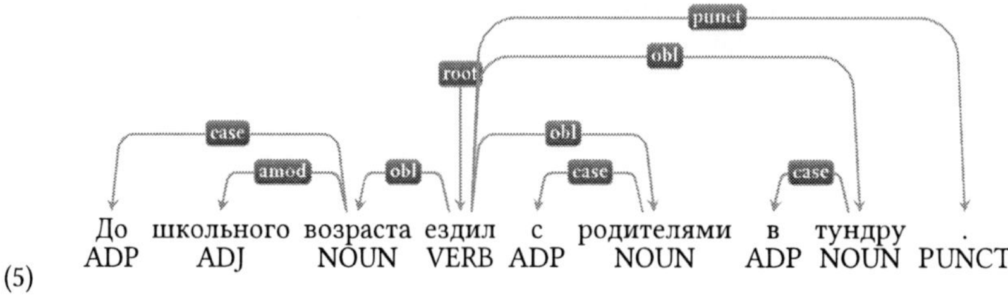

(5)

Based on these examples, we can conclude that a correctly analyzed dependency structure for the mixed utterance would be as presented in 6, as it effectively combines the relevant parts of the Russian and Komi annotations. As the applied annotation model is the same, the monolingual dependencies should not differ from multilingual ones.

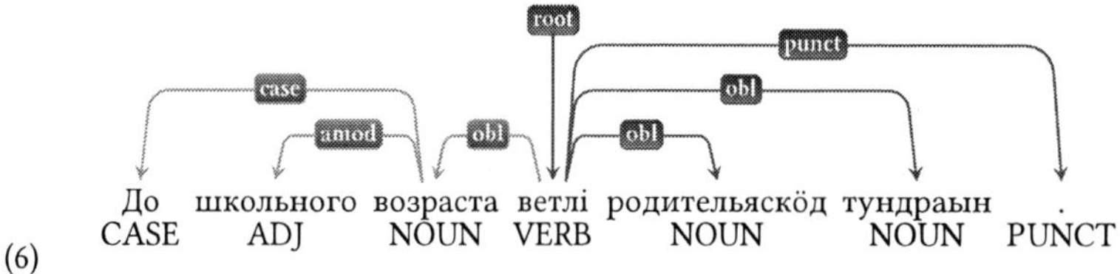

(6)

Although the Multilingual BIST-parser is trained with multilingual material, the goal has been primarily to parse the lesser resourced language. All earlier tests have been conducted using strictly monolingual data, although different assumptions can be made about the parallel structures in the languages included in the model. Applying the parser to data that truly contains syntactic constructions specific to only the individual languages within the same utterances reveals about the parser's ability to correctly identify structures of this type. If both distinctly Russian and Komi constructions can be parsed successfully within the same sentence, this indicates that the model is able to learn and deduce language-specific structures even when they co-occur. This would open up new possibilities for automatic analysis of such kind of data.

## 3  Related Studies

Multilingual dependency parsing aims at building a dependency tree for several languages using one and the same model. Three major approaches have been suggested for tackling such a task: 1) the cross-lingual annotation projection approach, 2) the joint modeling approach, and 3) the cross-lingual representation learning approach (cf. Guo et al., 2015). The main idea of the cross-lingual annotation projection approach is to project the syntactic annotations trough word alignments from a source language onto a target language (Mann and Yarowsky, 2001; Tiedemann, 2014). In a similar way, the joint modeling approach is carried out using projected dependency information for grammar inductions (Liu et al., 2013) and rule-based work (Naseem et al., 2010, 2012).

The cross-lingual representation learning method is focused on learning cross-lingual features by aligning (or mapping) feature representations (e.g. embedding) between the source and target languages. In general, cross-lingual representation learning can be divided into two approaches depending on whether or not the parser uses lexicalized features (e.g. word embedding). Since it is relatively easy to train a parser using supervised learning, many existing cross-lingual representation learning studies have been conducted with the delexicalized approach using POS tag-sets and word sequences (McDonald et al., 2011, 2013; Dozat et al., 2017). Such an approach includes training a dependency model with the source language (e.g. English), then processes the target language (e.g. French) using the model trained according to the source language. On the other hand, the lexicalized approach is able to adapt diverse lexical features while in training. The features adapted for the dependency parsing include cross-lingual word cluster features (Täckström et al., 2012), multilingual word embeddings (Guo et al., 2015, 2016; Ammar et al., 2016b,a) and language identification embeddings (Naseem et al., 2012; Ammar et al., 2016a).

From the perspective of code-switching, conversational code-switching problems have been studied mainly with regard to language identification (e.g. Solorio et al., 2014; Barman et al., 2014) and information extraction (e.g. Sharma et al., 2014) problems. This is because in order to process cross-lingual dependency parsing, language identification and morphological analysis for those languages must precede the processing. Ammar et al. (2016b) suggested that his multilingual model-transfer parser could be used to parse input with code-switching but were not able to conduct the experiment due to the lack appropriate test corpora.

## 4    Cross-Lingual Dependency Parsing

In this study, we invested our effort in developing the cross-lingual representation learning method with lexicalized features for the dependency parsing of code-switching scenarios. All the cross-lingual approaches discussed in Section 3, can be applied for our study, but in terms of the availability of language resources, cross-lingual representation learning is considered the best choice because of the lack of annotated corpora. Also in regard to the performance, existing studies have already shown that representation learning with lexical features performs better than the other models (Ammar et al., 2016a; Lim and Poibeau, 2017).

In this section, we describe two main ideas for parsing code-switching data using the cross-lingual representation learning approach. One of the main goals of our research is to build cross-lingual word embeddings based on supervised learning. The other is to find a way to address adapting cross-lingual word embedding in order to build a dependency parsing model.

## 4.1 Cross-Lingual Word Representations

As discussed in Section 3, adding lexical information for feature representations can improve performance in cross-lingual parsing. Various approaches have been investigated for the training of cross-lingual word embeddings mainly for resource-rich languages. Moreover, most of these approaches relied on the existence of a parallel corpus, especially for languages from the Indo-European family (cf. Ammar et al., 2016a; Guo et al., 2016). As we discussed earlier, however, this study focuses on code-switching scenarios in low-resource language data. Thus, we are constrained by the fact that there is no parallel corpus and no larger annotated dataset for training a dependency parser for the (low-resource) target language Komi. However, it must be noted that even for low-resource languages, we need raw texts as the minimum resource to train a word embedding. In this study, we trained a monolingual embedding for Komi by using raw text available in the public domain. The Komi texts used have been taken from the National Library of Finland's Fenno-Ugrica collection[4], and proofread versions of those Public Domain texts are available in FU-Lab's portal *Komi Nebögain*[5]. Niko Partanen has created a list of books included both in Fenno-Ugrica and FU-Lab[6], and the currently available data adds up to one million tokens. For the contact language Russian we have used pre-trained Wikipedia word embeddings published by Facebook and described in Bojanowski et al. (2016).

In a similar manner to the low-resource constraints, Artetxe et al. (2017) suggested a powerful method for projecting two monolingual embeddings in a single vector space with almost no bilingual data. Traditionally, the projection (or mapping) method for word embeddings requires a large parallel corpus or a bilingual dictionary in order to map two different word embeddings in a distributional space (Artetxe et al., 2016; Guo et al., 2015). However, Artetxe et al. (2017) showed a possible method for mapping two different embeddings based on the reinforcement learning approach with just 25 pairs of vocabularies but with almost no degradation of performance. The main idea in this method is to project two embeddings trained by different languages based on the linear transformation with bilingual word pairs.

The projection method can be described as follows. Let $X$ and $Y$ be the source and target word embedding matrix so that $x_i$ refers to $i$th word embedding of X and $y_j$ refers to $j$th word embedding of Y. And let $D$ is a binary matrix, where $D_{ij}$ = 1, if $x_i$ and $y_j$ are aligned. Our goal is then to find a transformation matrix $W$ such that $Wx$ approximates $y$. This is done by minimizing the sum of squared errors (following Artetxe et al., 2017), cf. 7.

(7)

$$\arg\min_{W} \sum_{i=1}^{m} \sum_{j=1}^{n} D_{ij} \|x_i W - y_i\|^2$$

The method is relatively simple to apply in our case because once we have a bilingual dictionary available, converting the dictionary as $D$ is not a problem. We followed Artetxe's 2017 mapping idea to train a bilingual word embedding for Komi-Russian using a bilingual dictionary. The size of the dictionary used for training is 7,642 pairs, and the projected word embedding is 5.9G. Those dictionaries and projected word

---

[4]https://fennougrica.kansalliskirjasto.fi
[5]http://komikyv.org
[6]https://github.com/langdoc/kpv-lit

embedding are accessible in a public repository.[7] Dictionary is extracted from Jack Rueter's Komi-Zyrian dictionaries that have translations to several languages.[8]

## 4.2 Cross-Lingual Dependency Parsing Model

As discussed in Section 3, the major idea of the cross-lingual representation learning method is to take aligned features, especially syntactic and lexical features. Since the Universal Dependencies (UD) (Nivre et al., 2017) model provides cross-linguistically consistent grammatical annotation, we do not need to consider aligning syntactic features among the languages (i.g., POS tags, dependency tags). However, in terms of the semantic point of view, ignoring lexical features may lead to a lack of semantic information not only in monolingual but also in multilingual dependency parsing.

A recent multilingual parsing experiment, the CoNLL 2017 shared task, has addressed dependency parsing for low-resource languages using a multilingual approach (Zeman et al., 2017). The main approach was cross-lingual representation learning, and most teams applied the delexicalized model to process the low-resource languages with around 20 samples of annotated sentences. However, the LATTICE team (Lim and Poibeau, 2017) suggested concatenating a bilingual word embedding as a lexicalized feature, which is mapped by a bilingual dictionary taken from Swadesh lists. In practice larger dictionaries would improve the result, and this has been done later, but the shared task had strictly specified resources. On the other hand, a small dictionary seems to be enough to align the embeddings reasonably well. All features, including lexicalized ones, are then fed into a bidirectional Long Short-Term Memory (LSTM) to take concatenated feature representations for each token. By using the concatenated features (vectors) as an input, Lim and Poibeau applied graph-based parsing, which views the parsing problem as a search for the best-scored tree graph.

As Lim and Poibeau (2017) suggested, the BiLSTM feature representation with lexicalized features is crucial for multilingual dependency parsing, particularly in low-resource scenarios. Since we assume that there are no UD corpora for low-resource languages, one common alternative approach is to take a training corpus from another language. Once we find a grammatically related language, we then simply train a dependency model with the mapped bilingual word embedding and a UD corpus of the related language. Although the training corpus is written in the related language, the system is possible to replace tokens with ones from the low-resource language by using pre-trained bilingual word embeddings, in which vocabulary items with the same meaning are mapped between two languages. LSTM is a specific type of Recurrent Neural Network (RNN), so it also has hidden layer with hidden vectors for each sequence, $h = (h_1, h_2, ..., h_n)$. If we look at the hidden layer in a sequence $i$, it is defined as in 8.

$$(8) \quad h_i = (W_{th}t_i + W_{hh}h_{i-1} + b_h)$$

The basic LSTM model is able to make use of the previous context based on the computation $W_{hh}h_{i-1}$ (to put it simply, we can think of $W_{hh}$ as a hidden input weight matrix and $h_{i-1}$ as the previous value of the hidden layer). Thus, BiLSTM can store contexts from the LSTM both in regular order ($LSTM_{forward}$) and inverse order ($LSTM_{backward}$). For further details on the LSTM model, see Huang et al. (2015) and Cho (2015).

---

[7] https://github.com/jujbob/multilingual-models
[8] https://victorio.uit.no/langtech/trunk/words/dicts/kpv2X/src

For the current study, we have extended the parser by Lim and Poibeau (2017) using the multilingual word embeddings proposed in Section 4.1. The bilingual dictionaries used in the word embedding alignment contained several thousands of word pairs, and the recent study by Artetxe et al. (2017) shows that the dictionary size we operate with should be large enough to reach a high level of alignment accuracy.

## 5 Experiment Design

The following section discusses in more detail the creation and use of the corpora used for training and testing.

### 5.1 Training Corpora

The applied tools have been developed specifically for parsing low-resource languages, and this study originates from the same background. The main part of training data consists of a Russian UD v2.0 corpus with 3,850 sentences[9], while the Komi part, which we have prepared, is only 40 sentences.

### 5.2 Testing Corpora

The early-stage Komi-Zyrian Universal Dependency corpus was used for the model training[10], as this makes the results comparable with our earlier studies and was readily available. All in all, the tests in this study were performed on three different subsets or variants of test corpora, which are described below. All of the data used is publicly available in the *IWCLUL* branch of the repository.

1. Monolingual written Komi test corpus: 80 sentences

2. Multilingual written Komi-Russian test corpus, based on the monolingual corpus but adapted to contain constructions comparable to those that occur in spoken data: 80 sentences

3. Spoken Komi test corpus, contains spontaneous code-switching and code-mixing: 25 sentences

Similar to our earlier research, the monolingual Komi testing corpus was used as one method for evaluating the baseline for the results. Another Komi corpus currently being built will eventually include more spoken data, however it is not directly comparable with the monolingual testing corpus as the examples are entirely different. The spoken language data, although dialectal, is still phonologically and morphologically close to the written language, and in this case the data were slightly normalized in order to harmonize the transcription conventions with the orthographic representation in the written corpora used.

As the kinds of constructions we were interested in analyzing tend to occur only in spontaneous spoken language, it was not possible to use a parallel corpus of written texts to compare the performance as such. Instead, another approach was adopted in which the code-switching-like elements were inserted into an originally monolingual testing corpus. It must be stressed that the Russian elements were not inserted

---

[9]https://github.com/UniversalDependencies/UD_Russian/releases/tag/r2.0
[10]https://github.com/langdoc/UD_Komi-Zyrian

randomly, but were carefully crafted to follow patterns observed in the real spoken data. The creation of mixed test corpus was helped by the large number of available translations for the texts used. To illustrate this, we can take one sentence that is part of the testing corpus:

(9)   *Шофер-ыс, том   зонка на,   дзик-ӧдз     растеряйтч-ис*       .
      driver-3SG  young boy    still totally-TERM get_confused-PST.3SG

      'Driver, still a young boy, got totally confused.'

As the same source book has translations into multiple minority languages of Russia, with the original Russian version, there is always access to multilingual versions of the same text segments. In this case the Russian version is as presented below:

(10)   *Водитель машин-ы, еще молодой парнишка, совсем растеря-л-ся.*
       driver      car-GEN   still young    boy        totally get_confused-PST.REFL

       'Driver, still a young boy, got totally confused.'

With translations available, it is possible to compare the examples into occurrences that there are in spoken language corpus that naturally contains intermixed Russian. Although the details vary, we can at least add pointers into example sentences in spoken corpus that contain *comparable* occurrences, although they naturally would never be identical, or comparable from only one point of view. The example sentence above has been restructured in following way, Russian in bold:

(11)   *Шофер-ыс, том   зонка на,* **совсем растеря-л-ся**.
       driver-3SG  young boy    still totally   get_confused-PST-REFL

       'Driver, still a young boy, got totally confused.'

The acceptability of the adapted sentences can be justified at least partly by the test corpus design, of which up to 35% originates from texts that have parallel variants in Russian. This has been very useful in order to examine how similar the sentences would be in different languages. Additionally, 40% of the testing corpus has been translated from Komi into Russian. In the majority of cases, the basic structure has indeed been so similar that the Russian and Komi versions should, to a large extent, display identical dependency structures with core relations, although the details still differ substantially. It is left outside the current investigation whether the translations that are present are the most natural ways to express these ideas in either of the languages, as the goal was primarily evaluate how the parser behaves in this kind of scenario.

In order to make these decisions explicit, the mixed corpus version has an additional metadata field *spoken_comparison*, which contains a link to the IKPD corpus of spoken language recordings that exhibits comparable Russian constructions. In this case we have pointed into examples where Russian adverb *совсем* is used on place of native Komi *дзик*, as well as recordings that exhibit insertions of Russian verb forms. The examples are not supposed to be identical, but illustrate that the modification bears some connection to what can be observed in real data. Some of the observed phenomena are relatively rare (although present) in Komi, but are described as common in other Uralic languages, such as Erzya, by Janurik (2017). The presence of

Russian items and their different types in either natural or artificial test corpora does not reflect the frequencies with which they occur larger spoken corpus, as no studies have been conducted that would provide metrics that could be used.

It has to be emphasized that the goal of this exercise has not been to create new data that would be directly useful for any other purposes, but to have a dataset that is comparable to the monolingual test corpus, and would be close enough to realistic phenomena that we observe in spoken data that we can use it to evaluate the parser's behaviour.

One of the available metrics comes from on-going research in which the items of Russian origin have been tagged in different text types. This examination shows that the rate of Russian items was, depending on the speaker, somewhere between 20%-40%, which is similar to the proportions used here.

## 6   Evaluation Strategy

The results are evaluated according to their LAS and UAS scores, but in order to analyze more precisely how the parser interacts with the constructions specific to Komi and Russian, we have examined some of these constructions in further detail. The recognition accuracy is also calculated separately for each dependency relation type. For evaluation purposes, the languages have been tagged into the misc-field of CONLL-U files, but the parser has not been aware of this information, and it is used only for evaluation.

There is a small portion of tokens occurring in the Komi corpus that are identical in form and function with corresponding Russian items. These are mainly particles and conjunctions. In the misc-field of the test corpus, these items have been classified with the tag "mixed", as their form and function are nearly identical in both languages. In addition to this, the "mixed" category also contains tokens that cannot be clearly defined as lexical items of either Komi or Russian, such as non-adapted Russian verb stems with Komi inflections.

Note that our analysis of a "mixed" category is also in line with the recent sociolinguistic description of similar contact-induced phenomena in Erzya (Janurik, 2017, 64, 89). According to this study, distinguishing between borrowing and code-switching is often very difficult in the case of Erzya and Russian. The same criteria seem to apply with regard to Komi-Russian language contact as well. Recent borrowings not displaying clear Russian morphology have therefore also been tagged as mixed, as the lack of phonological adaptation often makes them identical to the Russian alternatives, and using the Russian origin as the main criteria seems perfectly sensible.

The tokens that are unambiguously Russian and exhibit Russian morphology are tagged as Russian, so that it is possible to compare these parts of the corpus. The percentages of different languages across the testing corpora is as follows in Table 1.

The accuracy is also evaluated independently for a few grammatical structures in which the constituent order or relation type would differ in the two languages. In Komi noun phrases, nouns modify other nouns directly in the nominative, whereas in Russian, this would be accomplished using derived adjectives. In possessive constructions, the languages employ opposite strategies: possessor–possessed in Komi and possessed–possessor in Russian. Due the restrictions on the training data, it would be assumed that the parser would be more sensitive towards the Russian strategies, as the exposure to the Komi patterns has been minimal.

When evaluating the results, the possibility of mistakes remaining in training and

| file | corpus | kpv | mixed | rus |
|---|---|---|---|---|
| kpv-ud-test.conllu | written monolingual | 96.2% | 3.8% | - |
| kpv-ud-test-mixed.conllu | written artificially mixed | 70.2% | 2.3% | 27.5% |
| kpv-ud-ikdp.conllu | spoken | 50.2% | 9.9% | 39.9% |

Table 1: The compositional ratio of corpora between Komi (kpv), Russian (rus) and mixed.

testing data itself cannot be excluded. As there are very few annotated datasets for Komi, it is not always perfectly clear what would be the most adequate annotation or relation in every case. Further work with Universal Dependencies on smaller Uralic languages will certainly shed light also into best ways to analyze Komi data.

## 7   Results

The LAS and UAS scores of the tested corpora are presented in Table 2. The results varied significantly by epoch, and all tests were run for 10 iterations. The differences were particularly large within the spoken corpus, as the parsing accuracy of individual sentences had direct relation to the scores as whole, just because the number of analyzed tokens was so small. Addition of individual sentences would make scores fluctuate very much, whereas other corpora behave more consistently, which indicates that test corpus of approximately hundred sentences in the test corpus seems to be enough for consistency in results.

The test corpora containing more Russian produce slightly better results. The reason seems to be that the parser is more sensitive towards recognizing Russian, as both Russian training corpus and the word embedding used are significantly larger. Indeed, when the parser is run on the identical settings to Russian test corpus, the LAS score is almost 70,00. This happens even under scenario where the parser is specifically targeted to parse Komi, and will first try to look for tokens from Komi part of word embedding. The examination of language-tagged tokens showed that the dependency relation types were analyzed correctly on average 10% more often on Russian tokens than with Komi tokens. The difference in recognizing heads was even higher in favor of Russian. This seems to reflect the generally higher accuracy in respect to Russian, which is explainable by the larger resource portions used in training. On the other hand, preliminary tests done after the research for this paper was conducted indicated that simply building the Komi word embeddings from larger text corpus would improve the monolingual Komi score and bring those closer to one another.

One way to test the cross-linguistic applicability of the parser is to look into constructions that are specific only to one of the languages. Earlier mentioned uses of prepositions and postpositions in Russian and Komi seem to be properly recognized. In the manually mixed test corpus half of the adpositions were in Komi and half in Russian (13/13), and in the best epochs they contained only individual errors. The roots were located correctly 80% if the time. Table 3 presents the accuracy percentages for different dependencies in monolingual and mixed test corpora in . The spoken corpora is not presented here due to its small size and thereby sporadic number of different relations.

| Corpus | LAS | UAS |
|---|---|---|
| Written corpus | 51.34 | 67.73 |
| Artificially mixed corpus | 53.61 | 65.74 |
| Spoken corpus | 54.77 | 68.20 |

Table 2: The results of Labeled attachment scores (LAS) and unlabeled attachment scores (UAS) for Komi-Russian code-switching data (Artificially mixed corpus and Spoken corpus) and the regular scenario (only Komi). Komi word embedding size 1,0 million tokens.

| deprel | count kpv | correct in kpv | count mixed | correct in mixed |
|---|---|---|---|---|
| amod | 24 | 95.8% | 24 | 91.7% |
| case | 15 | 93.3% | 25 | 96% |
| advmod | 91 | 85.7% | 93 | 89.2% |
| root | 80 | 80% | 80 | 78.8% |
| conj | 10 | 70% | 10 | 80% |
| acl | 14 | 7.14% | 14 | 7.14% |
| xcomp | 21 | 66.7% | 21 | 71.4% |
| obj | 20 | 60% | 20 | 60% |
| cc | 23 | 60.9% | 23 | 56.5% |
| nsubj | 47 | 57.4% | 47 | 55.3% |
| mark | 7 | 57.1% | 7 | 71.4% |
| discourse | 9 | 55.6% | 9 | 66.7% |
| aux | 14 | 42.9% | 12 | 33.3% |
| nmod | 33 | 30.3% | 38 | 39.5% |
| advcl | 5 | 20% | 3 | 0% |
| ccomp | 1 | 100% | 1 | 100% |
| appos | 6 | 0% | 6 | 0% |
| cop | 3 | 0% | 3 | 0% |
| det | 5 | 0% | 5 | 0% |
| flat | 2 | 0% | 2 | 0% |
| iobj | 5 | 0% | 4 | 0% |
| obl | 47 | 0% | 46 | 19.6% |
| parataxis | 3 | 0% | 3 | 0% |
| vocative | 1 | 0% | 1 | 0% |
| fixed | 0 | 0% | 1 | 0% |

Table 3: The comparison to processed results between regular Komi corpus (Komi only) and the code-switching corpus (Artificially mixed corpus) for each dependency relations.

It seems that the rarer dependencies are also generally poorer in their accuracy, with many never being recognized correctly. As this is evaluation of just the best epoch, the accuracy of zero doesn't mean that the parser would never recognize this relation, but the poor accuracy seems to be consistent across tests. This may be connected to the small size of Komi training corpus which contained only 40 sentences, and thereby there are lots of relations which occur only sporadically there as well. However, the table Table 3 also shows that with some relations the accuracy is much better than for others.

One reason for high accuracy with adpositions could be explained by their very high frequency and relatively small number of distinct forms. Some attention has to be paid into the situation with obliques, which are almost uniformly parsed incorrectly in Komi test corpus. Within the Russian part of the mixed corpus the recognition accuracy increases, and this gain comes from the Russian part. In Komi part of the corpus obliques are most commonly parsed as nominal subjects. Across all training epochs this is most commonly mis-identified relation. Within Russian part the obliques are generally parsed correctly. In case of Russian the obliques are usually marked with prepositions and distinct case such as prepositional or dative.

In the monolingual Komi corpus and in Komi part of the mixed corpora very frequently mis-parsed relation was nominal subjects being analyzed as nominal modifiers. Right after this comes the analysis of nominal objects as nominal subjects.

Some of the results match fit typological differences between Komi and Russian. For example, noun modifiers in certain contexts were recognized much worse than could be expected. Even when constructions share lexical items with Russian, the parser systematically recognizes the first element as the head, probably reflecting Russian pattern where the order would be reversed, or the first component be an adjective and the relation thus *amod* instead of *nmod*.

As mentioned above, the adpositions were generally parsed correctly, irrespective of their language or direction. There were individual Komi postpositions which seemed to be often parsed incorrectly, but these were either used in non-prototypical way or were relatively rare otherwise. So rarer types were recognized worse, which may be related to the general difficulties in recognizing obliques as well, as those have hardly any prototypical form in which they appear in Komi.

# 8 Conclusion

According to our analysis, the Multilingual BIST-parser described in Lim and Poibeau (2017) is able to parse with comparable accuracy monolingual data and code-switching data. The analysis of parsing result of different dependency relation labels showed that some are recognized considerably more often than others, and especially with rarer relations the accuracy is suffering. There are some relations which show large differences between language pairs used in model training, such as obliques, but also cross-linguistically differently behaving categories, for example adpositions, which are recognized considerably well even when they occur in same sentences in code-switching data.

At the moment the main reason for relatively poor accuracy seems to be a lack of larger training corpus. At the moment the training has been done only with 40 sentences, which is by any standards very little. However, it is so small that comparable dataset could be easily created for virtually any language, and thereby the results are encouraging for extending this approach to new languages. Another aspect that needs more rigorous testing is the alignation and quality of word embeddings used. The currently used Komi embedding was built from one million token text corpus, and possibly an increase in the embedding size could already bring improvements to the performance. On the other hand, also Russian embeddings, although large, are from Wikipedia and could be improved by including wider variety of text types. Evaluating the minimum size that is needed for embeddings is also important in order to estimate how well suited the proposed method is for low-resource languages.

One additional concern is that as all training data and word embeddings are based on written data. Thereby there are many features of spoken language, such as discourse particles, which occur rarely if at all in any of these sources, even when the corpora would be relatively large. Although the discourse particles were in this case analyzed better than majority of the relations, there are still certainly numerous constructions that tend to occur mainly in spoken data. One of these are particular mixed forms which are likely never found in monolingual resources of these two languages, and thereby cannot directly benefit from the method tested in this paper. The IKDP Komi corpus counts approximately 300,000 tokens at present and training new word embeddings from this data alone doesn't seem reasonable right now. However, as regular transcription work increases the corpus size over time, reaching a million or more tokens should be reasonable in the foreseeable future. Meanwhile further experiments should be conducted on building word embeddings that mix spoken and written varieties, and thereby also contain spoken data with code-switching. Naturally, increasing the sizes of training and test corpora for Komi is also a foremost priority for our own future research.

## Acknowledgments

We want to express our gratitude to Marina Fedina, Jack Rueter, Trond Trosterud and Rogier Blokland for collaboration and continuous valuable feedback. Thanks are also due to two anonymous peer-reviewers for their useful comments. This work has been developed in the framework of the LAKME project funded by a grant from Paris Sciences et Lettres (IDEX PSL reference ANR-10-IDEX-0001-02). Thierry Poibeau is also partially supported by a RGNF-CNRS (grant between the LATTICE-CNRS Laboratory and the Russian State University for the Humanities in Moscow). This work has been carried out in collaboration with the project "Language Documentation meets Language Technology: The Next Step in the Description of Komi", led by Rogier Blokland, Niko Partanen and Michael Rießler and funded by Kone Foundation.

## References

Waleed Ammar, George Mulcaire, Miguel Ballesteros, Chris Dyer, and Noah A. Smith. 2016a. One parser, many languages. *CoRR* http://arxiv.org/abs/1602.01595.

Waleed Ammar, George Mulcaire, Yulia Tsvetkov, Guillaume Lample, Chris Dyer, and Noah A Smith. 2016b. Massively multilingual word embeddings. *CoRR* http://arxiv.org/abs/1602.01925.

Mikel Artetxe, Gorka Labaka, and Eneko Agirre. 2016. Learning principled bilingual mappings of word embeddings while preserving monolingual invariance. In *Proceedings of the 2016 Conference on Empirical Methods in Natural Language Processing*. www.aclweb.org/anthology/D16-1250.

Mikel Artetxe, Gorka Labaka, and Eneko Agirre. 2017. Learning bilingual word embeddings with (almost) no bilingual data. In *Proceedings of the 55th Annual Meeting of the Association for Computational Linguistics (Volume 1: Long Papers)*. pages 451–462. aclweb.org/anthology/P17-1042.

Utsab Barman, Amitava Das, Joachim Wagner, and Jennifer Foster. 2014. Code mixing: A challenge for language identification in the language of social media. In *Proceedings of The First Workshop on Computational Approaches to Code Switching*. pages 13–23.

Rogier Blokland, Marina Fedina, Niko Partanen, and Michael Rießler. 2009–2017. Izhva Kyy. In *The Language Archive (TLA)*, Max Planck Institute for Psycholinguistics. https://hdl.handle.net/1839/00-0000-0000-000C-1CF6-F@view.

Piotr Bojanowski, Edouard Grave, Armand Joulin, and Tomas Mikolov. 2016. Enriching word vectors with subword information. *CoRR* http://arxiv.org/abs/1607.04606.

Kyunghyun Cho. 2015. Natural language understanding with distributed representation. *arXiv preprint* http://arxiv.org/abs/1511.07916.

Timothy Dozat, Peng Qi, and Christopher D. Manning. 2017. Stanford's graph-based neural dependency parser at the conll 2017 shared task. In *Proceedings of the CoNLL 2017 Shared Task: Multilingual Parsing from Raw Text to Universal Dependencies*. Association for Computational Linguistics, Vancouver, Canada, pages 20–30. http://www.aclweb.org/anthology/K/K17/K17-3002.pdf.

Ciprian Gerstenberger, Niko Partanen, and Michael Rießler. 2017. Instant annotations in ELAN corpora of spoken and written Komi, an endangered language of the Barents Sea region. In *Proceedings of the 2nd Workshop on the Use of Computational Methods in the Study of Endangered Languages*, Association for Computational Linguistics, ACL Anthology, pages 57–66. http://www.aclweb.org/anthology/W17-0109.

Ciprian Gerstenberger, Niko Partanen, Michael Rießler, and Joshua Wilbur. 2016. Utilizing language technology in the documentation of endangered Uralic languages. *Northern European Journal of Language Technology* 4:29–47. https://doi.org/10.3384/nejlt.2000-1533.1643.

Jiang Guo, Wanxiang Che, David Yarowsky, Haifeng Wang, and Ting Liu. 2015. Cross-lingual dependency parsing based on distributed representations. In *Proceedings of ACL*.

Jiang Guo, Wanxiang Che, David Yarowsky, Haifeng Wang, and Ting Liu. 2016. A representation learning framework for multi-source transfer parsing. In *AAAI*. pages 2734–2740.

Zhiheng Huang, Wei Xu, and Kai Yu. 2015. Bidirectional lstm-crf models for sequence tagging. *arXiv preprint* http://arxiv.org/abs/1508.01991.

Boglárka Janurik. 2017. *Erzya-Russian bilingual discourse: A structural analysis of intrasentential code-switching patterns*. Ph.D. thesis, University of Szeged. http://doktori.bibl.u-szeged.hu/4097.

Sandra Kübler, Ryan McDonald, and Joakim Nivre. 2009. Dependency parsing. *Synthesis Lectures on Human Language Technologies* 1(1):1–127.

KyungTae Lim and Thierry Poibeau. 2017. A system for multilingual dependency parsing based on bidirectional lstm feature representations. In *Proceedings of the*

*CoNLL 2017 Shared Task: Multilingual Parsing from Raw Text to Universal Dependencies*. Association for Computational Linguistics, Vancouver, Canada, pages 63–70. http://www.aclweb.org/anthology/K/K17/K17-3006.pdf.

Kai Liu, Yajuan Lü, Wenbin Jiang, and Qun Liu. 2013. Bilingually-guided monolingual dependency grammar induction. In *ACL (1)*. pages 1063–1072.

Gideon S Mann and David Yarowsky. 2001. Multipath translation lexicon induction via bridge languages. In *Proceedings of the second meeting of the North American Chapter of the Association for Computational Linguistics on Language technologies*. Association for Computational Linguistics, pages 1–8. https://doi.org/10.3115/1073336.1073356.

Ryan McDonald, Slav Petrov, and Keith Hall. 2011. Multi-source transfer of delexicalized dependency parsers. In *Proceedings of the conference on empirical methods in natural language processing*. Association for Computational Linguistics, pages 62–72. https://www.aclweb.org/anthology/D11-1006.

Ryan T McDonald, Joakim Nivre, Yvonne Quirmbach-Brundage, Yoav Goldberg, Dipanjan Das, Kuzman Ganchev, Keith B Hall, Slav Petrov, Hao Zhang, Oscar Täckström, et al. 2013. Universal dependency annotation for multilingual parsing. In *ACL (2)*. pages 92–97. https://www.aclweb.org/anthology/P13-2017.

Tahira Naseem, Regina Barzilay, and Amir Globerson. 2012. Selective sharing for multilingual dependency parsing. In *Proceedings of the 50th Annual Meeting of the Association for Computational Linguistics: Long Papers-Volume 1*. Association for Computational Linguistics, pages 629–637.

Tahira Naseem, Harr Chen, Regina Barzilay, and Mark Johnson. 2010. Using universal linguistic knowledge to guide grammar induction. In *Proceedings of the 2010 Conference on Empirical Methods in Natural Language Processing*. Association for Computational Linguistics, pages 1234–1244.

Joakim Nivre, Željko Agić, Lars Ahrenberg, et al. 2017. Universal dependencies 2.0, CoNLL 2017 shared task development and test data. LINDAT/CLARIN digital library at the Institute of Formal and Applied Linguistics, Charles University. http://hdl.handle.net/11234/1-2184.

Kalika Bali Jatin Sharma, Monojit Choudhury, and Yogarshi Vyas. 2014. "I am borrowing ya mixing?" an analysis of English-Hindi code mixing in Facebook. *EMNLP 2014* page 116. https://www.aclweb.org/anthology/W14-3914.

Thamar Solorio, Elizabeth Blair, Suraj Maharjan, Steven Bethard, Mona Diab, Abdelati Hawwari, Fahad AlGhamdi, Julia Hirschberg, Alison Chang, et al. 2014. Overview for the first shared task on language identification in code-switched data. www.aclweb.org/anthology/W14-3907.

Oscar Täckström, Ryan McDonald, and Jakob Uszkoreit. 2012. Cross-lingual word clusters for direct transfer of linguistic structure. In *Proceedings of the 2012 conference of the North American chapter of the association for computational linguistics: Human language technologies*. Association for Computational Linguistics, pages 477–487. www.aclweb.org/anthology/N12-1052.

Jörg Tiedemann. 2014. Rediscovering annotation projection for cross-lingual parser induction. In *COLING*. pages 1854–1864.

Daniel Zeman, Martin Popel, Milan Straka, Jan Hajič, Joakim Nivre, Filip Ginter, Juhani Luotolahti, Sampo Pyysalo, Slav Petrov, Martin Potthast, Francis Tyers, Elena Badmaeva, Memduh Gökırmak, Anna Nedoluzhko, Silvie Cinková, Jan Hajič jr., Jaroslava Hlaváčová, Václava Kettnerová, Zdeňka Urešová, Jenna Kanerva, Stina Ojala, Anna Missilä, Christopher Manning, Sebastian Schuster, Siva Reddy, Dima Taji, Nizar Habash, Herman Leung, Marie-Catherine de Marneffe, Manuela Sanguinetti, Maria Simi, Hiroshi Kanayama, Valeria de Paiva, Kira Droganova, Héctor Martínez Alonso, Hans Uszkoreit, Vivien Macketanz, Aljoscha Burchardt, Kim Harris, Katrin Marheinecke, Georg Rehm, Tolga Kayadelen, Mohammed Attia, Ali Elkahky, Zhuoran Yu, Emily Pitler, Saran Lertpradit, Michael Mandl, Jesse Kirchner, Hector Fernandez Alcalde, Jana Strnadova, Esha Banerjee, Ruli Manurung, Antonio Stella, Atsuko Shimada, Sookyoung Kwak, Gustavo Mendonça, Tatiana Lando, Rattima Nitisaroj, and Josie Li. 2017. CoNLL 2017 Shared Task: Multilingual Parsing from Raw Text to Universal Dependencies. In *Proceedings of the CoNLL 2017 Shared Task: Multilingual Parsing from Raw Text to Universal Dependencies*. Association for Computational Linguistics.

# Building a Finnish SOM-based ontology concept tagger and harvester


Seppo Nyrkkö
University of Helsinki
seppo.nyrkko@helsinki.fi



### Abstract

I demonstrate here an experiment of word sense disambiguation method based on the Self-Organizing Map (SOM) and a pre-existing set of tools for analyzing text in Finnish. It is given a Semantic Web ontology as a reference model, and a related Finnish text corpus with sample term tagging related to the ontology concepts. The experiment is based on "OntoR", a previous experiment on SOM-based ontology term tagging for English. In this work the OntoR model is adapted to the Finnish language, and it is trained on a small text example with hand-picked concept annotations. This computational model can be considered useful for Information Retrieval and concept harvesting purposes in a specific domain where a limited training data set is available. The model adapted to Finnish text analysis stands on OMORFI and HFST morphological analysis, and uses the SOM-PAK library for unsupervised clustering, and ontology concept tagging and further for concept harvesting in Semantic Web ontology development.



### Tiivistelmä

Kehitän luonnollisessa kielessä ilmenevien sanojen merkitysten erotteluun sopivaa automaattista koneoppivaa työkalua. Laskennallinen malli perustuu itseoppivaan karttaan (SOM, Self-Organizing Map) ja annettuun suomenkieliseen semanttisen webin ontologiaan. Malli oppii tunnistamaan käsitteiden ilmenemistä mallitekstistä, johon on annotoitu (tagattu) malliksi aiemmin laaditun ongologian käsitteitä. Koe liittyy aiemmin englanninkielisten käsitteiden taggaamiseen liittyvään OntoR-koejärjestelyyn joka tutki tekstisyötteessä ilmenevien termien liittämistä SOM-kartan soluihin malliksi annetun annotoidun tekstiesimerkin avulla. Tällainen malli oppii annetun käsitemallin huomattavan niukalla esimerkkiaineistolla ja sopii käyttökohteisiin joissa ei ole tarjolla riittävän suurta datamäärää syvän oppimisen neuroverkkomallin opettamiseksi. Suomenkielisen kokeen morfologisen analyysin pohjalla on OMORFI- ja HFST-työkalut. Koneoppimisen toteuttava SOM-kartta lasketaan SOM-PAK-ohjelmistopaketin avulla. Kehitettyä laskennallista mallia käytetään käsitteiden tunnistamisen lisäksi myös uusien ontologiakäsitteiden ehdokkaiden löytämiseksi.


## 1   Introduction

Plain word-based keywords might be misleading in some Information Retrieval purposes. The Semantic Web ontologies can provide enhanced results in information search when multiple taxonomies of terms and keywords are used in the document




*Proceedings of the 4th International Workshop for Computational Linguistics for Uralic Languages (IWCLUL 2018)*, pages 18–25,
Helsinki, Finland, January 8–9, 2018. ©2018 Association for Computational Linguistics

database, for instance in medical or biological domain [1]. With automated ontology-concept tagging, a text database can be indexed incrementally to enhance queries defined by word-based examples or taxonomic identifiers. By referring to taxonomic concept identifiers in ontologies, both the tagging (indexing of terms and concepts) and Information Retrieval (search by terms or example phrases) can produce better precision in search results, compared to plain word-based keywords.

Text in Finnish is a challenge in Information Retrieval and automatic concept analysis due to its rich morphology and its marginal status in the existing forest of Semantic Web ontologies. By developing accessible and constitutive tools for analyzing morphologically rich languages, such as Finnish, the diverse work on automated and semi-automated concept tagging and multilingual ontology development will also become accessible. Also this way the methods developed for single languages can be evaluated in a foreign language or multilingual domain of the Semantic Web.

By using an automated concept tagging model, as aimed in the OntoR tool, it is possible to detect semantically significant features on tokens which link their usages to an ontology-based term. The detection of semantic features in the OntoR setup are based on a learning model, which is trained with data produced by a dependency parser program. The model described here also aims to disambiguate common words in special contexts where they are used as terms, as described in a Semantic Web ontology.

The utilized pre-processing software work with different levels (tokenization, lemmatisation, POS tagging and dependency parsing). The former English OntoR setup utilized the Stanford Parser PCFG model for English, but in this project I am using the OMORFI and HFST tools and UDPIPE tool adapted to the R environment.

Here the Finnish language is a very interesting challenge for dependency parsing since the word form disambiguation (e.g. lasta/lapsi) will be made in the R statistical programming environment, after the possible lemmas are parsed with HFST, but before estimation of the dependency graph with UDPIPE which will benefit from the lemma disambiguation. This project for adapting Finnish as the source language aims to normalize the set of pre-processing tools in a uniform model for analyzing concepts in multiple languages.

## 2   The Finnish OntoR experiment

This small demonstration aims to show how the Self-Organizing map method can work for unsupervised ontology term tagging and learning. The SOM is powerful in processing natural language since it can handle and learn on training data with a small set of significant outliers, and is robust in sense of accepting a noise component [2].

Neural network (NN) models for text-based learning are data-hungry when the model is trained with an unsupervised method. Word sense disambiguation require high-quality example training data, especially if the training data contains of homonyms and synonyms, reflecting real-life language. The concept detection method developed in the OntoR tool aims to be robust in cases of misspelled words and semantically equivalent alternatives by both a fuzzy character-based guessing (edit distance) technique and ontology-based semantic equivalence estimation. The out-of-lexicon words can be identified by a given synonym dictionary or applying typographic rules. Also the found words can be merged in the same concept by providing a synonym or a higher-class term (hypernym) in a Semantic Web ontology.

In contrast to most purely unsupervised neural network models, the OntoR model

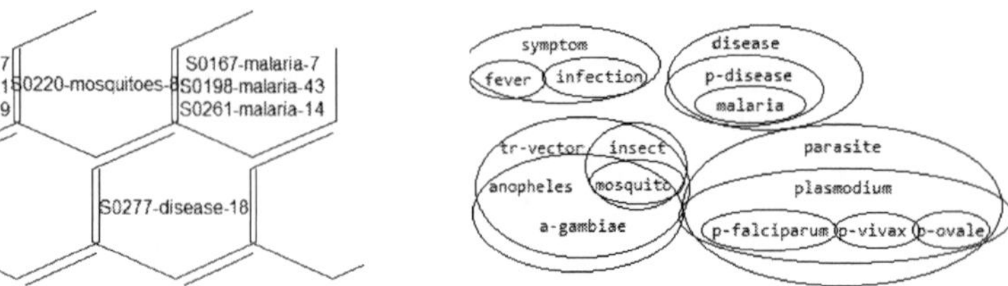

Figure 1: A detail of a Self-Organizing Map (SOM) and a related Venn diagram as a sample ontology for tagging terms

can be trained with a minimal training data set. For instance, the OntoR example development training data set for English contains a long Wikipedia article (9 500 words) and 100 related medical paper abstracts (24 000 words). This hand-picked development data set yielded a model capable of clustering a domain-related concept model, as sketched in Figure 1.

A previous, similar approach in English ontology concept term tagging has been done with the OntoR ontology term annotation tool, earlier developed in the EU MOLTO machine translation research project. Due to its open-to-develop nature it is very practical to extend its use by utilizing the existing Finnish morphological and syntactic analysis tools.

The OntoR was developed to use Stanford Parser for tokenization, lemmatization and extracting dependency information on natural language source text. The OntoR tool runs in the R statistical programming environment[3], using the CRAN library som, based on SOM-PAK[4], the Self-Organizing Map Program Package version 3.1.

## 2.1 Adapting OntoR to Finnish syntax

With this renovated experiment setup, I describe the required and planned steps to adapt the previously developed OntoR concept tagging model into a Finnish model for ontology concept tagging. As an extension to the previous OntoR experiment, I am now using HFST [5] and OMORFI [6] tools for Finnish corpus text lemmatization.

The developed syntactic analysis will use the Universal Dependencies (UD) data for Finnish [7]. For dependency arc computation, the Finnish OntoR model will be using the udpipe package for the R platform, instead of running the Stanford Parser model as an external process.

At the bootstrapping phase of adapting Finnish into the analysis model, I use 3-grams, which consists of the lemmatized base forms of the text node word, its previous and the following word. Practically this is done by adding "left" and "right" dependency arcs in the input sentence data. In a later step I intend to adapt the udpipe dependencies analysis developed in the UD project. This is expected to be equally powerful in expression, compared to the Stanford Parser PENN collapsed dependencies for English, which was used in the English OntoR setup.

In the development phase, a sample development corpus of 80 sentences were extracted from the Finnish wikipedia articles for Malaria and Protozoa (*fi:Alkueläimet*). A sample of this text in the OntoR environment can be seen in Figure 3. This aims at utilizing the same development ontology used for developing the English semantic model, shown in Figure 1.

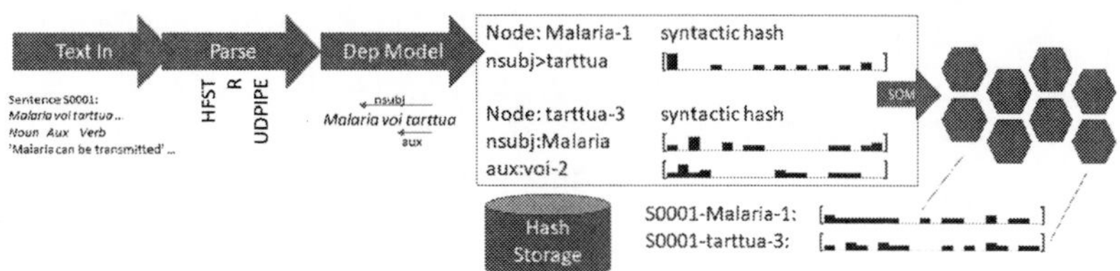


Figure 2: The workflow for producing semantic descriptors for syntactically analyzed text nodes.

## 2.2 Composing semantic feature vectors from syntactic arcs

Each *text node*, which is a specific occurrence of word in the source, gets a computed *semantic feature descriptor*. The which represents its observed syntactic neighborhood. The model generates *syntactic hash vectors* from syntactic dependencies, produced by the applied dependency parser and a random index generator. These hash vectors are composed into a weighted, distributional vector, used as the feature descriptor for the text node, which is practically the specific token in the sentence.

Since this is a probabilistic model, I chose random indexing as embeddings to represent lemmas and their typed syntactic dependencies. A random vector projection to a small dimension (20 at the first experiment) is applied to make computation affordable. The feature descriptors for text nodes are averaged from the set of their related syntactic hash vectors, and weighted by their inverse frequency. Similarly to the TF-IDF principle, a token occurring only a few times the weighting gives a large coefficient and commonly occurring tokens will get a smaller weight in the combined representation. The vector components are positive and L1-normed to sum of 1. A pipeline describing the feature generation process is shown in Figure 2.

This distribution-based numeric representation has been chosen over Euclidean vector-space models (such as word2vec) due to the requirements of statistical analysis: The components must be able to be interpolated, summed and weighted, so that presence of any components may be measured in a combined feature descriptor. Also the difference between two semantic feature descriptors can be measured by a L1-distance or an entropy based distance such as IRad (information radius).

A tuple consisting of a dependency attribute and its head/dependent word builds an individual indexed syntactic hash. Also, the reverse arc and their endpoint words produce indexed syntactic arcs. This way, both the head and dependent ends of arcs are given unique features.

In Fig. 3 is shown a screen capture of the OntoR user interface, used for examining a computed model of an ontology-related text and a selected set of text nodes. The user interface produces a coarse bar chart of evaluated semantic feature descriptors for the text nodes and the related syntactic hashes used in the computation.

## 2.3 Self-Organizing Map representing an ontology

The SOM model proves to be powerful in unsupervised learning of multidimensional vector input and can handle input vector spaces with multiple dense clusters and sparse outlier data points. It adapts its clustering structure to wide-scale multidimensional variance in the data set, and is robust in terms of accepting a noise component

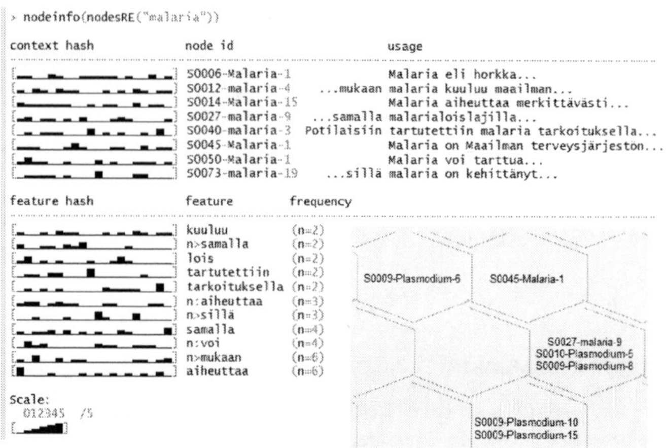



Figure 3: Screen shot from the OntoR environment, running in the R statistical programming environment. At the top, the semantic feature descriptors associated with token *Malaria* are printed. They represent the matching text nodes in the Finnish OntoR training data set, with a short word context of their usage. The node names are prefixed with a Snnnn- identifier which identifies the sentence number in the training data bank. The node names have a suffix -n which indicates the position of the token in the sentence, which is essential in cases of multiple word occurrences. Below are the syntactic hash vectors, which are used to build the semantic descriptors for text node related context. These are used in the composition of context descriptors, by weighted summing. An inverse frequency weighting is used so that an associated syntactic feature with low frequency (n) will cause a greater effect in the resulting context descriptor. Features occurring only once are not evaluated since they are taken only to provide noise to the training data. At this phase of development, a baseline lemmatisation is used instead of a dependency parse. *On the bottom right corner:* Some of the text nodes, aligned in the SOM space, as a result of the training process.

as part of the input. [2]

The OntoR setup demonstrates how ontology-based term structure is reflected on top the trained SOM map containing the keywords. A modified plot of the SOM map has been developed to explore the mapping of ontology term classes and super-classes over the machine-learned term model trained with the sample corpus. The SOM map can also be seen to reflect a Venn diagram representing an ontology concept space [8].

## 2.4  Observations on training the SOM classifier

The model can be given a sample ontology describing the domain of the training data set. The training ontology concepts are equipped with references to the training corpus. After the model is trained, the SOM model will reflect the found matching ontology concepts when a syntactic feature vector is presented to its feature space. Also, if a new term, a new spelling or synonym for an existing concept is detected, it is expected to appear near an existing concept tag in the SOM grid.

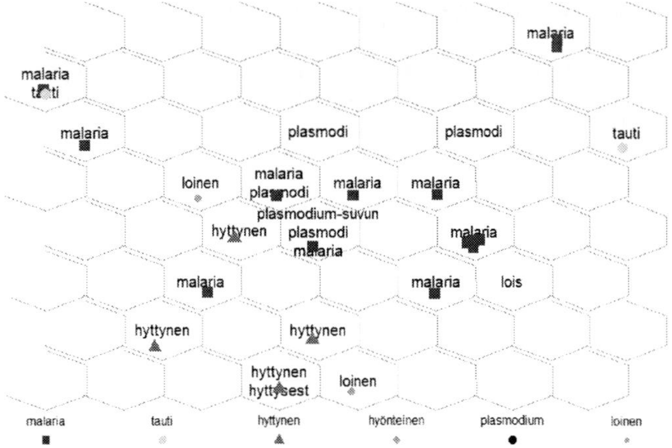


Figure 4: The SOM grid shown here demonstrates word contexts learnt from the development training data. The hexagonal cells are labeled with the associated terms, which are the words having a high frequency $n > 3$ in the training set. Each cell represents an averaged syntactic context, where the printed token is present. A cell may contain multiple tokens which appear in a similar syntactic context, and can be assumed to share some semantic features in common. Likewise, a token can appear in multiple cells, showing the syntactic context diversity of the specific token. An evaluation set of 20 sentences was separated from the development set of 80 sentences. The tokens selected for the evaluation are printed with their marking colors in the legend line at the bottom of the figure. The terms used in this evaluation plot were: *malaria, tauti* (en: disease), *hyttynen* (en: mosquito), *hyönteinen* (en: insect), *plasmodium, loinen* (en: parasite). These terms, evaluated in their sentence contexts are projected on a trained SOM model. The plot shows that the evaluation data points are located close to the "target" clusters.

For development purpopses, I split the early development data into an evaluation set (20 sentences) and a development set (60 sentences) at random. A screen capture of a SOM-based term clustering at the development phase is shown in Fig. 4. In this example, three pairs of sub-terms and super-terms from the evaluation data set are plotted on the trained SOM model. The word form similarity measurements are disabled in this experiment. This shows that the evaluation data point features are well estimated without prior knowledge of the labels in the training data set, only based on their semantic feature vectors. Surprisingly, some word sense disambiguation happens even without the trained UDPIPE model attached.

The sample data used in the current development corpus is insufficient for numeric evaluation. Currently, at the time of writing, I am integrating the full syntacic analysis with the UDPIPE into the Finnish OntoR system, and also I am adding a larger corpus extracted from medical domain articles. This work seems to lead into a promisingly interesting evaluation of word sense disambiguation with the SOM and into further research on harvesting terms and introducing them as new ontology concepts.

# 3 Related work and development discussion

The SOM maps can also be seen learning Boolean elementary reasoning with logical statements in a restricted artificial language, when the model is trained by appropriate domain-specific text. The related work by Letosa et al. [8] supports this approach for using SOM in clustering the tagged concepts in given input in a restricted language. The boundaries between dense clusters can be seen as analogies to branches in taxonomy trees.

The similarity model based on the semantic descriptor vectors is very promising for containing contextual information on a word occurrence. Similar research on similarity measures on hash vectors has been recently done, as in work by Wang et al. [9]

Important work on automated and semi-supervised ontology population and extension has been done in the CultureSampo [10] project. Their model is also based on word distribution models on analyzed text which makes comparison to this work relevant.

There is also previous work on concept mining for the Semantic Web with SOM, for example the work by Honkela et al. [11], where the emergent structure of an organized SOM reflects the structure of underlying information, used in the training process. Their research also shows that multiple layers of superclass layers can be seen as different-sized nested zones on the SOM grid. This is analogous to the approach used in the concept classification (and further semantic disambiguation) in the OntoR project.

The expressiveness of Semantic Web ontologies and their language independent concept schema exceed the information in plain monolingual keyword-based taxonomies. Semantic web ontologies can contain relation attributes outside the superclass-subclass-taxonomy, such as *belongs-to* or *caused-by* relations. Ontology concepts may also be annotated with human readable description and machine-readable annotated for logical reasoning applications (e.g. through a SPARQL based schema). This suggests a need for research towards bridging the Semantic Web over multiple languages.

As a future step, an evaluation scheme for successful ontology concept tagging must be considered when developing the OntoR model further towards the pre-founded Finnish ontology structures, such as in the FinnONTO [12] project, and towards cross-linguistic concept tagging. This will also benefit the work of building Semantic Web ontologies and extending previously built monolingual ontologies to cover new languages and usages in cross-lingual Information Retrieval.

## Acknowledgments

The development of the OntoR tool was initially funded by the EU MOLTO project at University of Helsinki. The experiment has been inspired by previous work on the SOM, lead by professor Timo Honkela. Timo has given beneficial feedback and ideas on this research subject.

## References

[1] Jouni Tuominen, Nina Laurenne, and Eero Hyvönen. Biological names and taxonomies on the semantic web–managing the change in scientific conception. *The Semantic Web: Research and Applications*, pages 255–269, 2011.

[2] Juha Vesanto and Esa Alhoniemi. Clustering of the self-organizing map. *IEEE Transactions on neural networks*, 11(3):586–600, 2000.

[3] R Core Team. *R: A Language and Environment for Statistical Computing*. R Foundation for Statistical Computing, Vienna, Austria, 2017.

[4] Teuvo Kohonen, Jussi Hynninen, Jari Kangas, and Jorma Laaksonen. Som pak: The self-organizing map program package. *Report A31, Helsinki University of Technology, Laboratory of Computer and Information Science*, 1996.

[5] Krister Lindén, Miikka Silfverberg, and Tommi Pirinen. Hfst tools for morphology–an efficient open-source package for construction of morphological analyzers. In *International Workshop on Systems and Frameworks for Computational Morphology*, pages 28–47. Springer, 2009.

[6] Krister Lindén, Erik Axelson, Senka Drobac, Sam Hardwick, Miikka Silfverberg, and Tommi A Pirinen. Using hfst for creating computational linguistic applications. In *Computational Linguistics*, pages 3–25. Springer, 2013.

[7] Sampo Pyysalo, Jenna Kanerva, Anna Missilä, Veronika Laippala, and Filip Ginter. Universal dependencies for finnish. In *Proceedings of the 20th Nordic Conference of Computational Linguistics, NODALIDA 2015, May 11-13, 2015, Vilnius, Lithuania*, number 109, pages 163–172. Linköping University Electronic Press, 2015.

[8] Jorge Ramón Letosa and Timo Honkela. Elementary logical reasoning in the som output space. In *International Conference on Artificial Neural Networks*, pages 432–437. Springer, 2010.

[9] Jingdong Wang, Heng Tao Shen, Jingkuan Song, and Jianqiu Ji. Hashing for similarity search: A survey. *arXiv preprint arXiv:1408.2927*, 2014.

[10] Tomi Kauppinen, Heini Kuittinen, Jouni Tuominen, Katri Seppälä, and Eero Hyvönen. Extending an ontology by analyzing annotation co-occurrences in a semantic cultural heritage portal. In *Proceedings of the ASWC 2008 Workshop on Collective Intelligence (ASWC-CI 2008), 3rd Asian Semantic Web Conference (ASWC 2008), Bangkok, Thailand*, pages 8–11, 2009.

[11] Timo Honkela and Matti Pöllä. Concept mining with self-organizing maps for the semantic web. In *WSOM*, pages 98–106. Springer, 2009.

[12] Eero Hyvönen, Kim Viljanen, Jouni Tuominen, and Katri Seppälä. Building a national semantic web ontology and ontology service infrastructure–the finnonto approach. In *European Semantic Web Conference*, pages 95–109. Springer, 2008.

# Sound-aligned corpus of Udmurt dialectal texts

Timofey Arkhangelskiy
Universität Hamburg / Alexander von Humboldt Foundation
timarkh@gmail.com

Ekaterina Georgieva
Research Institute for Linguistics
Hungarian Academy of Sciences
ekaterina.georgieva@nytud.mta.hu

## Abstract

The paper describes an ongoing effort aiming at building a sound-aligned corpus of Udmurt spoken texts. The corpus currently consists of about 3.5 hours of recordings, collected during fieldwork trips between 2014 and 2016. The recordings represent three dialect groups of Udmurt (Northern, Central and Southern). The recordings were transcribed with the help of native speakers. All morphological peculiarities characteristic of spoken or dialectal Udmurt were faithfully reflected, however, the transcription was somewhat normalized in order to facilitate morphological annotation and cross-dialectal search. The pipeline of our project includes aligning the texts with the sound in ELAN and annotating them with a morphological analyzer developed for standard Udmurt. We use automatic annotation as a much less time-consuming alternative of manual glossing and explore the resulting quality and the downsides of such annotation. We are specifically investigating how much and what kind of change the standard analyzer requires in order to achieve sufficiently good annotation of spoken/dialectal texts. The corpus has a web interface where the users may execute search queries and listen to the audio. The online interface will be made publicly available in 2018.

## Kivonat

Ezen tanulmányban egy pilot projektet mutatunk be, amely célja egy hanganyagot tartalmazó udmurt nyelvjárási korpusz építése. A készülő korpusz 2014 és 2016 között végzett terepmunkák során gyűjtött, jelenleg körülbelül 3,5 órányi lejegyzett hanganyagból áll, amely az udmurt nyelv fő nyelvjáráscsoportjait (északi, közép- és déli nyelvjárásait) mutatja be. A hangfelvételek lejegyzése udmurt anyanyelvi beszélők segítségével történt. A lejegyzés hűen tükrözi a hangfelvételeken előforduló, az udmurt nyelvjárásokra vagy az udmurt beszélt nyelvre jellemző morfológiai jelenségeket. A lejegyzés azonban fonetikai szempontból bizonyos mértékben sztenderdizálva lett annak érdekében, hogy megkönnyítse a szövegek morfológiai elemzését és a több nyelvjárásra kiterjedő keresést. A szövegek feldolgozása a következő lépésekből áll: a szövegek ELAN-nal való lejegyzése (amelynek során a legjegyzett szöveg időben illesztve lesz a hanganyaghoz),





*Proceedings of the 4th International Workshop for Computational Linguistics for Uralic Languages (IWCLUL 2018)*, pages 26–38,
Helsinki, Finland, January 8–9, 2018. ©2018 Association for Computational Linguistics

majd az udmurt irodalmi nyelvre fejlesztett morfológiai elemzővel való annotálá-
sa. A korpuszépítés során az automatikus annotálás mellett döntöttünk, amellyel
sok idő megspórolható a manuális annotáláshoz képest. Cikkünkben megvizsgál-
juk az automatikus annotálás alkalmazhatóságát, különös tekintettel arra, hogy
milyen mértékű és típusú módosításokat kell elvégezni az irodalmi udmurt nyelvre fejlesztett morfológiai elemzőn, hogy az a beszélt nyelvi és nyelvjárási szövegek elemzésére is alkalmas legyen. A korpusz online felülettel rendelkezik, amely
lehetővé teszi a felhasználók számára az adatok lekérdezését és a hanganyag meg-
hallgatását. Az online felületet a 2018-as év folyamán nyilvánossá tervezzük ten-
ni.

### Аннотация

В этой статье описывается текущий проект, в рамках которого плани-
руется создать звуковой корпус устных текстов на удмуртских диалектах.
Наш корпус в настоящий момент включает около 3,5 часов расшифрован-
ных записей на трёх группах удмуртских диалектов (северные, средин-
ные и южные), которые были собраны в ходе экспедиций 2014–2016 гг.
Все тексты были расшифрованы с помощью носителей. Все морфологиче-
ские особенности устных/диалектных текстов точно отражены в расшиф-
ровке, однако с фонетической точки зрения расшифровки были стандар-
тизованы, чтобы облегчить морфологическую разметку и одновременный
поиск в текстах на разных диалектах. Обработка данных в нашем проекте
включает в себя выравнивание расшифровок со звуком с помощью ELAN
и их автоматическую морфологическую разметку с помощью стандартно-
го удмуртского анализатора. Мы рассматриваем автоматическую разметку как намного менее затратную альтернативу ручному глоссированию и
проводим оценку качества и минусов такой разметки. В особенности мы
рассматриваем вопрос о том, насколько сильно и как именно необходимо
изменить стандартный анализатор, чтобы добиться достаточно качествен-
ной разметки устных/диалектных текстов. Корпус имеет веб-интерфейс,
через который пользователи могут задавать поисковые запросы и прослу-
шивать фрагменты аудио. Этот интерфейс будет открыт для общего досту-
па в 2018 году.

# 1 Introduction

This paper summarizes the preliminary results and the future directions of building a
linguistic corpus of spoken texts from different Udmurt dialects.

Udmurt belongs to the Permic branch of the Uralic language family. Udmurt is
spoken mainly in the Udmurt Republic, but also in the Republic of Tatarstan, the
Republic of Bashkortostan, Perm Krai, Sverdlovsk Oblast and Kirov Oblast. According
to the Russian Census of 2010, there are about 325,000 speakers of Udmurt.[1] The
EGIDS level of Udmurt is 5, i.e. it is a *developing language*, which means that "[t]he
language is in vigorous use, with literature in a standardized form being used by some
though this is not yet widespread or sustainable".[2] Standard Udmurt has an official
orthography based on the Cyrillic script. This orthography is taught in schools and is
familiar to most Udmurt speakers, regardless of their dialect.

As far as the existing corpora of Udmurt are concerned, we would like to mention three recent projects aiming at building linguistic databases for Udmurt, namely

---

[1] http://www.gks.ru/free_doc/new_site/perepis2010/croc/Documents/Vol4/pub-04-05.pdf
[2] https://www.ethnologue.com/language/udm

the Udmurt Corpus, the Beserman Corpus and the UraLUID database. The Udmurt Corpus[3] contains about 7.3 million tokens from mostly newspaper texts written in standard Udmurt. The Beserman Corpus[4] consists of transcribed oral texts in the Beserman dialect of Udmurt (currently, its size is about 65,000 tokens). The UraLUID database[5] encompasses both Udmurt texts collected in the $19^{th}$ century as well as text samples from two Udmurt blogs (the aim of this project was to create a database containing at least 4000 tokens of these two types of Udmurt texts, see Simon and Mus 2017).

Our goal is to process fieldwork recordings collected between 2014 and 2016. During these fieldwork trips, we collected contemporary spoken language material, hence, the corpus is aimed to represent the spoken varieties of Udmurt. Additionally, it is noteworthy that the recordings do not exemplify the standard Udmurt language but rather its dialects. In this way, our corpus is a further step in the corpus building efforts for Udmurt.

Needless to say, spoken texts are an irreplaceable source of valuable data for linguists. This is especially true in the case of endangered and under-documented languages like Udmurt. This highlights the importance of making fieldwork data open and reusable for the researchers, and possibly, for the native speaker community as well.

However, collecting and transcribing recordings is an extremely long and expensive process. The traditional approach to compiling spoken corpora includes aligning the transcription with the recording and then manually annotating the texts in Toolbox or FLEX (for Beserman Udmurt see Arkhangelskiy et al. 2017; for Enets see Khanina 2017). In this case, the annotation is by itself quite time-consuming and, in case of small-scale project like ours, could keep researchers and fieldwork linguists from processing and sharing their data. Hence, we took a different approach, namely to sound-align the recordings manually, but annotate them automatically. This approach to text processing has been advocated in several recent language documentation projects, e.g. in the Ustya Basin Russian project (Waldenfels et al., 2014) as well as in the Saami and Komi documentation project (Blokland et al., 2015), since it has two advantages: first, it is much less time-consuming, and second, the corpus built in this way can still be used for many research purposes.

In this paper, we discuss the workflow of our ongoing project and the obstacles we faced in the process. The paper is organized as follows. In Section 2, we present the Udmurt data used in the corpus with special reference to the metadata of the recordings. Then, in Section 3, we turn to the text processing steps, namely transcription and morphological annotation. We present the transcription used in the corpus and discuss several problematic cases in connection to it. As for the morphological annotation, we used a morphological analyzer originally developed for standard Udmurt. Given the fact that the corpus contains dialectal data, we had to make some adjustments to the analyzer, which is another novelty of the project presented in this paper. We specifically discuss the difficulties dialectal data pose with respect to morphological annotation (Section 4). Finally, we briefly describe the main features of the user interface of the corpus in Section 5.

---

[3]http://web-corpora.net/UdmurtCorpus/search/
[4]http://beserman.ru/corpus/search/
[5]http://www.nytud.hu/depts/tlp/uralic/dbases.html

| Collection point | Dialect | Speaker(s) | Duration |
|---|---|---|---|
| Alnash district, Udmurtia | Southern | VE; EE | 33:30 |
| Alnash district, Udmurtia | Southern | LP; EE | 29:02 |
| Grakh district, Udmurtia | Southern | OK; IK; MK | 53:54 |
| Grakh district, Udmurtia | Southern | ESj | 09:40 |
| Grakh district, Udmurtia | Southern | VK; IK | 27:09 |
| Izhevsk, Udmurtia | Central | EL | 08:28 |
| Izhevsk, Udmurtia | Central | SSh | 06:10 |
| Izhevsk, Udmurtia | Northern | OS | 04:53 |
| Balezino district, Udmurtia | Northern | TS; TaS | 09:15 |
| Balezino district, Udmurtia | Northern | TS; ES | 34:24 |
| Kukmor district, Tatarstan | Southern Peripheral | EK; KK | 22:33 |

Table 1: The Udmurt fieldwork recordings used in the corpus

## 2 Data

The Udmurt recordings used in this corpus were collected by Ekaterina Georgieva during three fieldwork trips conducted between 2014 and 2016 in the Republic of Udmurtia (and partly in the Republic of Tatarstan). All audio data were recorded in .wav format. The data represent different dialects of Udmurt, which we briefly overview below.

The dialects of the Udmurt language are divided into four main groups, namely the Northern, Central, Southern and Beserman dialect groups (Kelmakov, 1998, p. 41–44). The Southern dialect group is further divided into Southern dialects (spoken in the southern parts of the Republic of Udmurtia) and Southern Peripheral dialects (spoken in the Udmurt diasporas in Tatarstan, Bashkortostan, etc.).

Additionally, a division is made between "standard Udmurt" and its vernacular varieties (Edygarova, 2014). Standard Udmurt is used mainly in written form. As for the vernacular varieties of Udmurt, Edygarova (2014) distinguishes between local and cross-local vernacular varieties. The local varieties of Udmurt show features of a particular dialect, while in the cross-local varieties, features of mixed dialect and standard forms occur (Edygarova, 2014, p. 379).

Taking into account these facts, we assume that the fieldwork recordings used in the corpus represent the spoken varieties of Udmurt (that differ from its written variety, i.e. standard Udmurt) as well as exemplify certain dialectal features characteristic of the speakers' dialects. Nevertheless, they often contain standard forms alongside the dialectal ones. For example, in the texts, we find infinitives in both -n (dialectal) and -ni̯ (standard), with the standard variant being slightly more frequent.

Now let us now take a closer look at the recordings used in our corpus. At present, the recordings collected during the fieldwork conducted in July and August 2014 are being processed. Below, we overview some basic metadata of these recordings, such as the place of recording, the dialect recorded, the speakers participating in the interviews and the duration of the recording, see Table 1. As can be seen from the table, the corpus is meant to cover (to a varying degree) the main dialects of Udmurt: Northern, Central, Southern and Southern Peripheral.

During the fieldwork trips, the semi-structured interview method was chosen. This format gave the speakers some freedom in the course of the interview. This was needed in order to ensure the right settings for a natural recording. It should be also emphasized that Udmurt was the only medium of the interviews. The interviews cover different genres, such as narratives, informal conversations between speakers, description of customs, etc.

Furthermore, the recordings fall into two groups regarding the number of speakers participating in the interview. In some of the recordings, only one native speaker was interviewed by the (non-native) fieldwork linguist, while in other recordings, the informant(s) was/were interviewed with the help of another native speaker. In the latter case, the result was a group conversation (featuring two or three native speakers and the linguist).

## 3  Text processing

In this section, we present the steps of processing the recordings. First, we discuss transcription and related issues. Then we proceed to the morphological analysis, for which we used the analyzer developed for standard Udmurt with some necessary adjustments. More specifically, we evaluate the applicability of this analyzer to dialectal data.

### 3.1  Transcription

The recordings were transcribed and time-aligned in ELAN[6]. ELAN allows to create complex annotations for audio and video files. The annotations are organized in a layered structure, in so-called *tiers*. The audio files were utterance/sentence-level time-aligned. Currently, the annotation of the recordings consists of two types of tiers: transcription and fieldwork notes. In each recording, there is a separate transcription and notes tier for each of the speakers (including the interviewer).

The first step of processing the audio files was the transcription. The transcription was carried out with the help of native speakers (in some cases, a speaker of the relevant dialect or one of the participants in the recording in question). Given the fact that we are dealing with spoken language recordings showing dialectal features, we had to make some principal decisions regarding the transcription we used. Let us mention a couple of problems in oral texts: assimilations, colloquial forms, unfinished words, hesitations, dialectal morphological features, etc. Below, we summarize the the decisions we have made regarding the transcription used in the corpus. Our goal was to apply these principles throughout, as consistency is one of the keys properties of corpus building.

First of all, it should be emphasized that we did not aim at providing a phonetic transcription. Hence, we chose the Cyrillic script used in the case of standard Udmurt, and not the Finno-Ugric Transcription System/Uralic Phonetic Alphabet[7] or the International Phonetic Alphabet. This made the transcribed texts consistent with the standard Udmurt texts and also facilitated the morphological analysis of the transcribed files. This choice was also motivated by the fact that our aim was to create a valuable and useful corpus with limited resources and within a relatively short period of time.

In contrast to other Cyrillic-based transcriptions of Udmurt oral texts (Kelmakov, 1998), we do not mark certain phonological processes, such as assimilations and non-standard stress patterns. For example, in this text collection, the regressive assim-

---

[6]https://tla.mpi.nl/tools/tla-tools/elan/

[7]http://std.dkuug.dk/jtc1/sc2/wg2/docs/n2419a.pdf

ilation is transcribed, as in the verb forms like *tod-sko* (know-PRS.1SG) used in the Northern dialects, which is realized as *totsko* or *tocko*. Based on our data, it seems that the devoicing always applies, hence, we prefer to transcribe this verb form simply as *тодско* instead of *тотско* or *тоцко*. This transcription has the advantage that we do not need to add a stem allomorph *tot* of the verb *todini* (to know). Additionally, we also normalize certain colloquial forms, such as *бенэть* and *капказьын* to *бен ведь* and *капка азьын*, respectively. However, we do mark the actual realization of these colloquial forms in angle brackets (see in Table (2)). Hence, our decision in most cases is to adhere to the standard orthography with some exceptions that we discuss below.

The most important exception is the transcription of dialectal morphological features. Since our goal was to test whether the standard Udmurt morphological analyzer can deal with dialectal morphology, morphological features were always transcribed according to their actual realization in the recordings. Moreover, our data show that both the standard and the dialectal forms can be used in the same dialect or even by the same speaker, for example, as mentioned above, we find infinitives in both *-n* (dialectal form) and *-ni* (standard form). Hence, it was necessary to mark the actual realization of the infinitive suffix.

Furthermore, we did not normalize dialectal lexical items, such as *gid'* (pigsty) and *ţiriśen* (since), corresponding to *gid* and *dịriśen*, respectively. In Section (4), we will discuss how these lexical items have to be processed morphologically.

The third major deviation from the standard Udmurt orthography concerns the transcription of compounds. We would like to stress that the standard orthography is very inconsistent with respect to compounds: some of them are written as one word, others are written with a hyphen, but most of them are written as two words. Moreover, the descriptive studies are also inconclusive of what exactly counts as a compound in Udmurt (Fejes, 2005). Hence, we decided to hyphenate all potential instances of compounding in the corpus.

Our transcription approach resembles the one adopted by (Waldenfels et al., 2014). On the one hand, we do not standardize the text on morphological level, so that the users can search for dialectal morphological features. On the other hand, we standardize the spelling to a certain extent to make it consistent throughout the corpus. This approach gives us two advantages. First, it minimizes the changes we have to make to the standard Udmurt morphological analyzer in order to apply it to our data. Second, it allows the users to search certain morphemes, words and lemmata in all dialects at once, while otherwise they would have to take into account all possible phonetic variants. Since the corpus has sound alignment, the users can still research dialectal phonetics by listening to the examples they find, regardless of the simplifications in the transcription.

Additionally, we chose to mark certain discourse and extralinguistic elements in the transcription.[8] This was motivated not only by the fact that we aimed at transcribing the recordings as precisely as possible, but also by the fact that we aimed at building a multi-purpose corpus. The conventions we adopted are listed in Table (2). It should be emphasized that we transcribed only those discourse elements that occurred inside the utterances. External noise, such as coughing, laughing, etc. that occurred between the utterances were not transcribed. A further convention of our transcription is that sentences start with lower case letters, and capitals are used only to mark proper names.

---

[8]We are grateful to Katalin Mády and Uwe Reichel for their suggestions regarding this part of the transcription.

| Symbol | Description |
|---|---|
| <P> | unfilled pause |
| <B> | breathing |
| <S> | lipsmack |
| <L> | laugh |
| <N> | non-human noise |
| <H:xx> | filled pause, such as ыы, öö, ааа |
| <H:> | verbal realization of hesitation that cannot be captured with phonemes |
| <H> | hesitation, interruption after a word |
| <%> | non-understandable speech |
| <CF:xx> | colloquial form |
| xx<A> | aborted articulation of a word; written without a blank |
| xx<F> | foreign word (not used for Russian loanwords); written without a blank |
| . | finished utterance |
| no punctuation mark | unfinished utterance |
| , | used according to the intuition of the annotator |
| ? | question |
| ! | exclamation |

Table 2: Transcription symbols

Below we provide an example of an utterance from the corpus. In this utterance, several discourse tags can be seen, as well as the compound *ǯek-kišet* (tablecloth) which is transcribed with a hyphen as *жöк-кышет*.[9]

(1)  20140811; Balezino district; TS

*кыше<A>  жöк-кш<A>  жöк-кышетъёсыз вань-а öвöл-а шуса <B> тйнь озь <CF:тнёзь>, кöня штука, тйнь та сюанлэн, мынам, жöк-кышетэ.*

## 3.2  Morphological analysis

The morphological analysis was carried out using an open-source rule-based morphological analyzer used previously for processing written texts in standard Udmurt[10]. The rules it uses consist of a dictionary, where the lexemes are listed together with their stems, part-of-speech tags and Russian translations, and a formalized description of the morphology.

Before processing the texts, we compiled a frequency list of word forms from our texts and manually added to the dictionary about 30 lexemes that were absent there, but frequent in the texts. This list included dialectal variants of several frequent words, such as the postposition *śajen* instead of *śamen* (in some way/language), the particle *bon*, several place names discussed in the texts, as well as the deictic adverb series with the stem *so-* (these correspond to the *o*-adverbs in standard Udmurt).

---

[9]The question clitic *a* is also hyphenated, as required by the standard orthography.
[10]https://github.com/timarkh/uniparser-grammar-udm/

After the morphological analysis, part of the ambiguity was removed with the help of a small set of Constraint Grammar rules (Bick and Didriksen, 2015). These rules have also been developed for standard Udmurt and cover only several prominent cases where the ambiguity can be eliminated with near-total accuracy.

Statistics regarding the quality of morphological analysis were calculated based on a pilot portion of texts, which contains about 2,500 words in the Southern dialect (30 minutes of sound). Initially, the proportion of the tokens that did not receive any analysis reached 13.9%. However, after performing the small dictionary enhancement described above, this proportion fell to 10.1%, which nearly equaled the proportion for the written texts in standard Udmurt (9.5%)[11]. In accordance with the Zipf's law, half of this improvement could have been achieved by adding only four new lexical entries.

The results of the morphological annotation in the case of Udmurt dialectal texts can be explained by two opposite trends. On the one hand, our texts have higher proportion of lexemes and features characteristic of spoken/dialectal Udmurt, which are not recognized by the analyzer. On the other, the speakers use more basic vocabulary without the complex neologisms one often encounters in standard Udmurt, and especially, in the Udmurt newspaper texts, which makes it easier for the analyzer. The ambiguity rate, about 1.4 analyses per analyzed token, was also approximately equal to that of the written texts. Although these results are preliminary and may be imprecise due to the size of the test corpus, they show that in general, it is possible to use the standard analyzer with minimal additions to process dialectal oral texts.

According to a very rough estimate, dialect and spoken features account for around 25% of the unanalyzed tokens. The rest consists of Russian loanwords (45%), proper names (15%) and standard Udmurt vocabulary handled incorrectly by the parser due to the incompleteness of the dictionary or the morphological description (also 15%). The 25% dialect-specific unanalyzed tokens will be discussed in more detail in the next section.

## 4 Problems with processing dialectal data

During text processing of dialectal data, several problems might arise. These concern the dialectal vocabulary and morphology, and to some extent, the orthography. Below, we summarize the main obstacles we had to face while processing Udmurt dialectal texts, and the solutions we came up with.

### 4.1 Dialectal vocabulary

One of the most obvious obstacles to processing dialectal data is the vocabulary, which may differ from that of the standard language. However, in reality, differences in vocabulary do not constitute a big problem. Dialectal nouns and verbs occur sporadically in standard Udmurt texts, they usually appear in standard Udmurt dictionaries, thus, many of them have been already included in the dictionary of the analyzer. For instance, when processing Southern texts, we added the noun *ajšet* (apron). Although this noun is marked as dialectal in Kirillova's (2008) dictionary, it could and should

---

[11]The figures for both corpora were calculated by the authors in November 2017. Currently, the proportion of unanalyzed tokens is less than 5% in both of them due to an enhancement of the analyzer dictionary, which was performed later.

have already been added to the dictionary of the analyzer because it appears 193 times in the corpus of standard Udmurt.

Dialectal variants of words are more problematic. Dialectal variants in our case included stems that were slightly different from their standard Udmurt counterparts, such as *ńil'* instead of *ńįl'* (four); *gid'* instead of *gid* (pigsty); and *nal/nnal* instead of *nunal* (day). There are two possible approaches regarding these cases. The first is to include them in the dictionary as separate entries. The second one is to list them in the existing entries as stem variants. We chose to adhere to the latter strategy. For example, the word *nal* is assigned the lemma *nunal* and can be found as one of its forms in the corpus. Nevertheless, it is still possible to find all words with the stem *nal-* because the segmentation of words into morphemes is stored in the analyzed files.

Furthermore, adverbs and words that belong to closed grammatical classes are especially problematic. We added to the dictionary words belonging to several closed classes, such as series of deictic adverbs in *so-*, particles (e.g. *ginek* (only)) and postpositions (e.g. *tįriś* (since)). All of them have standard Udmurt counterparts, but are better analyzed as separate entries. Although these words constitute less than half of the lexemes we needed to add, they account for the majority of unanalyzed words in terms of token frequency.

## 4.2 Dialectal morphology

Dialectal morphology constitutes a double problem for the annotation. On the one hand, most words with dialectal suffixes simply will be left unanalyzed because they are absent from the morphological description of the analyzer. On the other hand, adding all of these suffixes may give rise to another problem, namely morphological ambiguity. This happens in cases when the dialectal morpheme homophonous with another morpheme used in standard Udmurt.

The solution that we applied in most of these cases was to add the lacking suffix to the grammatical description of the analyzer. In some of the cases, we also had to make changes to the dictionary, by adding stem allomorphs to certain lexemes. Finally, when we were dealing with the features that could increase ambiguity, we introduced additional constraints. Below, we list the suffixes we had to add in order to analyze the Southern texts, with special reference to the potential ambiguity.

- **Epenthetic *-j-* in an intervocalic position.** This concerns primarily the plural marker, which has the form *-os* after vowels and *-jos* after consonants in the standard language. In Southern texts, due to the epenthesis, the suffix *-jos* might be used in both cases. This variation never leads to ambiguity.

- **Dialectal variants of case markers:** *-iś* (*-įś* in standard Udmurt) for the elative and *-ťi* instead of *-ti* for the prolative. Both do not lead to ambiguity.

- **Converb in *-kį* (*-ku* in standard Udmurt).** Does not lead to ambiguity.

- **Converb in *-sa* instead of *-įsa.** Both variants exist in the standard language, but, just as with the infinitive marker, *-sa* is restricted to the non-*a*-stems. In Southern texts, *-sa* can be used with all stems. This variant does not lead to ambiguity.

- **Plural negative verbal form in *-ele* (*-e* in standard Udmurt), used with non-*a*-stems. Does not lead to ambiguity.

- **Assimilated iterative suffix** *-ća* instead of *-ja*, following *-t*. This variant should not lead to ambiguity. Since this suffix is not fully productive, it occurs in both the dictionary and the grammar components of the analyzer. The combinations of verbal stems with the *-ja* suffix are stored in the dictionary. However, its quite frequent combination with the causative suffix, *-(e)t-ja*, is stored in the grammar component. Therefore, unlike other cases on this list, this dialectal morphological feature should be handled by both adding the suffix to the grammar and adding stem variants to the dictionary.

- **Colloquial verb forms**. A handful of frequent verb forms have widespread colloquial versions, e.g. *šuko/ško* instead of *šu-iśko* (say-PRS.1SG). We added these forms to the dictionary as separate entries with standard lemmata.

- **Infinitive in** *-n/-in* instead of the standard Udmurt suffix *-ni/-ini*. The *-n/-ni* variant attaches to the stems ending in *-a*, while *-in/-ini* attaches to all other stems. Since *-in* is the standard Udmurt locative marker, this can lead to ambiguity in cases when there is a nominal stem homonymous with a verbal stem. There are quite few such pairs, but they include frequent words, such as *ul-in* (live-INF vs. under-LOC), or *zor-in* (rain:V-INF vs. rain:N-LOC). The situation could be partly amended by the Constraint Grammar rules, since there are not so many frequent contexts where an infinitive could appear. There is, however, a bigger problem with the *a*-stems because *-n* is the standard Udmurt nominalization suffix for these stems, cf. *uža-n* (work-INF vs. work-NMLZ). The derivation of *n*-nominalizations in Udmurt is fully productive and very frequent.

- **Non-standard morphophonology of** *-śk-*. In Udmurt, *-śk-* is used as a present tense marker as well as a passivizing/intransitivizing suffix. Descriptively, it has been observed that this suffix can have different morphological realizations in the Udmurt dialects (Kelmakov, 1998, p. 147–150). We will explore the consequences of this dialectal variation with respect to the processing of the oral texts.

In the presence of the suffix *-śk-*, the preceding *-d/-t* is elided regardless of its morphological status. This can give rise to several problems:

1. First, we have to add stem variants for all verbs ending in *-d/-t*: *tod+śko* might be realized as *to-śko* (know-PRS.1SG).

2. Second, the biggest problem stems from the fact that passive can be – and frequently is – preceded by the causative suffix *-(e)t-*. The causative suffix might be elided, too, which leads to ambiguity. For instance, the verb form *todma-śk-i-dǐ* can represent two different cases: (i) recognize-PASS-PST-2PL or (ii) recognize-CAUS:PASS-PST-2PL, in the latter of which the causative suffix has been elided. This kind of ambiguity can be partly resolved by rules if there is transitivity information in the dictionary, since intransitive verbs can only have impersonal 3SG passive forms. We have manually added transitivity information to the dictionary. However, in the case of transitive stems or 3SG forms, the ambiguity will remain. Currently, the analyzer does not annotate these transitive verb forms as containing a zero causative to avoid significant amount of ambiguity that would follow. Consequently, the form *todmaśkidǐ*, which actually contains a causative suffix in our corpus, is treated incorrectly by the analyzer.

It should be noted that the same phonological process sometimes works even in the cases where the segment *-śk-* is part of the stem and not a suffix, as with the dialectal verb *uśk̦in̦i* (look), standard form of which is *ućk̦in̦i*. Therefore, we have to locate such verbs in the dictionary and add stem variants for them as well.

Below, we summarize our preliminary notes regarding the morphological peculiarities of the Northern texts, which we have started processing. The Northern dialects share some of the non-standard features described above (epenthetic *-j*, infinitive in *-n*, shortened verbal forms, converbs in *-sa*, consonant assimilation before the suffix *-ja*). Here we only touch upon some of the features absent in Southern texts.

- **A series of personal-local case markers, e.g. *-n̦e*.** Personal-local suffixes are a combination of the marker *-n̦-* with one of the spatial cases, and convey the meaning 'at/to/from/through one's place' (Teplyashina, 1981). They do not lead to ambiguity.

- **Frequentative suffix *-ill̦-* instead of *-il̦-*.** Does not lead to ambiguity.

- **Limitative converb in *-ććoź* instead of *-toź*.** Does not lead to ambiguity.

- **Non-standard forms of *-śk-*.** The suffix *-śk-*, as it was stated above, has several dialectal variants. In the Northern texts, it often appears as *-sk-* and devoices the preceding consonant. Unlike its Southern counterpart, the Northern variant does not pose a problem to the analysis if the transcription is somewhat standardized, e.g. when *todsko* (know-PRS.1SG) is spelled as *тодско* rather than *тоцко* or *тотско*, cf. Section 3.

- **Non-standard forms of personal and reflexive pronouns.** Certain case forms of personal and, especially, reflexive pronouns used in the Northern texts are non-standard, such as *mil'emesti̦* (we.ACC) with the standard form being *mil'emi̦z*. Since these forms of the pronouns are morphologically irregular, all of them need to be stored in the dictionary. We added the dialectal form to the dictionary as well, which did not lead to any ambiguity.

## 4.3 Orthography

Apart from lexical and grammatical challenges, there are also challenges related to orthography. The cases that involve non-standard tokenization are especially problematic. A large share of these cases is represented by compounds which consist of two nominal stems, or by complex numerals. Nominal compounds are frequent in Udmurt, and all but a relatively small number of them are written as two separate words according to the standard orthography. When we transcribed compounds, we wrote them with a hyphen regardless of their lexicalization degree and stress pattern. We took a similar approach in the case of numerals like *kiź odig* (twenty-one), which are always written as separate words in standard Udmurt, but are hyphenated in the corpus. Although hyphenation of all compounds and numerals diverges from the official orthography and does not capture the difference between lexicalized and non-lexicalized compounds, it allows the users to easily find all such instances and decide for themselves.

## 5    User interface

Our corpus will be accessible for the linguistic community through an online web-interface.[12] We use the open source *tsakorpus* platform, which was developed by Timofey Arkhangelskiy and is available under an MIT license[13]. Each ELAN file is passed through morphological analyzer and Constraint Grammar disambiguator. The analyzed file is stored in JSON format, which is then uploaded to an Elasticsearch database. The functions of the web interface include: search by word, lemma, Russian translation, grammatical tags and their combinations; search with regular expressions; search for specific allomorphs of a morpheme; multi-word search; and selecting texts based on metadata values. Users are able to see or download sentences that contain the requested words, listen to the sound aligned with the sentence, get frequency lists of words, and chart word distribution e.g. by dialect. Source Cyrillic orthography and automatically transliterated Uralic Phonetic Alphabet representation are supported. The interface is available in English and Russian, but other languages can be easily added to this list. Currently, we are testing the interface. We intend to make it publicly available in 2018.

## 6    Conclusions

In this paper, we presented an ongoing project in the course of which we are going to develop a sound-aligned corpus of spoken texts in Udmurt dialects. Our workflow consists of transcribing and aligning the texts in ELAN using (mainly) standard orthography, automatic morphological analysis with partial rule-based disambiguation, and publishing the recordings online using a publicly available web interface. Standardization of orthography enables cross-dialectal search and facilitates automatic processing of the texts. We demonstrated that a morphological analyzer for the standard language works sufficiently well for our data, and can be relatively easily adjusted for the annotation to be comparable in quality to that of the standard Udmurt texts. We also outlined the obstacles we faced in the process. Some of them are caused by the inconsistencies of the standard orthography, while others stem from the ambiguity introduced by dialectal variants of morphemes. We believe that the same workflow can be applied by other researchers who have dialectal recordings at hand to efficiently produce valuable dialectal corpora with relatively small investments of time or resources.

## Acknowledgments

We are immensely indebted to the native speakers who participated in the fieldworks and helped our work.

## References

Timofey Arkhangelskiy, Natalia Serdobolskaya, and Maria Usacheva. 2017. Corpus-oriented lexicographic database for Beserman Udmurt. *Acta Linguistica Academica* (64):397–415.

---

[12]For the moment, we do not intend to make the source ELAN files available to the general public.

[13]https://bitbucket.org/tsakorpus/tsakonian_corpus_platform/overview

Eckhard Bick and Tino Didriksen. 2015. CG-3 — Beyond Classical Constraint Grammar. In *Proceedings of the 20th Nordic Conference of Computational Linguistics, NODALIDA 2015, May 11-13, 2015, Vilnius, Lithuania.* Linköping University Electronic Press, Linköpings universitet, 109, pages 31–39.

Rogier Blokland, Marina Fedina, Ciprian-Virgil Gerstenberger, Niko Partanen, Michael Rießler, and Joshua Wilbur. 2015. Language Documentation meets Language Technology. In *Septentrio Conference Series.* pages 8–18.

Svetlana Edygarova. 2014. The varieties of the modern Udmurt language. *Finnish-Ugrische Forschungen* (62):376–398.

László Fejes. 2005. *Összetett szavak finnugor nyelvekben.* Ph.D. thesis, Eötvös Loránd Tudományegyetem.

Valentin V. Kelmakov. 1998. *Kratkij kurs udmurtskoj dialektologii.* Izdatelstvo Udmurtskogo universiteta, Izhevsk.

Olesya Khanina. 2017. Digital resources for Enets. *Acta Linguistica Academica* (64):417–433.

L. E. Kirillova, editor. 2008. *Udmurtsko-russkij slovar.* Izhevsk.

Eszter Simon and Nikolett Mus. 2017. Languages under the influence: Building a database of Uralic languages. In *Proceedings of the Third International Workshop for Computational Linguistics of Uralic Languages.* pages 10–24.

Tamara I. Teplyashina. 1981. O novyx udmurtskix padezhax. In *Congressus Quintus Internationalis Fenno-Ugristarum, Turku.* 20 (27), Pars VI, pages 285–292.

Ruprecht von Waldenfels, Michael Daniel, and Nina Dobrushina. 2014. Why standard orthography? Building the Ustya River Basin corpus, an online corpus of a Russian dialect. In *Computational Linguistics and Intellectual Technologies. Papers from the Annual International Conference "Dialogue".* 13, pages 720–728.

# Automatic Generation of Wiktionary Entries for Finno-Ugric Minority Languages


Zsanett Ferenczi
Research Institute for Linguistics
Hungarian Academy of Sciences
ferenczi.zsanett@nytud.mta.hu

Iván Mittelholcz
mittelholcz.ivan@nytud.mta.hu

Eszter Simon
simon.eszter@nytud.mta.hu



### Abstract

The research presented in this paper aims to generate online content and help to revitalize the digital functions of some Finno-Ugric (FU) minority languages. The practical objective of the research was to create bilingual dictionaries for six FU minority languages (Udmurt, Komi-Permyak, Komi-Zyrian, Meadow Mari, Hill Mari and Northern Saami) paired with four major languages which are important for these communities (English, Finnish, Hungarian, Russian) and to deploy the enriched lexical material on the web in the framework of the collaborative dictionary project Wiktionary. We give an overview of the workflow in which Wiktionary entries were fully automatically generated from automatically created and manually validated translation units. We also give a thorough evaluation, whose results show that we would multiply the number of Wiktionary entries in the aforementioned FU minority languages.



### Tiivistelmä

Tutkimuksen tavoitteena on tuottaa digitaalista sisältöä usealle suomalais-ugrilaiselle vähemmistökielelle, ja edistää niiden kielten elvytystä, eli pelastaa niiden uhanalaisia kieliä häviämiseltä. Tutkimuksen käytännöllisenä tavoitteena oli luoda kaksikielisiä sanakirjoja kuudelle suomalais-ugrilaiselle vähemmistökielelle (nimittäin udmurtille, komipermjakille, komisyrjäänille, niittymarille, vuorimarille ja pohjoissaamelle), yhdistettynä neljään, näille yhteisöille tärkeisiin kieliin (englanti, suomi, unkari ja venäjä). Automaattisesti luodut, sitten käsin tarkastetut, ja morfologisien ja ääntämistietojen kanssa vahvistetut käännökset ladattiin Wikisanakirjaan. Artikkelissa pyrittiin esittelemään koko prosessi tarkasti, minkä aikana Wiktionary-artikkelit luotiin kokonaan automaattisesti. Tutkimuksessa esittelemme myös, miten onnistuisimme moninkertaistamaan Wikisanakirjassa jo olemassa olevien edellä mainittujen suomalais-ugrilaisten vähemmistökielien sanojen lukumäärää.







*Proceedings of the 4th International Workshop for Computational Linguistics for Uralic Languages (IWCLUL 2018)*, pages 39–50,
Helsinki, Finland, January 8–9, 2018. ©2018 Association for Computational Linguistics

**Kivonat**

A cikkben bemutatott kutatás célja, hogy kisebbségi finnugor nyelvek számára nyelvi erőforrásokat állítson elő, melyek segíthetik ezeket a veszélyeztetett
nyelvi közösségeket a revitalizálási folyamatokban. A kutatás során kétnyelvű
szótárakat állítottunk elő olyan nyelvpárokra, melyeknél a forrásnyelv az udmurt,
komi-permják, komi-zürjén, mezei mari, hegyi mari és északi számi nyelvek egyi-
ke, míg a célnyelv az angol, finn, magyar és orosz közül kerül ki. Az automatikusan előállított, majd kézzel ellenőrzött fordítási párok kiejtési és morfológiai
információkkal kiegészítve kerülnek feltöltésre a Wiktionarybe. A cikk bemutat-
ja a teljes munkafolyamatot, amelynek során a Wiktionary-bejegyzések teljesen
automatikusan előállnak. Egy alapos kiértékelésben megmutatjuk azt is, hogy az
általunk létrehozott bejegyzésekkel megsokszorozható a fent említett finnugor
nyelvű szavak száma a célnyelvi Wiktionary-kiadásokban.

# 1   Introduction

The research presented in this paper is part of a project whose general objective is to
provide linguistically based support for several small Finno-Ugric (FU) digital communities to generate online content and help to revitalize the digital functions of some FU
minority languages. The practical objective of the project is to create bilingual dictionaries for six FU minority languages (Udmurt, Komi-Permyak, Komi-Zyrian, Meadow
Mari, Hill Mari and Northern Saami) paired with four major languages which are important for these communities (English, Finnish, Hungarian, Russian) and to deploy
the enriched lexical material on the web in the framework of the collaborative dictionary project Wiktionary.

Even for widely used languages, freely available professional online multilingual
lexical data are scarce; exceptions being BabelNet (Navigli and Ponzetto, 2012) and
open wordnets in a variety of languages, such as Multilingual Central Repository
(Atserias et al., 2004) and MultiWordNet (Pianta et al., 2002). Smaller communities are
often left to their own devices, which can manifest in their affinity towards mastering
other languages to be able to translate or localize information that is unavailable in
their native language.

In the current global economic and information space, we interact via new types
of media, applications of which are e.g. Facebook, Twitter, YouTube, Wikipedia and
other Wikimedia-related initiatives. Social media, powered by Web 2.0 technology
– which actively involves language technology –, are becoming extremely popular,
not only in the Western world where they typically originate from, but also among
virtually any speech communities with internet connection. The new concepts that
are brought to the smaller language communities – such as speakers of FU minority languages – are likely impact everyday lives to a bigger extent than in the case
of larger speech communities, shifting new segments of native language use towards
"globalized" language use. It is an empirical question to what extent, and which dimensions of the language of these speech communities – having been heavily affected
by neighboring or dominating language contacts already – will be pervaded (or even
corrupted) by the usage of new media.

Wiktionary[1] is a collaborative multilingual dictionary project, a sister project of
Wikipedia, available under the same license (CC-BY-SA 3.0 and GNU Free Documentation License). It aims to describe all words of all languages. It has editions in sev-

---

[1] https://www.wiktionary.org/

eral languages using definitions and descriptions in the given language. Entries that are being maintained by a large active digital community are typically fully-fledged, whereas entries in the language domain of a small community can be very sparse, or missing. This situation can be improved by applying language technology methods and automatically creating Wiktionary entries. Using the Wiktionary infrastructure, lexical entries across FU and widely used language versions of Wiktionary can be interlinked. This will enable user communities to access rich, networked lexical material.

The aforementioned FU languages are under-resourced, hence we could not collect enough data for building parallel and comparable corpora, on which the standard dictionary building methods are based. Therefore, conducting experiments with alternative methods was needed. We made experiments with several lexicon building methods utilizing crowd-sourced language resources, such as Wikipedia and Wiktionary (see Section 2). Completely automatic generation of clean bilingual resources is not possible according to the state of the art, but it is possible to create certain lexical resources, termed proto-dictionaries, that can support lexicographic and NLP work. Proto-dictionaries contain candidate translation pairs produced by bilingual dictionary building methods.

Once the proto-dictionaries were prepared, they were merged for each language pair and repeated lines were filtered out. These files were then the object of manual validation by native speakers and linguist experts of the languages. These validated dictionaries containing translation units were the input of generating new Wiktionary entries which were created fully automatically. As the last step of the project, we upload the entries to Wiktionary.

The rest of the article is as follows. In Section 2, the workflow of generating the translation units is shortly presented. Section 3 gives an overview of the process how the Wiktionary entries are generated from the previously created translation units. In Section 4, the steps of uploading the newly created entries are described. We conducted a thorough evaluation of the coverage for proto-dictionaries created by us, which is described in Section 5. The article ends with some conclusions and plans for future work in Section 6.

## 2   Generating the Translation Units

For the creation of the proto-dictionaries, we applied several lexicon building methods utilizing Wikipedia and Wiktionary. For more details on the dictionary creating methods we used, see Benyeda et al. (2016) and Simon and Mittelholcz (2017) – here we only provide a short description.

Wikipedia is not only the largest publicly available database of comparable documents, but it also can be used for bilingual lexicon extraction in several ways. Following Erdmann et al. (2009), we created bilingual dictionaries from Wikipedia title pairs using the interwiki links.

Besides Wikipedia, Wiktionary is also considered as a crowd-sourced language resource which can serve as a source of bilingual dictionary extraction. Although Wiktionary is primarily for human audience, the extraction of underlying data can be automated to a certain degree. Following Ács et al. (2013) and Ács (2014), we applied the `Wikt2dict` tool[2] in two modes. First, we parsed the English, Finnish, Russian and Hungarian editions of Wiktionary and extracted translations from the so-called

---

[2] `https://github.com/juditacs/wikt2dict`

translation tables for the small FU languages we deal with. Second, the collection of translation pairs were expanded with a triangulation method, which is based on the assumption that two expressions are likely to be translations, if they are translations of the same word in a third language.

Besides the proto-dictionaries created by us, the large merged files for the Northern Saami–{English, Finnish, Hungarian} language pairs also contain proto-dictionaries which were not created by us but were downloaded from the Opus corpus (Tiedemann, 2009). These dictionaries contain word pairs from the automatic word alignment created with GIZA++ and the Moses toolkit.

Once the proto-dictionaries were prepared, they were merged for each language pair and repeated lines were filtered out. These raw dictionary files were then the object of manual validation by native speakers and linguist experts of the languages. The instructions for the validators were as follows. The source and the target word must be a valid word in the language concerned, they must be dictionary forms, and they must be translations of each other. If the source word is not a valid source language word, the word pair is treated as wrong. If the source word is a valid word but not a dictionary form, the correct dictionary form should be manually added. If the target word is a good translation of the source word but is not a dictionary form, similarly to the former case, the correct dictionary form should be added. If the target word is not a good translation, a new translation should be given.

The validated dictionaries, however, were not fully clean and ready-to-use, thus several checking and correcting steps were required. As a sanity check, we checked whether the dictionary contains a source and a target word, whether any cells contain suspicious characters, etc. As a consistency check, cases when the target word was provided with a dictionary form as well as a new translation and cases when the source word was treated as wrong but a new translation were added for the target word were filtered out. A cross-language consistency check was also done, in which we checked whether source words were treated consistently in all languages. At the end of this workflow, we got the validated dictionaries containing the translation units, which served then as the input of the evaluation and the newly generated Wiktionary entries.

## 3   Generating the Wiktionary Entries

The manually validated word pairs were used as the source material of newly created potential Wiktionary entries, which contain several obligatory elements. These elements containing morphological and phonetical information were generated fully automatically. For example, in the case of the Northern Saami–English language pair, the Northern Saami word would be an entry in the English Wiktionary: the title of the entry would be the Northern Saami word, while its English definition would be its English translation equivalent.

Each language edition of Wiktionary has its own rules that describe how to create new entries. These determine the structure of the entries and the pieces of information which must be included in each entry. From these descriptions of the four Wiktionary editions into which our entries were uploaded, a generalized description was created that contains the word itself, its language, its POS tag, and its translation equivalent. The only information missing from that list is the POS tag, which could be gathered from morphological analyzers available for these languages. Additional information can also be added to the entries, such as etymology or phonetic (IPA) transcription, however, these are not compulsory elements. IPA transcription is also included in our entries, since these FU languages have freely available tools that provide phonetic transcription and we wanted to enrich the Wiktionary entries with as many pieces of linguistic information as possible applying only automatic tools.

## 3.1 Providing POS Tags

New Wiktionary entries cannot be created without applying templates, which are provided for several word categories including POS classes. Therefore, providing the correct POS tag of a word is essential for generating a Wiktionary entry for that word. POS tags can be gathered from the output of morphological analyzers available for the languages we deal with. However, these are only words without context, thus the standard morphosyntactic disambiguation techniques based on contextual information cannot be used. Therefore, we had to find alternative ways for disambiguation, see Section 3.2.

There are available morphological analyzers for all languages we deal with that we could use to get POS tags for the words. We used the morphological analyzers of Giellatekno[3] for all of the source languages and for Finnish and Russian of the target languages. For Hungarian, we used the emMorph morphological analyzer (Novák et al., 2016), which is also based on the Helsinki Finite-State Technology[4] infrastructure just like the Giellatekno analyzers. For English, we used the hunmorph toolkit (Trón et al., 2005) with English-specific aff and dic files created from English lexicon and grammar files of morphdb, an open source morphological database (Trón et al., 2006). Since we work with different kinds of morphological analyzers providing different output formats, a kind of normalization of tags was needed. Having the normalized tagset, there is no difference in the format of analyses, so that the tags can be used in further steps without having different notations for the same POS tag.

Due to the fact that morphological analyzers only give analysis for single words, multi-word expressions (MWEs) had to be handled differently. In these cases, the last element of the MWE was split, and the MWE was temporarily substituted by its last word. The hypothesis behind this solution is that FU languages are typically head-final languages, thus the head follows its complements, i.e. the head is at the end of the phrase. Therefore, if we get the POS tag of the last element of the phrase, we will know the POS tag of the whole phrase. However, English and Russian are said to be strongly head-initial languages, moreover, even the FU phrase is not always head-final, thus the last element of a MWE in our dictionaries is not always the head. Handling of this phenomenon is described in Section 3.2.

Some validators inserted the particle 'to' before the English translation of verbs. This particle was removed from the input of the morphological analyzer but was kept as a background info and was used in the disambiguating step. The English analyzer gives back many possible analyses for a single word, since most of the English words can be a noun and a verb at the same time. There are cases when the disambiguation is difficult or almost impossible without this extra information. In the English Wiktionary, the 'to' particle must be included in the definition before each English verb, therefore they are later pasted back before the verb.

The output of this process contains five columns that consist of the source word, its possible POS tags, the target word, its possible POS tags and a column that contains information about the 'to' particle.

---

[3] http://giellatekno.uit.no
[4] https://hfst.github.io/

## 3.2 Disambiguating the POS Tags

Disambiguating the POS tags happens in circles. First, we only consider the morphological information of the given word. The second step of the POS disambiguation is a horizontal comparison, when the POS tags of a source word and the POS tags of the corresponding target word are compared, and we get the disambiguated POS tag from this comparison. The third step is a vertical comparison, in which the sets of POS tags added to a word acting as a source word in more translation units are compared.

### 3.2.1 Considering the Morphological Information

Not only the POS tag of the output of the morphological analyzers are utilized, but we keep the lemma, and information on the case and the number. When a word has more than one analysis, a decision has to be made, and these pieces of morphological information can help in this process.

A kind of filtering is possible based on the assumption that the lemma and the input word are the same. Since only dictionary forms were sent to the analyzers, those tags that are the analysis of a non-dictionary form are rejected. For example, in Hungarian, the dictionary form is the nominative singular form in the case of nouns and adjectives and the present 3rd person singular indefinite form in the case of verbs. For example, if the input word is *várat*, the possible analyses are vár [/N] + at [Acc], and vár [/V] + at [_Caus/V] + [Prs.NDef.3Sg], thus the POS tag can only be V (verb), since the other one is an accusative word form, not a dictionary form.

However, there are cases when none of the lemmas is equal to the input word. In the case of MWEs, the lemma is only the last element of the input word, and therefore they must match at the end of the string. If none of the analyses matches the conditions, the set of possible POS tags is left empty.

A filtering happens at the end of this stage, because there are cases when a word gets more than one POS tag, and yet, it can contain redundant information. We keep the POS tags that are the most precise ones, e.g. if the set of POS tags contains both N and Prop (proper noun), then N is removed from the set.

### 3.2.2 Horizontal Comparison

In this step, the disambiguation of POS tags happen based on the comparison of the POS tag set of the source word and that of the target word. A translation pair has two sets of possible POS tags, and assuming that the words participating in a translation pair belong to the same POS, these tags can be reduced in number.

However, it is not correct in all cases. Not all source words has a one-word translation in the target language, and in such cases, the validator gave a MWE that seemed to be the most correct translation of the source word. Since MWEs may not have the head at the end of the phrase, they do not belong to the same POS as the original word.

Within the horizontal comparison, we investigate the intersection of the POS tag set of the source word and that of the target word. The following cases come from this comparison.

When the intersection of the two sets does not contain any POS tags, a decision has to be made in order to get some results for those translation units as well. Once, if the analyzer did not provide any output for the source word, it is the target word that determines the POS tag of the translation. Second, if the set of POS tags of the target word is empty, the source word is the one that determines. In those cases, when neither of the words has a possible tag, the translation candidate has to be removed, because no correct POS tag can be provided.

Another possible difficulty is that a single POS tag cannot be determined because of the fact that English and Hungarian phrases were split up by the last space, and although in Hungarian the head of a phrase is likely to be at the end, in English it is only so in some noun phrases. If the target word is a MWE, the target language is English, and the possible POS tags do not contain the N tag, these candidates are removed from the list of possible Wiktionary entries.

If the intersection of the two sets contains only one element, it is treated as the correct POS tag for that translation pair. If a correct POS tag is found, the result is saved into a list with the source word, because it may be used in the vertical comparison.

When the translation pair has more than one POS tag in common, the number of common tags is tried to be reduced by some rules. One of them is based on that the verbs of the FU languages have a particular ending (e.g. Northern Saami verbs end with '-t'), so if the source word has this verb ending, and the V tag is found among the common tags, then the source word is possibly a verb and is marked as that.

The number of the common POS tags can also be reduced for verbs, if the fifth column in the input contained the word 'TO'. It means that the validator inserted an extra 'to' before the English target word. Since it is a manually added information, it is assumed to be a reliable information about the POS of the word.

### 3.2.3 Vertical Comparison

When the sets of the POS tags of the source word and that of the target word have only one POS tag in common, the result is saved in a list with the source word, and it can be used for disambiguation. This is based on the observation that if a source word occurs in more than one translation unit, its corresponding target words are synonyms in most of the cases. Therefore, we assumed that the source word has the same POS tag in all of the translation units. When two sets have more than one POS tag in common, it is checked whether the source word has a former meaning with only one possible tag.

There are, however, cases when each translation unit with the same source word has multiple POS tags. In this case, the aforementioned method cannot be used, but those can still be disambiguated, if their sets are compared. For example, the Komi-Permyak word *ань* has three different equivalents in English: *female*, *mother*, and *woman*. These words have different sets of POS tags, namely *female* is marked as a N and as an A (adjective), while *mother* and *woman* have the tags N and V. The intersection of these three sets is undoubtedly N. A specific case of this is when the source word and the target word also have more POS tags, and all of them are correct. For example, the Meadow Mari word *нарынче* ('yellow') is an adjective and a noun, just like in English. In these cases, both tags are kept.

This process outputs three columns: the source word, the target word, and the correct POS tag. If a translation unit has more than one POS tag, the first two columns are repeated, thus it is treated as a new translation unit.

## 3.3 Adding IPA Transcription

The next step was to gather phonetic transcription to enrich the content of Wiktionary entries. We used the Mari Web Project's automatic transcription tool (Bradley, 2017) for generating IPA transcription for Hill Mari, Meadow Mari, Komi-Permyak,

Komi-Zyrian, and Udmurt. For Northern Saami, we used an FST compiled from the
`text2ipa` source files of the Giellatekno infrastructure[5].

All of the source FU languages has a transcription tool available, so every source
word was sent to the tool and the result was saved so that it could be used when
generating entries. The only problem occurred when the string contained digits and
when proper nouns were sent to the transcription tool. Since the pronunciation of
proper nouns might differ from the phonetics of the language, IPA transcription was
not added to entries having only a proper noun as POS tag or entries having a digit
in the source word.

### 3.4 Putting the Bits Together

Having all pieces of information, the next step is putting them together thus generating the final entries to be uploaded to Wiktionary in the last step. Although different
editions of Wiktionary have different rules determining the structure of the articles, it
was possible to create a template that covers all four editions to which the generated
entries would be uploaded. (Consider that the languages called as target languages so
far are now the languages of the Wiktionary editions to which the entries containing
source words are to be uploaded.)

Before generating actual entries, it must be checked whether the word already
exists in Wiktionary, and some further modifications concerning the existing data
also had to be made. First, those words that already exist in the given edition of
Wiktionary are filtered out: entries for those words which are in the last Wiktionary
dump are not generated. Second, if a source word has more than one translation,
the translation units can have the same POS tag, and in this case, they must be listed
under the same POS header. If the translation unit has more than one POS tag, the
translation must be repeated under each POS header in the entry.

After having extracted the words to be uploaded and having the list of translations
for each POS tag, entries can be created. Each entry has a headword which is the
source word. When uploading to Wiktionary, Pywikibot (see Section 4) will create
a page that has the same name as this headword. Each entry contains one or more
POS headers, and one or more translations under each header. If a source word is an
existing word in more languages, then these two (or more) entries have to be merged
and listed under the same headword. At the end of this step, an output file is created
which meets the requirements of the input file of `Pywikibot`.

## 4 Uploading the Entries

Uploading multiple entries to Wiktionary can be automated. MediaWiki has a bot
called Pywikibot[6], that can automate work on MediaWiki sites such as Wiktionary
or Wikipedia. This library has a script called `pagefromfile`[7], which allows to create
pages on Wiktionary (or other MediaWiki sites) from text files. That script reads the
file and recognizes the template that can be configured, and it will create Wiktionary
entries according to these. Each page must be separated by some characters, and each
headword is used to define the name of the page. We run it with the option `--safe`,


[5]`https://victorio.uit.no/langtech/trunk/langs/sme/src/phonetics/`
[6]`https://www.mediawiki.org/wiki/Manual:Pywikibot`
[7]`https://www.mediawiki.org/wiki/Manual:Pywikibot/pagefromfile.py`

which means that if a certain page already exists, the bot will not upload or refresh the existing page but skips it.

Fully automated uploading of large amounts of newly created Wiktionary entries is however not supported in the Wiktionary community. We have to ask the administrators of each Wiktionary edition to allow us to upload our entries. Unfortunately, we did not get the permission from all Wiktionary editions, therefore, now we can only provide numbers based on the last downloaded Wiktionary dumps, see Table 1.

## 5   Evaluation

The manual validation and correction of the automatically generated proto-dictionaries has a twofold aim. First, the performance of dictionary creating methods can be compared. For more details on the results, see Simon and Mittelholcz (2017). Second, we get the number of word pairs which can be used for upload to the Wiktionary. In this section, we provide a thorough evaluation of generating Wiktionary entries.

Measuring of the coverage of a dictionary is far from trivial. It can be measured by comparing it to a word list of a corpus, or to a frequency list generated from a corpus. Or, it can be measured by comparing the number of its entries to that of another – ideally hand-crafted – dictionary. Since our newly created word pairs are to be transformed into Wiktionary articles, for this purpose, here we used Wiktionary, which is not an expert-built lexicon but manually edited by thousands of contributors.

Table 1 contains the figures for this evaluation. We use ISO 639-3 language codes for the individual languages: koi: Komi-Permyak, kpv: Komi-Zyrian, mhr: Meadow Mari, mrj: Hill Mari, sme: Northern Saami, udm: Udmurt; eng: English, fin: Finnish, hun: Hungarian, rus: Russian. However, several Wiktionary editors do not differentiate between individual languages but use macrolanguage codes (chm for Mari languages, kom for Komi languages), therefore we had to merge the dictionaries for the two Mari and for the two Komi languages.

The first column of the table ('all') shows the total number of word pairs gathered with all methods for the language pair. As can be seen, hundreds or thousands of translation candidates were generated for each language pair. However, not all of these word pairs are correct translation candidates, therefore we needed to extract the useful word pairs from the merged dictionary for each language pair. The second column ('useful') shows the number of useful word pairs which comprise all word pairs except of the ones in which the source word is not a valid word, since correct dictionary forms and translation equivalents were manually added by human validators.

As mentioned above, our Wiktionary articles are generated fully automatically. The POS tag of an entry is a compulsory element of an article, which is gathered from the output of morphological analyzers through several disambiguating steps, as detailed in Section 3.1 and 3.2. The number of the useful word pairs drops in line with the increase of source language words for which we could not provide a POS tag. Before uploading new entries, it must be checked whether an entry with the same word already exists in Wiktionary. If yes, it also decreases the number of uploadable word pairs. Column 'remain' contains the decreased number of the word pairs ready to upload. We have also got the number of the source language words already existing in the target language Wiktionary ('wikt'), along with the number of the words being in both lists ('comm'). These numbers come from the Wiktionary dumps[8] and are

---

[8]Wiktionary dumps used in the evaluation: eng: 06-Nov-2017, fin: 05-Nov-2017, rus: 07-Nov-2017, hun:

"theoretical" numbers in the sense that they are not the numbers of actually uploaded entries, which can only be known after uploading.

From the columns 'wikt' and 'comm', the number of brand new entries ('new') created by us can be easily counted, along with a kind of coverage ('cover'), which is a ratio of the number of common words to the number of words already being in Wiktionary, thus it is the degree of overlap with Wiktionary. Consider that the coverage for each language pair drops as the size of the relevant Wiktionary grows. The last column ('improv') contains the ratio of the number of the new Wiktionary entries to one of the already existing ones which shows the improvement in the amount of Wiktionary entries of the given source language in the given target language edition of Wiktionary.

| langs | all (#) | useful (#) | remain (#) | wikt (#) | comm (#) | new (#) | cover (%) | improv (%) |
|---|---|---|---|---|---|---|---|---|
| kom–eng: | 2,153 | 2,111 | 656 | 54 | 25 | 631 | 46.30 | 1,168.52 |
| kom–fin: | 1,169 | 1,162 | 687 | 42 | 27 | 660 | 64.29 | 1,571.43 |
| kom–hun: | 1,063 | 1,025 | 699 | 152 | 35 | 664 | 23.03 | 436.84 |
| kom–rus: | 1,155 | 1,148 | 673 | 465 | 223 | 450 | 47.96 | 96.77 |
| chm–eng: | 4,883 | 4,883 | 1,671 | 347 | 53 | 1,618 | 15.27 | 466.28 |
| chm–fin: | 3,578 | 3,578 | 1,905 | 443 | 213 | 1,692 | 48.08 | 381.94 |
| chm–hun: | 2,589 | 2,589 | 1,634 | 34 | 12 | 1,622 | 35.29 | 4,770.59 |
| chm–rus: | 2,542 | 2,542 | 1,497 | 848 | 202 | 1,295 | 23.82 | 152.71 |
| sme–eng: | 6,041 | 5,556 | 2,531 | 4,073 | 882 | 1,649 | 21.65 | 40.49 |
| sme–fin: | 7,100 | 6,463 | 2,862 | 817 | 422 | 2,440 | 51.65 | 298.65 |
| sme–hun: | 4,969 | 4,509 | 2,392 | 206 | 146 | 2,246 | 70.87 | 1,090.29 |
| sme–rus: | 4,373 | 4,172 | 2,034 | 306 | 237 | 1,797 | 77.45 | 587.25 |
| udm–eng: | 2,087 | 2,069 | 754 | 32 | 15 | 739 | 46.88 | 2,309.38 |
| udm–fin: | 1,700 | 1,694 | 828 | 55 | 45 | 783 | 81.82 | 1,423.64 |
| udm–hun: | 1,204 | 1,198 | 739 | 128 | 69 | 670 | 53.91 | 523.44 |
| udm–rus: | 1,226 | 1,211 | 578 | 644 | 247 | 331 | 38.35 | 51.40 |

Table 1: Results for the language pairs.

# 6 Conclusion and Future Work

Wiktionary is not only used for extracting data from it, but we want to give our results back to the community, thus translation pairs enriched with obligatory pieces of linguistic information are to uploaded as new entries into Wiktionary. Before uploading new entries, it is needed to be checked whether an entry with the same word already exists in Wiktionary. From this, the number of brand new entries created by us can be easily counted, along with a kind of coverage and improvement in the number of Wiktionary entries. As can be seen from the results, the latter is very impressive, thus, with our dictionaries, we would multiply the number of Wiktionary entries in the aforementioned FU minority languages. Since automatic uploading of entries is

06-Nov-2017.

not supported by the Wiktionary community, we have to ask for permission to upload our newly created entries into Wiktionary.

We provide freely available professional online multilingual lexical data for digital communities of some FU minority languages with Wiktionary entries. However, lexical data can be provided in several other ways. We plan to make them available in standard data formats (e.g. `tsv`, `XML`) which are easy to apply in further lexicographic or NLP subtasks. We also want to convert our data into the data format following the conventions of linguistic linked open data and provide them via our web site or via the repositories of dictionary families such as Giellatekno and Apertium.

## Acknowledgments

The research reported in the paper was conducted with the support of the Hungarian Scientific Research Fund (OTKA) grant #107885. We are grateful to the reviewers for their valuable comments.

## References

J. Ács. 2014. Pivot-based multilingual dictionary building using Wiktionary. In *9th Language Resources and Evaluation Conference*. ELRA, Reykjavik.

J. Ács, K. Pajkossy, and A. Kornai. 2013. Building basic vocabulary across 40 languages. In *6th Workshop on Building and Using Comparable Corpora*. ACL, Sofia, pages 52–58.

J. Atserias, L. Villarejo, G. Rigau, E. Agirre, J. Carroll, B. Magnini, and P. Vossen. 2004. The MEANING Multilingual Central Repositoryse. In *Proceedings of the Second International Global WordNet Conference (GWC'04)*. Brno, Czech Republic.

Ivett Benyeda, Péter Koczka, and Tamás Váradi. 2016. Creating seed lexicons for under-resourced languages. In *GLOBALEX 2016 workshop*. ELRA, Portorož.

Jeremy Bradley. 2017. Transcribe.mari-language.com. *Acta Linguistica Academica* 64(3):369–382. https://doi.org/10.1556/2062.2017.64.3.3.

M. Erdmann, K. Nakayama, T. Hara, and S. Nishio. 2009. An Approach for Extracting Bilingual Terminology from Wikipedia. *ACM Transactions on Multimedia Computing, Communications, and Applications* 5(4):1–17.

Roberto Navigli and Simone Paolo Ponzetto. 2012. BabelNet: The automatic construction, evaluation and application of a wide-coverage multilingual semantic network. *Artificial Intelligence* 193:217–250.

Attila Novák, Borbála Siklósi, and Csaba Oravecz. 2016. A new integrated open-source morphological analyzer for Hungarian. In *Proceedings of the Tenth International Conference on Language Resources and Evaluation (LREC 2016)*. European Language Resources Association (ELRA), Paris, France.

Emanuele Pianta, Luisa Bentivogli, and Christian Girardi. 2002. MultiWordNet: Developing and Aligned Multilingual Database. In *Proceedings of the First International Conference on Global WordNet*. Mysore, India, pages 293–302.

Eszter Simon and Iván Mittelholcz. 2017. Evaluation of Dictionary Creating Methods for Under-Resourced Languages. In Kamil Ekštein and Václav Matoušek, editors, *Text, Speech and Dialogue*. Springer International Publishing, Prague, Czech Republic, volume 10415 of *Lecture Notes in Artificial Intelligence*, pages 246–254.

Jörg Tiedemann. 2009. News from OPUS - A collection of multilingual parallel corpora with tools and interfaces. In Nicolas Nicolov, Galia Angelova, and Ruslan Mitkov, editors, *Recent Advances in Natural Language Processing V: Selected Papers from RANLP 2007*, John Benjamins, Borovets, pages 237–248.

Viktor Trón, Gyögy Gyepesi, Péter Halácsy, András Kornai, László Németh, and Dániel Varga. 2005. Hunmorph: Open Source Word Analysis. In *Proceedings of the ACL Workshop on Software*. Association for Computational Linguistics, Ann Arbor, Michigan, pages 77–85.

Viktor Trón, Péter Halácsy, Péter Rebrus, András Rung, Péter Vajda, and Eszter Simon. 2006. Morphdb.hu: Hungarian lexical database and morphological grammar. In *Proceedings of the Fifth International Conference on Language Resources and Evaluation (LREC'06)*. pages 1670–1673.

# Development of an Open Source Natural Language Generation Tool for Finnish

Mika Hämäläinen
University of Helsinki
Department of Modern Languages
`mika.hamalainen@helsinki.fi`

Jack Rueter
University of Helsinki
Department of Modern Languages
`jack.rueter@helsinki.fi`

## Abstract

We present an open source Python library to automatically produce syntactically correct Finnish sentences when only lemmas and their relations are provided. The tool resolves automatically morphosyntax in the sentence such as agreement and government rules and uses Omorfi to produce the correct morphological forms. In this paper, we discuss how case government can be learned automatically from a corpus and incorporated as a part of the natural language generation tool. We also present how agreement rules are modelled in the system and discuss the use cases of the tool such as its initial use as part of a computational creativity system, called Poem Machine.

## Tiivistelmä

Tässä artikkelissa esittelemme avoimen lähdekoodin Python-kirjaston kieliopillisten lauseiden automaattista tuottamista varten suomen kielelle. Kieliopilliset rakenteet pystytään tuottamaan pelkkien lemmojen ja niiden välisten suhteiden avulla. Työkalu ratkoo vaadittavan morfosyntaktiset vaatimukset kuten kongruenssin ja rektion automaattisesti ja tuottaa morfologisesti oikean muodon Omorfin avulla. Esittelemme tavan, jolla verbien rektiot voidaan poimia automaattisesti korpuksesta ja yhdistää osaksi NLG-järjestelmää. Esittelemme, miten kongruenssi on mallinnettu osana järjestelmää ja kuvaamme työkalun alkuperäisen käyttötarkoituksen osana laskennallisesti luovaa Runokone-järjestelmää.

## 1   Introduction

Natural language generation is a task that requires knowledge about the syntax and morphology of the language to be generated. Such knowledge can partially be coded

---



The source code is released in GitHub `https://github.com/mikahama/syntaxmaker`



*Proceedings of the 4th International Workshop for Computational Linguistics for Uralic Languages (IWCLUL 2018)*, pages 51–58,
Helsinki, Finland, January 8–9, 2018. ©2018 Association for Computational Linguistics

by hand into a computational system, but part of the knowledge is better obtained automatically such as case government for verbs.

Having a computer create poetry automatically is a challenging task. Even more so in the context of a morphologically rich language such as Finnish which makes generating grammatical sentences, even when they are not creative, a challenge. Therefore having a syntactically solid system as a part of the poem generation process is extremely important.

In this paper, we present an open-source tool for producing syntactically correct Finnish sentences. This tool is used as a part of an NLG pipeline in producing Finnish poetry automatically. The poem generation part of the pipeline is out of the scope of this paper.

## 2   Related work

Previously in the context of poetry generation in Finnish (Toivanen et al., 2012), the problem of syntax has been solved by taking a ready-made poem, analyzing it morphologically and replacing some of the words in it, inflecting them with the morphology of the original words. This, however, does not make it possible to generate entirely new sentences, and it fails to take agreement or government rules into account, instead it expects agreement and government to be followed automatically if words with sufficient similarity are used in substitutes.

Another take on generating Finnish poetry in a human-computer co-creativity setting (Kantosalo et al., 2015) was to use sentences extracted from the Project Gutenberg's children's literature in Finnish. These sentences were treated as "poetry fragments" and they were used to generate poems by combining them together in a randomized fashion. This method indeed gives syntactically better results than the one described in (Toivanen et al., 2012), as it puts human-written sentences together, but it doesn't allow any variation in the poem apart from the order of the sentences in the poem.

Reiter (1994) identifies four different steps in an NLG pipeline. Those are content determination, sentence planning, surface generation, and morphology and formatting. In the content determination step, an input is given to the NLG system, e.g. in the form of a query to obtain desired information from the system. Based on this query, a semantic representation is produced addressing the results to the query. In other words, this step decides what information is to be conveyed to the user in the final output sentence, but also how it will be communicated in the rhetorical planning of the sentence.

The sentence planner will then get the semantic representation as input and produce an abstract linguistic form which contains the words to be used in the output and their syntactic relations. This step bears no knowledge of how the syntax will actually be realized, i.e., agreement or government rules, instead it applies the chosen words and how they are related to one another.

The last two steps of the pipeline deal with the actual realization of the syntax in the sentence. It is the task of the surface generator to handle the linguistic expression of the abstract linguistic structure. It means resolving agreement, forming questions in a syntactically correct manner, negation and so on. The actual word forms required are produced in the morphology step.

# 3   The Finnish NLG tool

The tool, Syntax Maker, described in this paper focuses on the surface generation step of the NLG pipeline described by Reiter (1994). It is used as a part of a complete NLG pipeline for producing Finnish poetry and is currently in place in the Poem Machine[1] system. This tool was made as a part of the poem generation system in order to solve the problem of creating novel, grammatical sentences not tackled by the previous Finnish poem generators. Taking an NLG point of view hasn't been studied before in the case of Finnish poetry, which is a shame since Finnish, unlike English, has a rich morphosyntax. This rich morphosyntax must be given proper attention if the computational creativity system is to be given more freedom to produce sentences of its own, using its own choice of words in a sentence that might cause other words around them to undergo morphological change as dictated by agreement and government.

Syntax Maker only knows the morphology needed in the level of tags. For example, it knows what case to use for a noun and what person to use for a verb. Actual morphological forms are generated using Omorfi (Pirinen et al., 2017).

## 3.1   Syntactic representation

Syntax Maker is designed to take the abstract linguistic structure of a sentence as its input. This structure consists of part-of-speech specific phrases each of which have their head word in lemmatized form. The phrases are nested under each other so that the highest possible root of the tree is a verb phrase.

When the phrases are nested together, they need to be added in proper slots to fulfill the requirements of agreement and government. For example, a noun phrase that is to act as a direct object of a verb phrase has to be nested in the verb phrase slot *dir_object*. In dealing with verb phrases, Syntax Maker automatically deduces the possible slots based on the verbs used as heads. In other words, Syntax Maker, determines the valency of a verb automatically and assigns values such as transitive, ditransitive or intransitive. On an abstract level, the phrases and their structures are defined manually.[2]

Using phrase structures gives us an easier way to implement the needed functionalities. Since the structure of phrases is similar for different parts-of-speech, we can reuse the same code across different parts-of-speech. The division into part-of-speech specific phrases gives us more freedom in expressing their peculiarities such as agreement and government rules and what kind of phrases can be nested under them. These structures come with a predefined word order, but it's not enforced by Syntax Maker. In other words, the word order in a phrase can be shuffled at will without losing the government or agreement information. Even with an altered word order, Syntax Maker can resolve the proper morphology correctly. The phrase structures are defined in JSON outside of the source code of Syntax Maker written in Python.

## 3.2   Handling government

Case government rules for adpositions have been hand coded. This can be attributed to the fact that there is only a very limited number of adpositions in Finnish, and it takes little time for a native speaker to write down the case required of a noun

---

[1] `http://runokone.cs.helsinki.fi/`

[2] These structures are available on `https://github.com/mikahama/syntaxmaker/blob/master/grammar.json`

phrase when it serves as complement to a given adpositional phrase. The analogous treatment of verbs, however, would be overly time consuming and laborious, and hence this has been automated.

As Finnish is an accusative language, the object is marked with a specific case. The case used depends on the verb in question and thus has to be specified for each verb separately. We obtain the case government information together with verb transitivity automatically from The Finnish Internet Parsebank (Kanerva et al., 2014) syntactic bi-grams.

Each line of the automatically parsed Parsebank bi-gram data consists of two word forms connected by a syntactic relation in the order in which they appeared in the sentence. These word forms are accompanied by their lemma, part-of-speech, morphology and syntactic annotation.

To extract the cases in which nouns have been linked to verbs, we look for lines in which the first word form has *V* as its part-of-speech tag and the second word form has *N* part-of-speech and *NUM_Sg* in its morphology. The reason why we limit the search to singular nouns only is that, in Finnish, a verb that takes its object in genitive in singular, takes it in nominative in plural, e.g. *syön kakun* and *syön kakut* but not **syön kakkujen*. Therefore taking plural objects into account as well would introduce more undesired complexity. Furthermore, we ignore all nouns where the lemma and word from are the same. This is done because the noun in question would then either be in the nominative, which is not an object case, or it will have been given an improper analysis in which case no lemmatization has been performed. Examples of this kind of wrong analyses in the corpus are *kattella/kattella/N/NUM_Sg* and *kasteleen/kasteleen/N/NUM_Sg*. For each bi-gram filling these criteria, we store the lemma of the verb and the case the related noun was in. This gives us a dictionary[3] of verbs and frequencies for noun cases associated with each verb.

The resulting dictionary is then used to determine the transitivity of a verb and the most frequent case for its object(s). This dictionary consists also of a plethora of non-verbs such as *Ljubuški* and *Dodonpa* as a result of erroneous parsing in the Parsebank data. This, however, causes no problems in the system because the dictionary also contains a extensive number of real, lemmatized verbs. Given that Syntax Maker operates on the level of surface generation, it is not actively involved in choosing the words in the NLG task. This means that, unless Syntax Maker is specifically instructed to use a non-verb it happens to know as a verb, it won't. This noise in the verb noun case dictionary, however, has no real effect on the grammaticality of the generated sentences.

The transitivity and most frequent case of the object is determined for a given verb by the verb noun case dictionary. The system is coded to accept the genitive, partitive, elative and illative as possible direct object cases and the essive, translative, ablative, allative and illative cases as indirect object cases. When the system defines whether a verb can take a direct object, it requires the relative frequency of one of the direct object cases to be above 23% of all the possible cases the verb has been seen with. For ditransitivity, the threshold is 18% for an indirect object case. Ditransitivity will not be considered if the verb is determined not to have a direct object. These threshold values have been adjusted by hand after looking at the performance of the system with a handful of verbs used in testing.

The genitive serves another use in Finnish syntax in addition to marking the direct

---

[3] The verb-noun case dictionrary is released on `https://github.com/mikahama/syntaxmaker/blob/master/verb_valences_new.json`

object. If the most frequent direct object case is genitive, we preform an additional check to see that it really is being used as an object function. The verb has to also has enough partitive case, over 23%, so that we can safely say that genitive indeed can be used as an object. This is because in Finnish, verbs that take their direct object in the genitive, also accept partitive in certain contexts such as in the expression of differences in aspect or negation.

## 3.3  Modelling agreement

Agreement, unlike government, is something that does not need to be extracted from a corpus. It is a rather straightforward thing and can be modelled with hand-written rules. In Finnish the predicate verb agrees in person and number with the subject, and adjective attributes agree in case and number with the head noun.

Since all the phrase types in our system are modelled in a similar way, it is easy to introduce agreement rules in the phrase structures. In a phrase structure, we define a key that is either *parent* referring to the parent phrase of the current phrase or a key to the list of *component*. Component lists all the possible syntactic positions for nested phrases such as *subject* or *dir_object*. Even though there aren't many agreement relations in Finnish, by modelling them in the external grammar file, we hope to make it easier to add more languages to the system in the future.

When Syntax Maker produces a sentence, it starts to process the syntactic tree phrase by phrase. For each phrase, it looks at the defined agreement relationship and copies the morphological information from the phrase defined to be agreed with. The agreement relation in the grammar file states the morphological tags which should be copied, for example in the case of an adjective phrase, the tags are *CASE* and *NUM*.

## 3.4  Modifying the verb phrase

Apart from just providing basic grammaticality by resolving agreement and government, Syntax Maker also provides means to modify verb phrases to produce more complex, yet grammatical sentences.

Syntax Maker can be used to negate sentences. When a sentence is negated, a new phrase with the head *ei* is added to the components of the verb phrase as *aux*. The new phrase has an agreement relation *parent->subject: PERS, NUM* and the verb phrase containing the predicate verb is tagged as *NEG* so that it will be conjugated as such when the full sentence is produced as text. The case of the direct object is also changed to partitive if the most frequent direct object case of the verb is genitive, in compliance with Finnish grammar.

Mood and tense are also handled by Syntax Maker. In the case of the prefect, the auxiliary verb *olla* is set as the new head of the verb phrase and the old head is moved to a new subordinate phrase with the part-of-speech value *PastParticiple* and agreement *parent->subject: NUM*. This makes sense from the point of view of Syntax Maker since *olla* is the verb that is conjugated normally while the participle form only agrees with the number of the subject. Other auxiliary verbs can be added in a similar fashion, where the auxiliary verb substitutes the original head and the verb is moved to a nested phrase with the morphology required by the auxiliary verb.

Passive voice is handled by creating a dummy phrase as a subject with the morphological tags *PERS = 4* and *NUM = PE*. This will automatically make the verb agree with the dummy phrase's morphology and produce the correct form as output. Also,

if the verb takes its direct object in genitive, the government rule is changed so that
the direct object will be in the nominative.

A sentence can also be turned into an interrogative one. This adds an additional
morphological tag *CLIT = KO* to the head of the verb phrase and moves it to the
beginning of the whole sentence. Syntax Maker does not produce punctuation, so a
question mark has to be appended to the end of the sentence at a different level in the
NLG pipeline.

## 4   Evaluation

In this part, we evaluate how accurately Syntax Maker can produce verb phrases. We
limit this evaluation to the automatically extracted information used by Syntax Maker
because it is more prone to errors than the hand written rules. This means that we are
evaluating two things in the generated output: the predicted valency i.e. how many
objects the verb can take and the predicted case for the object.

In order to do the evaluation, we take a hundred Finnish verbs at random from the
Finnish Wiktionary[4]. These verbs are then given as input to Syntax Maker to produce
verb phrases out of them. The valency and object cases are then checked by hand to
conduct the evaluation phase.

|  | too low | too high | correct |
|---|---|---|---|
| **valency prediction** | 28% | 5% | 67% |

Table 1: Accuracy in predicting valency

Syntax maker predicts the number of objects correctly 67% of the time and 28%
of the time too low. This is acceptable in the task of poem generation where we
are interested in generating syntactically correct poems. Having too few objects in
the generated output only creates an ellipsis that doesn't result in incorrect syntax.
However, in other NLG tasks outside of the scope of poem generation, the objects
might be important and thus having a higher accuracy is something to work towards.

|  | case correct | case incorrect | no object |
|---|---|---|---|
| **object case prediction** | 50% | 4% | 46% |

Table 2: Accuracy in predicting object case

In the test set, Syntax Maker produced a wrong case only 4% of the time. 46% of
the verbs were either truly intransitive or didn't take an object according to Syntax
Maker. In other words, by just taking into account the transitive verbs recognized by
Syntax Maker, the accuracy reached to 93%. This means that Syntax Maker is very
good at coming up with the correct case but not as good at determining the valency
accurately.

## 5   Future work

At the current state, Syntax Maker doesn't handle all parts of the Finnish grammar.
For instance, it doesn't have the functionality to express aspectual difference by alter-

---

[4] From a Wiktionary dump on https://dumps.wikimedia.org/fiwiktionary/

ing between genitive and partitive objects. In addition, it has only a limited knowledge of the transitivity of verbs. Novel automated ways should be studied to solve this shortcoming.

In the future, Syntax Maker should be tested as a part of the NLG pipeline in uses other than poetry generation as well. This might reveal new requirements for the system that do not appear in the task of poetry generation. This might also reveal missing functionalities both in the generation of syntax and the API provided by the library that are needed in other NLG tasks.

Including small Uralic languages in this tool is also in our interest for the future. This is because having an NLG system would be especially useful in the case of minority languages, for example in generation of news automatically in these languages.

## 6 Conclusions

In this paper we have presented an open source Python library called Syntax Maker. The library was made to be used as a low-level syntax producer in a new NLG pipeline for producing Finnish poetry and is currently in place in a computational creativity system known as Poem Machine[5]. By embracing the notion of separation of concerns in the software architecture of the system, Syntax Maker can be used in a multitude of contexts outside of computational creativity applications as an all-purpose tool for producing grammatical Finnish. To achieve this goal, a method for extracting the information needed to resolve verbal agreement automatically was presented and evaluated.

## Acknowledgments

This work has been supported by the Academy of Finland under grant 276897 (CLiC)

## References

Jenna Kanerva, Juhani Luotolahti, Veronika Laippala, and Filip Ginter. 2014. Syntactic n-gram collection from a large-scale corpus of internet finnish. In *Proceedings of the Sixth International Conference Baltic HLT*.

Anna Kantosalo, Jukka Toivanen, and Hannu Toivonen. 2015. Interaction evaluation for human-computer co-creativity: A case study. In *Proceedings of the Sixth International Conference on Computational Creativity*. pages 276–283.

Tommi A Pirinen, Inari Listenmaa, Ryan Johnson, Francis M. Tyers, and Juha Kuokkala. 2017. Open morphology of finnish. LINDAT/CLARIN digital library at the Institute of Formal and Applied Linguistics, Charles University. http://hdl.handle.net/11372/LRT-1992.

Ehud Reiter. 1994. Has a consensus nl generation architecture appeared, and is it psycholinguistically plausible? In *Proceedings of the Seventh International Workshop on Natural Language Generation*. INLG '94.

---

[5] Poem Machine can be used on `http://runokone.cs.helsinki.fi/`

Jukka Toivanen, Hannu Toivonen, Alessandro Valitutti, and Oskar Gross. 2012. Corpus-based generation of content and form in poetry. In *Proceedings of the Third International Conference on Computational Creativity*.

# Guessing lexicon entries using finite-state methods

Kimmo Koskenniemi
University of Helsinki
Department of Modern Languages
`kimmo.koskenniemi@helsinki.fi`

### Abstract

A practical method for interactive guessing of LEXC lexicon entries is presented. The method is based on describing groups of similarly inflected words using regular expressions. The patterns are compiled into a finite-state transducer (FST) which maps any word form into the possible LEXC lexicon entries which could generate it. The same FST can be used (1) for converting conventional headword lists into LEXC entries, (2) for interactive guessing of entries, (3) for corpus-assisted interactive guessing and (4) guessing entries from corpora. A method of representing affixes as a table is presented as well how the tables can be converted into LEXC format for several different purposes including morphological analysis and entry guessing. The method has been implemented using the HFST finite-state transducer tools and its Python embedding plus a number of small Python scripts for conversions. The method is tested with a near complete implementation of Finnish verbs. An experiment of generating Finnish verb entries out of corpus data is also described as well as a creation of a full-scale analyzer for Finnish verbs using the conversion patterns.

### Tiivistelmä

Artikkelissa esitellään menetelmä, jonka avulla käyttäjä voi määrittää LEXC-leksikkoon sopivia uusia hakusanoja. Menetelmässä kuvataan kukin taivutusluokka säännöllisten lausekkeiden avulla. Samoja lausekkeita voidaan käyttää toisaalta tavanomaisen sanakirjan sanaluettelon konversioon ja toisaalta yksittäisten hakusanojen määrittämiseen siten, että käyttäjä antaa haluamansa hakusanan eri muotoja, kunnes hakusana on yksiselitteisesti määrätty. Arvaaminen voidaan suorittaa myös korpuksista kerättyjen tietojen avulla, jolloin oikea hakusana löytyy nopeammin. Myös pelkän sanalistan perusteella voidaan arvata hakusanoja. Menetelmä on toteutettu käyttäen HFST:n äärellistilaisten transduktorien työkaluja ja erityisesti käyttäen niitä Python-ohjelmointikielestä käsin. Lisäksi on tehty muutamia lyhyitä Python-skriptejä, joilla tietoja muunnetaan eri muodoista toisiinsa. Menetelmää on testattu soveltamalla sitä lähes kattavaan suomen kielen verbien taivutusmalliin. Menetelmiä on kokeiltu alustavasti toisaalta hakusanojen automaattiseksi muodostamiseksi tekstikorpuksen sanalistasta ja toisaalta täysimittaisen suomen kielen verbien morfologisen jäsentimen muodossa.



*Proceedings of the 4th International Workshop for Computational Linguistics for Uralic Languages (IWCLUL 2018)*, pages 59–77,
Helsinki, Finland, January 8–9, 2018. ©2018 Association for Computational Linguistics

# 1    Introduction

Creating lexical entries is an important and time consuming task for any language. For lesser resourced languages with a rich morphology the task is particularly relevant. Building a lexicon requires often not only plenty of time and labour but also specific training. Thus, there is an obvious need for automating this task.

This paper describes the process of generating entries for computational morphological analysis in the framework of finite-state morphology and it uses the concepts of the Xerox/HFST LEXC lexicons, for more information see (Beesley and Karttunen, 2003). Inflection classes (the declinations and conjugations) refer to traditional dictionaries, where the inflection of lexemes is characterized by model words and numbers or other identifiers referring to those model words. Dictionaries often list many more inflection classes than there are different types of LEXC entries. LEXC can generalize the entries by relying on TWOLC or XFST rules which take care of the regular differences in the shapes of stems.

Several topics are discussed in this paper, including:

- How to describe inflection classes with regular expression patterns, i.e. how to formalize what kinds of syllable structures and phonological alternations are characteristic to each inflection class.

- How the regular expressions can be used for converting dictionary word lists with inflection class codes into lexical entries of a LEXC lexicon.

- How to reuse the same regular expressions for guessing all possible LEXC entries for a given single inflected word form.

- How to use such a mapping for selecting the correct LEXC lexicon entry by prompting the user for further forms of the same lexeme.

- How the same data for affixes and their sequencing can be reused for building ordinary morphological analyzers, lexicon converters and entry guessing.

- How to use the mapping for guessing in order to automatically deduce entries out of a corpus.

The idea here is to build a finite-state model of inflecting unknown lexemes roughly as was proposed by Ken Beesley and Lauri Karttunen (2003). For Finnish, their model could produce the following two results for a Finnish word form *puramme* ('we unpack', 'we disassemble'):

```
puramme --> purkaa V+PRES+ACT+PE2
            puraa+V+PRES+ACT+PE2
```

The first result would be the correct analysis and the second analysis proposes a nonexistent lexeme. But actually both results are ambiguous because neither of them tells how the lexemes are inflected. The final *a* of the stem has two possibilities in both results: either it alternates with *o* or it disappears in past tense. Thus there are four possible entries behind the analysis. One of the hidden entries is what we want.

For the purposes of lexicon entry guessing, we need an equally general method which is prepared to accept almost any surface word but would output lexical entries instead of the base forms and morphosyntactic features. A lexical entry consist of a lexical representation and a name of a continuation sub-lexicon. The lexical representation consist of phonemes and morphophonemes (here we always use braces for morphophonemes, e.g. {aoe}).[1] The name of a continuation sub-lexicon (e.g. /v) determines the set of possible endins and possible less regular pieces of the stems. The mapping we are building could map e.g.:

```
puramme --> pur{kØ}{aoe} /v
            pur{kØ}{aØe} /v
            pur{aoe} /v
            pur{aØe} /v
```

The program would then prompt the user for further inflected forms of the same lexeme. In this way the user can soon narrow down the possibilities to the desired single lexicon entry without any detailed knowledge of the codes or conventions of the lexicon.

The work is done in the finite-state two-level framework in the spirit of the original (Koskenniemi, 1983) version and in particular the so called simplified two-level model as presented in (Koskenniemi, 2013b). Helsinki Finite-State Transducer Tools (HFST) were used for the implementations of the finite-state transducers (FST) described in this paper, for more information on HFST see (Lindén et al., 2011) and various sites in the net, e.g. `http://hfst.github.io`.

## 2   Previous and related research

The interactive method for guessing presented here was inspired by Aarne Ranta's Grammatical Framework (GF) system where a similar functionality was implemented, see (Ranta, 2011) and (Détrez and Ranta, 2012). They presented so called *smart paradigms* which have been implemented in GF. Smart paradigms perform a mapping that is similar to the mapping described in this paper but do it in a different way.

Several other approaches have been proposed for the assisting or automating entry generation. Beesley and Karttunen (2003) presented a way to recognize unknown words using regular expressions in a LEXC lexicon as was mentioned above, and in this way cover an inflection class by each expression. The present paper elaborates this approach further and explains how one can generate such expressions in an principled way and how to connect the mechanism into the LEXC lexicon of normal morphological analysis and how to use such a generator in practice.

Huldén (2014) and Ahlberg et al. (2015) discuss how paradigms or inflectional tables can be used for finding or forming entries which is a topic beyond the scope of this paper where the inflection is assumed to be already known.

A recent paper (Esplà-Gomis et al., 2017) presents methods for a task quite relevant to that of this paper. In those papers, inflection classes (i.e. declinations and conjugations) are considered to consist of a set of affixes which are directly concatenated with the single stem of the lexeme. In contrast to this, GF is prepared to have lexemes with several stems, and so does the present approach. In addition, the present approach uses morphophonemes in order to describe regular variations within stems, and therefore a very small number of distinct classes is needed. In some languages,

---

[1] This morphophoneme indicates that in that position there may be either an *a* or an *o* or an *e* depending on the context. Inflection classes usually determine what kinds of phoneme alternations are present in lexemes in that class and what sets of affixes can be attached to them.

e.g. several Sami languages, a large portion of inflection is represented as stem alternations instead of and in addition to using suffixes. The approach presented in this paper is intended to be applicable even to languages with such characteristics. (Esplà-Gomis et al., 2017) present also methods for for optimizing the yes/no queries for the user. These or similar methods could be applied on top of the solutions in this paper but that is not discussed in this paper.

## 3   Regular expressions for inflection classes

In order to generate lexical entries interactively or from comprehensive word lists, we construct a model which characterizes the inflection classes by describing the common features and alternations in each class. It will be shown that with a single description, one one may solve two tasks : (1) converting a dictionary word list with base forms and class numbers into LEXC lexical entries and (2) guessing LEXC lexical entries out of inflected word forms as was discussed above.

The first mapping transforms dictionary headwords and their inflection class codes into LEXC entries (as sequences of symbols) e.g.:

```
p u r k a a V02*  -->  p u r {kØ} {aØe}  /v
```

The transformation can be represented equivalently as a sequence of symbol pairs where the left symbol is transformed into the right symbol:

```
p:p u:u r:r k:{kØ} a:{aØe} a:0 V02*:/v
```

or in an abbreviated form where pairs (e..g. *p:p*) of identical symbols are represented by a single symbol (*p*) without the colon:

```
p u r k:{kØ} a:{aØe} a:0 V02*:/v
```

The inflection code *V02** indicates that the entry is a verb of the second inflection class and that the stem is subject to consonant gradation. The example expresses the fact that the fourth phoneme of the dictionary word, *k*, must be replaced with a morphophoneme *{kØ}*. The morphophoneme tells that in that position *k* alternates with nothing (Ø).[2] At the end of the stem of the dictionary word, the final vowel *a* alternates with zero Ø and *e*. All these facts can be deduced by studying verbs with the inflection code *V02**, i.e. studying the shapes and what kinds of alternations occur in those verbs.

A LEXC lexicon consists of sub-lexicons containing entries for affixes and lexemes. The lexemes are in the sub-lexicon where everything starts and the guessing of such entries is the topic of this paper. Each entry typically corresponds to a morpheme. A morpheme is represented as a pair of its morphophonemic representation and a name of a sub-lexicon containing those morphemes (or entries) which may occur immediately after this morpheme. This name of the next sub-lexicon is often called the *continuation class* of a lexeme.

The inflection class also determines the continuation class, e.g. */v* (which indicates here that all verbal endings are attached directly to the stem). The association between a inflection code (e.g. *V02**) and a continuation class (e.g. */v*) could be included as a

---

[2] We use an arbitrary symbol (Ø) to denote deletion or epenthesis. In morphophonemes and within two-level rules it is always a concrete symbol, not an epsilon which would correspond to the empty string. In this way, one has a better control over epenthesis and deletions. The Ø symbols will be removed only after the rule component has been applied.

part of the regular expression but it proved to be better to represent as a separate two-column table, which is used both in building the converter and the guesser.

In order to generalize the patterns we need to define some common component expressions, e.g. vowels and consonants:

```
Vo = [a|e|i|o|u|y|ä|ö];
Co = [b|c|d|f|g|h|j|k|l|m|n|p|q|r|s|t|v|w|x|z];
```

For Finnish words, we need an expression for the mapping of gradating consonant clusters (as they appear in the dictionary words) into the corresponding morpho-phonemic representations (as they will be in the LEXC entry).

```
Gs = [(l|r|n) k k:{kØ}|(l|r) k:{kØ}|n k:{kg}|
      m p:{pm}|(l|r) p:{pv}|(l|r|m) p p:{pØ}|
      (h) t:{td}|l t:{tl}|n t:{tn}|r t:{tr}|(l|r|n) t t:{tØ}];
```

One might generalize the above transformation example by noticing that the initial part of the word is the same in the dictionary word and in the LEXC entry part. Near the end of the dictionary word there is a strong grade of a gradating consonant cluster but in the LEXC entry there is a corresponding morphophoneme. At the very end, there is the infinitive ending, (here) *a* which has to be removed, and the the code of the inflection class which has to be replaced by the corresponding continuation class. For our example, the following simple mapping could do the conversion:

```
[Co|Vo]* Gs a:{aØe} a:0 VO2*:/v
```

Such a simple expression might work correctly when converting dictionary words but usually one wants to describe the inflection classes in more detail according to the syllable structure and other characteristics shared by all words in that class. The more precisely the expression separates lexemes in its class from those in other classes, the better the expression serves its purpose. Precise characterizations help the building of the lexicon by finding atypical entries in the dictionary and possible mistakes in the data. Accurate expressions also help the guessing process to converge faster.

A short Python script was made for reading in expressions for all verbal inflection classes and for transforming the expressions into a converter LEXC lexicon. The converter lexicon implements the mapping from dictionary entries into actual Finnish LEXC entries. Each expression forms the first part of one converter lexicon entry and this part maps dictionary entries of that class into a morphophonemic representation. The second part of the converter lexicon entry is the inflection identifier used here as a name of a sub-lexicon. A small sub-lexicon of the transformer lexicon is produced out of the separate table that was mentioned above. Each line of that table is converted into a sublexicon to which the expression entry continues. This arrangement allows one to experiment with different types of converted lexicons e.g. one which is very permissive and useful for old or dialectal texts and others which are more normative by excluding less common ending allomorphs of each inflectional class. Below is a fraction of the generated LEXC for conversion:[3]

```
LEXICON Root
< Co* Vo+ (Sy1)* Co* [o|ö|u|y] [a:0|ä:0] > VO1 ;
< Co* Vo+ (Sy1)* Gs [o|ö|u|y] [a:0|ä:0] > VO1* ;
< Co* Vo+ (Sy1)* Co+ [a:%{aØe%} a:0|ä:%{äØe%} ä:0] > VO2 ;
```

---

[3]The curly brackets were used in the expressions as such but in LEXC they must be protected or quoted with a per cent sign (%). The Python script adds the per cent signs.

```
< Co* Vo+ (Sy1)* Gs [a:%{aØe%} a:0|ä:%{äØe%} ä:0] > VO2* ;
< Co VV t:%{tds%} [a:%{aØe%} a:0|ä:%{äØe%} ä:0] > VO3 ;
< Co VV t:%{tds%} [a:%{aØe%} a:0|ä:%{äØe%} ä:0] > VO4 ;
```

The above lexicon is then compiled into a FST, stored and used by another Python
script which performs the conversion. This script can be applied to a test set of representative dictionary entries or to a full scale list of all dictionary list words. In order
to have full control of possible failures of the expressions, the script uses the lookup
mode so that it finds not only the appropriate result but also knows when the expressions fail to give any results. So, in addition to the resulting LEXC entries, also a
control list is produced for verification and debugging. Potential errors in the source
data (dictionary entries) as well as in the expressions can be found in this way.

The patterns and definitions are given as a file of comma separated values (CSV)
(possibly by editing with a spreadsheet and then saving in this format). The patterns
and definitions are extracted from there using a short Python script which formats
the data into the LEXC format and collects any multicharacter symbols needed for
the definitions in the header part of the resulting LEXC file. This CSV file can then be
reused for other purposes. The following are samples from a full-scale description of
patterns for Finnish verbs according to the inflection class codes used in the *Reverse
dictionary of Modern Standard Finnish* (Tuomi, 1980), see Figure 1.[4]

## 4    Reusable affix data

Converters and guessers are not meaningful in isolation. In order to know into what
format the dictionary entries have to be converted, one needs to have at least a small
test TWOLC lexicon and the associated rules. The test lexicon defines the target for
the conversion and the guessing. It ought to include example lexemes from all inflection classes and define what affixes may be attached to the stems and in which
combinations. The rules[5], in turn, make the test lexicon operational so that the morphophonemic alternations and the combinations of stems and affixes can be validated.
The design of a LEXC lexicon and rules is beyond the scope of this paper except that
parts of the test lexicon can be reused in the guesser. Thus, one would benefit from
combining the writing the analyzing and the guessing lexicons.

Both the normal morphological analyzer and the guesser need a description of
inflectional morphemes (affix entries), their shapes and the ways in which they may
combine with each other. The structures of these two lexicon systems is rather iso-
morphic, i.e. the entries and the sub-lexicons correspond directly to each other, even
if the entries are a bit different.

LEXC lexicons are technically a *collection of sub-lexicons* where each sub-lexicon
has a *name* and a *set of entries*. For each lexeme (or root morpheme) and each affix (or
inflectional morpheme) , there is an entry in some sub-lexicon. Each entry consists
formally of three components: (1) *input string*, (2) *output string* and (3) the name of
the *continuation sub-lexicon* from which the next entry is chosen:

---

[4]All Python scripts and the CSV files mentioned in this section are freely available at Github: `https:`
`//github.com/koskenni/twolex`. The HFST used in these Python scripts was loaded according to the
instructions at `https://pypi.python.org/pypi/hfst`

[5]In this paper, two-level rules were used and the morphophonemes were established according to the
principles of the simplified two-level model. The method for conversions, guessing and the reuse of affix
data is independent of the kind of rules one uses.

```
ID,NEXT,MPHON,COMMENT
,V01,<Co* Vo+ Co+ [o|ö|u|y] [a:0|ä:0]>,PUNOA
,V01*,<Co* Vo+ Gs [o|ö|u|y] [a:0|ä:0]>,KUTOA
,V02,<Co* Vo+ (Co+ Vo+)* Co+ [a:{aØe} a:0|ä:{äØe} ä:0]>,MUISTAA
,V02*,<Co* Vo+ (Co+ Vo+)* Gs [a:{aØe} a:0|ä:{äØe} ä:0]>,HUUDAHTAA
,V03,<Co VV t:{tds} [a:{aØe} a:0|ä:{äØe} ä:0]>,HUUTAA
,V04,<Co VV t:{tds} [a:{aØe} a:0|ä:{äØe} ä:0]>,SOUTAA
...

,V09,<(Co) [Vo|VV] Co+ a:{aoe} a:0>,KAIVAA
,V09*,<(Co) [Vo|VV] Gs a:{aoe} a:0>,KATTAA
,V10,<Co [Vo|VV] Co+ a:{aoe} a:0>,HAASTAA
,V10*,<(Co) [Vo|VV] Gs a:{aoe} a:0>,MALTTAA
,V11,<Co a i s t a:{aoe} a:0 >,PAISTAA
,V11*,<Co [a|i|a a|a i] [Gsk|Gst] a:{aoe} a:0 >,VIRKKAA
,V12,<Co a a r t:{trs} a:{aoe} a:0>,SAARTA
,V13,<(Co) Vo+ Co+ e:{eiØ} [a:0|ä:0]>,LASKEA
,V13*,<(Co) Vo+ Gs e:{eiØ} [a:0|ä:0]>,KYLPEÄ
,V13*,<(Co) Vo+ Gsj e:{eiØ} [a:0|ä:0]>,SULKEA
,V14,<t u n t:{tns} e:{eiØ} a:0>,TUNTEA
,V15,<p o t:{tds} e:{eiØ} a:0>,POTEA
,V16,<l ä h:0 t:0 e:0 ä:0>,LÄHTEÄ
,V17,<Co* Vo+ Co+ i:{iØ} [a:0|ä:0]>,SALLIA
,V17*,<Co* Vo+ Gs i:{iØ} [a:0|ä:0]>,LEMPIÄ
,V17,<Co* Vo+ (Sy1)* [k s|p s] i:{iØ} [a:0|ä:0]>,KÄVELEKSIÄ
,V17*,<Co* Vo+ (Sy1)* [h t:{td}] i:{iØ} [a:0|ä:0]>,PUIKKELEHTIA
,V18,<n a i:{iØ} d:0 a:0>,NAIDA
,V18,<Co o i:{iØ} d:0 a:0>,VOIDA
,V18,<(p) u i:{iØ} d:0 a:0>,UIDA PUIDA
,V18,<Co* Vo+ (Sy1)* [o|ö] i:{iØ} d:0 [a:0|ä:0]>,VOIDA
,V19,<s a a:{VØ} d:0 a:0>,SAADA
,V19,<j ä ä:{VØ} d:0 ä:0>,JÄÄDÄ
,V20,<m y y:{VØ} d:0 ä:0>,MYYDÄ
,V21,<Co [u:{uØ} o d:0 a:0|y:{yØ} ö d:0 ä:0]>,JUODA SYÖDÄ
,V22,<v i:{iØ} e d:0 ä:0>,VIEDÄ
,V23,<k ä y:0 d:0 ä:0>,KÄYDÄ
,V24,<Co* [Vo|VV] Co* (a|ä) i s 0:{eØ} t:0 [a:0|ä:0]>,NUOLAISTA
,V24,<Co* [Vo|VV] (Sy1) Co*  s 0:{eØ} t:0 [a:0|ä:0]>,NOUSTA SEISTÄ
,V24*,<Co* [Vo|VV] Gw (a|ä) i s 0:{eØ} t:0 [a:0|ä:0]>,LAUAISTA
,V25,<Co [Vo|VV] l 0:{eØ} l:0 [a:0|ä:0]>, TULLA NIELLÄ
,V26,<Co [Vo|VV] r 0:{eØ} r:0 [a:0|ä:0]>,PURRA PIERRÄ
,V27,<Co [Vo|VV] n 0:{eØ} n:0 [a:0|ä:0]>,PANNA MENNÄ
...

,V32,<j u o | p i e | s y ö>,JUOSTA juo-kse/v
,V33,<n ä | t e>,NÄHDÄ nä-ke/v
,V34,<Co* Vo+ (Sy1) Co+ [a|ä|o|ö|u|y|e] t:0 [a:0|ä:0]>,ALETA ale-ne/v
,V34*,<Co* Vo+ (Sy1) Gw [a|ä|o|ö|u|y|e] t:0 [a:0|ä:0]>,KYETÄ ale-ne/v
,V34*,<Co* Vo+ (Sy1) Gwj e t:0 [a:0|ä:0]>,KYETÄ ale-ne/v
,V35,<Co* Vo+ (Sy1)* Co* [a|ä] t:0 [a:0|ä:0]>,SALATA sala-V/v
,V35*,<Co* Vo+ (Sy1)* Gw [a|ä] t:0 [a:0|ä:0]>,AIDATA sala-V/v
,V35*,<Co* Vo+ (Sy1)* Gwj ä t:0 ä:0>,AIDATA sala-V/v
...

,V37,<Co* [Vo|VV] Co+ i t:0 [ä:0|a:0]>,SELVITÄ selvi-A/v
,V37*,<Co [Vo|VV] Gw i t:0 [ä:0|a:0]>,SIITÄ selvi-A/v
,V38,<Co* [Vo|VV] Co+ [o t:0 a:0|ö t:0 ä:0]>,KOHOTA koho-A/v
,V38*,<Co* [Vo|VV] Gw [o t:0 a:0|ö t:0 ä:0]>,TAUOTA koho-A/v
...
```

Figure 1: Regular expression patterns for Finnish verbs

```
INPUT:OUTPUT CONT;
```

Either the input or output string can be empty, and also here, only one of them needs to be given if they are identical. If both are empty strings, even the colon may be omitted.

In the framework used in Beesley and Karttunen (2003), the input string is the final base form of the lexeme or for affixes, it consists of the morphosyntactic features of each affix. The output string is the (morph)phonological shape of the affix. In order to reduce the number of entries for morphemes, morphophonemic forms are used. Then one may let the rules take care of the different shapes the affixes have when combined with different stems or other affixes.

The present approach uses the three components of an entry in different ways depending on whether an analyzer or a guesser is made. E.g. an entry for the ending for conditional mood in analysis could be:

```
+COND+ACT:isi Person;
```

where the INPUT consists of the morphosyntactic features *+COND* and *+ACT*, the OUTPUT (or morphophonemic representation) is *isi* and the next morpheme is in a lexicon *Person*.

In affixes for guessing the components OUTPUT and CONT are the same as for the analysis but the INPUT component is an empty string, e.g.:

```
:isi Person;
```

Let us move to *lexeme entry classes*. An entry class corresponds to one or several similar inflection classes (as used in the dictionaries). For lexemes of such a class, stems are not fully related to each other via simple phonological rules. E.g. a Finnish verb *salata* ('hide', 'keep in secret') belongs to a common inflection class where the stems are e.g. *salaa-, salas-, sala-, salat-, salan-*. One may simplify the rule component by splitting such lexemes in two parts: (1) a truncated stem which is constant or phonologically regular for a lexeme and (2) stem endings which are common to all lexemes in this lexeme entry class. Both parts may themselves contain regular phonological alternations such as vowel harmony or consonant gradation.

For each lexeme entry class, a sub-lexicon is established and it lists the end parts of the stems in such a class. A sub-lexicon corresponding to a lexeme entry class is common to all lexeme entries of this class and the lexeme entries all continue to this sub-lexicon. The actual sub-lexicon used in the analysis of words inflected like *salata* could be as follows:

```
LEXICON sala-A/v
{nt}{dlnrtØ}{aä}:{VØ} v0;
{nt}{dlnrtØ}{aä}:s    v1;
{nt}{dlnrtØ}{aä}:{VØ} v2;
{nt}{dlnrtØ}{aä}:{nt} v3;
```

In this example, *sal-A/v* is the name of this sub-lexicon, *v0* is the sub-lexicon for present tense forms, *v1* is the sub-lexicon for the past tense morpheme, *v2* for conditional morpheme and *v3* is the sub-lexicon where infinitives and participial morphemes reside. The base form for verbs is traditionally the first infinitive which is in sub-lexicon *v3*. The INPUT component (for analysis) consists of whatever must be added to the truncated stem (i.e. *{nt}* is added) in order to form the v3 stem. It is

given here followed by the common morphophonemic form of the infinitive ending
*{dlnrtØ}{aä}*.[6] The OUTPUT component consists of the final parts of morphophonemic
representations of the different stems.

In the guesser version, all this information is not needed. Instead, the INPUT
that is needed here, consists of the name of the continuation class itself (defined as a
multicharacter symbol and preceded by a space that has been quoted with a per cent
sign).

```
LEXICON sala-A/v
% sala-A/v:{VØ} v02;
% sala-A/v:s v1;
% sala-A/v:{nt} v3;
```

Some linguists think that complex lexicons in LEXC format are not convenient for
humans to edit.[7] Therefore, it is a practical idea to create and edit those parts of the
lexicon in a simple tabular form by using e.g. some spreadsheet calculator. From the
internal format of spreadsheet calculators, one may store the data as comma separated values (CSV) which are easy to process with small Python scripts. One may use
slightly different scripts in order to produce either normal LEXC entries for morphological analysis or entries modified for the guesser or other purposes. Below is the
source CSV data for the above examples for *sal-A/v* sub-lexicons:

```
ID       , NEXT, MPHON, FEAT, BASE
sala-A/v, v0  , {VØ} ,     , {nt}{dlnrtØ}{aä}
        , v1  , s    ,     , {nt}{dlnrtØ}{aä}
        , v2  , {VØ} ,     , {nt}{dlnrtØ}{aä}
        , v3  , {nt} ,     , {nt}{dlnrtØ}{aä}
```

In a similar manner, the CSV entries of actual affixes can be in the same tabular
format, e.g. the conditional ending:

```
ID, NEXT      , MPHON, FEAT     , BASE
v2, Person neg , isi  , V COND ACT,
```

For analysis, INPUT comes from the FEAT column, and OUTPUT from the MPHON
column. There are two sub-lexicon names in the NEXT column and therefore two
separate entries are produced into the LEXC lexicon. For guessing, in inflectional
endings, INPUT will be empty but otherwise the entry will be similar whereas the
lexicons for inflection classes will be slightly different. In them, the INPUT is the
name of the sub-lexicon (and OUTPUT as in analysis). Short Python scripts perform
all simple conversions that are needed.[8]

## 5   Producing the FST for guessing

Now we know how to make the sub-lexicons for affixes and the special sub-lexicons
for each lexeme entry class. When converting dictionary headwords into lexeme en-

---

[6]The infinitive ending may be in several shapes (*-a, -ä, -ta, -tä, -da, -dä, -la, -lä, -na, -na, -ra, -rä*), but
the forms are fully determined by the phonological properties of the preceding stem and easily handled by
a rule.

[7]Especially the handling of so called flag diacritics requires duplication and results in less readable
LEXC source files. Moreover, there are no convenient ways to parametrize the LEXC files so that one could
compile different versions out of the same source file.

[8]All Python scripts and the CSV files mentioned in this section are freely available at Github: `https://github.com/koskenni/twolex`.

tries in Section 3, each pattern had an inflection class code and there was a separate table associating the inflection class and the lexeme entry class so that the pattern and the sub-lexicons could produce a lexeme entry with the proper continuation class. We use the same pattern data when building the regular expression entries for guessing.

In the conversion, the expressions themselves were transformations from the dictionary head word into a morphophonemic representation of the lexeme entry. For the guesser, we only need the output part of this mapping. For transforming the conversion patterns into guessing patterns, a small Python script was made. The script changed the regular expressions in the definitions and in the regular expressions patterns so that any symbol pair was replaced by the output part only, e.g.:

```
p:{pv}   -->  {pv}
a:0      -->  0
```

The result was an output projection of the initial transduction. It was formatted according to the conventions required by LEXC and compiled together with the affixes in a respective format. The compiled lexicon FST was then compose-intersected with the two-level rules. The inverse of this was then minimized and optimized for lookup so that it could be used for looking up possible entries for any verb form, e.g.:

```
$ hfst-lookup -i guesser.fst
> hakkeroiden
hakkeroiden     hakkero     haravo-i/v   0,000000
hakkeroiden     hakkero{i0} /v           0,000000
```

The hfst-lookup program reads a word form (*hakkeroiden*) at a time and looks the FST for any matches and prints them (*hakkero haravo-i/v* and *hakkero{i0} /v*) together with the input word. In addition, the program prints a weight of the results (which is not yet used in the guessing but probably one can find useful ways to incorporate weights into the process).

## 6   Selecting the correct entry interactively

In Section 5 we ended up with a FST which maps any inflected word form into a set of possible LEXC entries. Neither the XFST scripts not the HFST command line tools lend themselves for the kind of looping and testing that one would need for interfacing the guessing FST with a human user in a natural way. Fortunately, this is quite easy when using the HFST that is embedded in Python 3.

A very simple script can read in the FST produced as above. In a loop, the program can read in a word form and search the FST for any entries which were associated with it. Searching can be done with an efficient lookup function which produces the results in a form that the script can easily test. If there still are several entries remaining, the script asks for another form of the same word. An intersection of the new and the previous set of results is calculated. If only one result remains, that is the answer. If several results remain, then the user must enter a further form.

The above procedure solves the problem in most cases but not in all. Two tentative lexical entries can overlap so that one generates all forms which the other one does but it generates some additional forms which the other does not. The user can then find the solution if the entry which she is searching has a lager set of forms. If the correct entry would have only forms also acceptable for the other entry, the problem cannot be solved by just entering more forms. In this situation, the user needs to enter a negative example, i.e. a form which would be allowed by the wrong candidate lexeme but not by the correct. The program, then, subtracts the entries corresponding to such a word-form.

The following is an example where the user enters *brassata* and *brassasin* in order to narrow down the possible LEXC entries. The negative example *brassajaa* (prefixed with a minus sign) resolves the problem that the two tentative entries (*sala-A/v* and *pala-V/v*) are overlapping so that the former is included in the latter.

```
ENTER FORMS OF A WORD
brassata
    {'brassa ale-ne/v', 'brassa sala-A/v', 'brassa pala-V/v',
     'brassat{t∅}{a∅e} /v', 'brassat{a∅e} /v'}
brassasin
    {'brassa sala-A/v', 'brassa pala-V/v'}
-brassajaa
    {'brassa sala-A/v'}
RESULT:
brassa sala-A/v ;
```

As the reader can readily see, the script is just a starting point which can be made more sophisticated, c.f. (Esplà-Gomis et al., 2017). Instead of just accepting correct or incorrect forms from the user the program might generate critical forms and ask the user whether they are correct or not. Forms which are valid inflected forms of one but not all tentative entries are useful in this respect. There are several possibilities in selecting which forms to ask.

One could make the guesser more helpful by restricting the inflectional forms to so called principal parts i.e. a minimum set of forms which is still sufficient for determining the correct entry. With this restriction, one can use the guesser FST together with its inverse. The given word form goes through the guessing FST and results in a set of tentative entries. Each of the entries is fed to the inverse FST. In this way one gets a set of principal forms for each entry candidate. These lists could be shown to the user who then can select one list and thus the underlying entry.

One may also process the sets of forms of each lexeme candidate and hide common word forms. One idea is that a sequence of word forms would be presented in a particular order. The sequence would only contain forms which are not common to all tentative entries. At the top of the list would be those forms which belong to the least number of entries. The user would then respond by telling which is the first acceptable form of the target entry. If all forms in front of that one are marked as negative examples then the interaction between the program and the user might converge even more rapidly.


## 7   Corpus-assisted guessing of entries

A list of all word forms occurring in a large corpus is quite valuable when choosing among different possible entry candidates. The correct entry is more likely to have some word forms in the corpus than the entries for non-existing lexemes. After the first step when the user has given a word form to the guesser, the program has a set of alternative entries which could generate that word form, e.g.:

```
rääkkäsi
    {'rääkkä sala-A/v', 'rääkkäs{äØe} /v',
     'rääkkäs{eØ} /v', 'rääk{kØ}ä sala-A/v'}
```

Let us consider each of these entries in turn. The set of word forms occurring in the
corpus which are also generated by the entry is interesting.[9] What happens if one
feeds these word forms into the algorithm described above. The algorithm may find
a unique solution if the set contains enough forms. Such solutions are likely to be
the correct ones we are looking for. Sometimes there may several possibile answers
because the corpus contains forms of other (similar looking) lexemes and even typing
errors. In case there are many (unique) solutions, one can choose the one having the
largest set of word forms or the program might ask the user to choose the correct one.

The plain algorithm would require another word form in order to proceed. The
corpus-assisted algorithm would find the solution right away from the first word form:

```
rääkkäsi
        CORPUS CONTAINS: { rääkättiin, rääkkään,
            rääkkäävät, rääkäten, rääkännyt, rääkätty,
            rääkättäisi, rääkätään, rääkkäisi, rääkätä,
            rääkkäsi, rääkkää }


===================
rääk{kØ}ä sala-A/v ;
===================
```

Using the HFST finite-state tools, it is easy to implement the enhanced guesser.
We already have $G$, a FST which maps a word form into the set of possible entries
$\{e_1, ..., e_k\}$. We must prepare the corpus data in advance in order to support the
interactive guessing of the entries. The distinct word forms (types) occurring in a
corpus can be easily produced as a list. This list can be converted into a FSA, say $W$
using the *hfst-strings2fst* command line tool. The composition $C = W \circ G$ maps each
word form in the corpus into the entries which could generate them. The inverse of
this mapping, $H = C^{-1}$ gives us the word forms in the corpus that an entry could
generate. This mapping $H$ is used in the corpus-assisted version of the entry guesser.
See Appendix A for some examples of corpus-assisted for Finnish verbs guessing are
given. It appears that such methods could be used for building lexicons for lesser
resourced languages.

## 8  Guessing entries from a corpus

One can modify the computer-assisted guessing so that it works without human in-
tervention. The input side (projection) of the transducer H accepts all entries that
we need to consider. It is a finite-state machine and it can easily be converted into
a plain list (of strings). Once this is done, the algorithm may proceed by considering
each entry at a time and test whether the entry ought to be accepted or not.

The mapping $H$ which was defined above, maps every entry $e$ into those word
forms occurring in the corpus which the entry would accept. As in the previous section, we evaluate the goodness of an entry $e$ in $E$ by using the set of word forms in

---

[9]One could simply choose the entry with the longest list but here we wish to stress the correctness of
guesses.

$H(e_i)$ and by feeding them into the algorithm and see whether the list makes the algorithm to converge into exactly one entry. If successful, we have a good candidate for an entry. If unsuccessful, we have not enough evidence to exclude the other candidate entries because some of them also generate all word forms in the list.

An experiment of this method is described in Appendix B. The results were encouraging although the guesser only covered verbs and all noun and adjective forms presented harmful noise to the procedure. For a random sample of word form types taken out from a large text corpus of Finnish, the method provided some 77 % correct results when using very simple criteria. Further research on the topic is clearly needed. One could assign weights to the affixes and use them when excluding less likely entries.[10]

One could easily combine the information from a corpus with the interactive guessing. A word form given by the user would first be expanded to a set of tentative entries. Then, each tentative entry would be tested against the corpus in order to see whether the corpus would give conclusive evidence for exactly one of the entries. In such cases, the entry could be directly selected and the interaction would be faster. Even partial evidence could be utilized byt that would probably need some further research and testing.

## 9   Experiment with Finnish verbs

The examples presented in the preceding sections were taken from an experiment with Finnish verb morphology. There was a long term interest to deal with older Finnish texts and therefore the *Reverse Dictionary of Modern Standard Finnish* (RDMSF) which reflects the language in the first half of the 20th century was taken as the basis rather than *Kielitoimiston sanakirja* (KS) which reflects the present day use. RDMSF allows more liberal use of ending allomorphs and stem variants than the KS. The extra forms are readily understood even by present day speakers but seldom used any more although they are quite commonly found in earlier texts.

The examples in the preceding sections were made using a the RDMSF conjugation tables and example words of the dictionary and two-level rules and a lexicon with verbal ending which had been prepared earlier for other purposes. A couple days were spent in establishing 78 regular expression patterns for the 45 conjugations used in RDMSF. A Unix makefile was prepared to control the use of a number of small command line and Python scripts. In this way, it was convenient to rebuild the FSTs for conversion, analysis and guessing.

The test set of selected entries was converted using the conversion FST. The resulting entries were then combined with verbal affixes and compose-intersected with the rule FSTs. The string pairs represented by this FST was produced in a human readable form. The list consisted of pairs of base form plus features and and the corresponding surface form:

```
. . .
iätä+V+INF1+NOM:iätä
iätä+V+INF2+ACT+INE:iätessä
iätä+V+INF2+ACT+MAN:iäten
```

---

[10]HFST-LEXC has a facility for weighted entries and these would automatically propagate to the mappings that were described above. The same applies to the FSA for word form types in the corpus whose frequencies could be utilized when assigning weights to them.

```
iätä+V+INF2+PSS+INE:iättäessä
iätä+V+PAST+ACT+1PL:ikäsimme
iätä+V+PAST+ACT+1SG:ikäsin
iätä+V+PAST+ACT+2PL:ikäsitte
...
```

The list was checked manually and some errors were detected in the affix tables and one in the rules. After modifications, the test data appeared to be clean of errors.

The conversion was tested against the full list of 16,000 verb entries in the dictionary. The test revealed some points where the patterns had to be made more general in order to accept less typical verb entries in some conjugations. The analysis was tested superficially by entering word forms randomly picked up from *Nykysuomen sanakirja* (Sadeniemi, 1951–1961) and verifying that the results were correct. The same kind of testing was done with the guesser.

## 10    Further work

There is a plan to continue the present work and produce a full scale Finnish morphological analyzer and guesser which could be used for various purposes, including the analysis of Finnish texts from the 19th century. The present approach makes such an analyzer quite flexible for extending and tuning. One could easily add and change inflectional patterns so that the historical endings and stem patterns would be better covered. The kind of a morphophonemic lexicon which is used in this approach lends itself also to applications within historical linguistics and comparing related languages with each other, cf. (Koskenniemi, 2013a). Whereas the existing open source morphological analyzer OMORFI of Pirinen (2015) is designed for a wide coverage lexicon and is normative, the proposed one OFITWOL would be permissive and descriptive. OMORFI aims at excluding old and dialectal inflections whereas OFITWOL aims at including them, cf. the arguments in Koskenniemi and Kuutti (2017).

Handling Finnish dialects by using the morphophonemic lexical representations would also be an interesting topic to study. It is not always possible to relate word forms in standard Finnish with forms in dialects because a word form alone does not contain the relevant information. Morphophonemes combine the information of the various stems of a lexeme and various forms of affixes. These morphophonemic forms might contain the sufficient information for generating old or dialectal forms of Finnish out of the morphophonological representations of OFITWOL.

## References

Malin Ahlberg, Markus Forsberg, and Mans Hulden. 2015. Paradigm classification in supervised learning of morphology. In *Proceedings of the 2015 Conference of the North American Chapter of the Association for Computational Linguistics: Human Language Technologies*. Association for Computational Linguistics, Denver, Colorado, pages 1024–1029. http://www.aclweb.org/anthology/N15-1107.

Kenneth R. Beesley and Lauri Karttunen. 2003. *Finite State Morphology*. Studies in Computational Linguistics, 3. University of Chicago Press. Additional info, see: `www.stanford.edu/~laurik/fsmbook/home.html`.

Grégoire Détrez and Aarne Ranta. 2012. Smart paradigms and the predictability and complexity of inflectional morphology. In *Proceedings of the 13th Conference of the European Chapter of the Association for Computational Linguistics*. Association for Computational Linguistics, Avignon, France, pages 645–653. http://www.aclweb.org/anthology/E12-1066.

Miquel Esplà-Gomis, Rafael C. Carrasco, Víctor M. Sánchez-Cartagena, Mikel L. Forcada, Felipe Sánchez-Martínez, and Juan Antonio Pírez-Ortiz. 2017. Assisting non-expert speakers of under-resourced languages in assigning stems and inflectional paradigms to new word entries of morphological dictionaries. *Language Resources and Evaluation* 51(4):989–1017.

Måns Huldén. 2014. Generalizing inflection tables into paradigms with finite state operations. In *Proceedings of the 2014 Joint Meeting of SIGMORPHON and SIGFSM*. Association for Computational Linguistics, Baltimore, Maryland, pages 29–36. http://www.aclweb.org/anthology/W14-2804.

Kimmo Koskenniemi. 1983. *Two-level Morphology: A General Computational Model for Word-Form Recognition and Production*. Number 11 in Publications. University of Helsinki, Department of General Linguistics.

Kimmo Koskenniemi. 2013a. Finite-state relations between two historically closely related languages. In *Proceedings of the workshop on computational historical linguistics at NODALIDA 2013; May 22-24; 2013; Oslo; Norway*. Linköping University Electronic Press; Linköpings universitet, number 87 in NEALT Proceedings Series 18, pages 53–53. http://www.ep.liu.se/ecp/article.asp?issue=087&article=004&volume=.

Kimmo Koskenniemi. 2013b. An informal discovery procedure for two-level rules. *Journal of Language Modelling* 1(1):155–188. http://jlm.ipipan.waw.pl/index.php/JLM/article/view/62.

Kimmo Koskenniemi and Pirkko Kuutti. 2017. *K + K = 120: Papers dedicated to László Kálmán and András Kornai on the occasion of their 60th birthdays*, Research Institute for Linguistics, Hungarian Academy of Sciences, chapter Indexing Old Literary Finnish text, page 32 p.

Krister Lindén, Erik Axelson, Sam Hardwick, Tommi A. Pirinen, and Miikka Silfverberg. 2011. Hfst – framework for compiling and applying morphologies. In Cerstin Mahlow and Michael Piotrowski, editors, *Systems and Frameworks for Computational Morphology 2011 (SFCM-2011)*. Springer-Verlag, volume 100 of *Communications in Computer and Information Science*, pages 67–85.

Tommi A. Pirinen. 2015. Development and use of computational morphology of finnish in the open source and open science era: Notes on experiences with omorfi development. *SKY Journal of Linguistics* 28:381–393.

Aarne Ranta. 2011. *Grammatical Framework: Programming with Multilingual Grammars*. CSLI Publications, Stanford. ISBN-10: 1-57586-626-9 (Paper), 1-57586-627-7 (Cloth).

Matti Sadeniemi, editor. 1951–1961. *Nykysuomen sanakirja*, volume 1–6. Werner Söderström Osakeyhtiö, 4 edition.

Tuomo Tuomi. 1980. *Suomen kielen käänteissanakirja / Reverse Dictionary of Modern Standard Finnish*. Number 274 in Toimituksia. Suomalaisen Kirjallisuuden Seura, 2 edition.

# A    Test of corpus-assisted guessing of entries

The assisting corpus used here was a list of word forms starting with *r* from the SKTP collection of texts[11]. The lists used here consists of some 115,000 word form types. Only a small portion (less than 1/10) of them was actually forms of verbs. The word forms that were tested as input were manually selected from another list, the Finnish PAROLE corpus. Some forms occurring six times in the Parole corpus were picked up and fed to the program. Nouns, nominal derivations and also verb forms with clitic particle were excluded from the selection. This unsystematic, small and biased test gave very promising results, i.e. the correct solution was found directly:

```
ryöstäen
    (1) << ryöst{äØe} /v >> ryöstää, ryöstivät, ryöstetä,
    ryösti, ryöstävät, ryöstä, ryöstetään, ryöstetty,
    ryöstänyt, ryöstäen, ryöstettiin, ryöstettävä, ryöstäessä,
    ryöstän, ryöstämme, ryöstäisi
===============
ryöst{äØe} /v ;
===============


rakasti
    (1) << rakast{aØe} /v >> rakastettava, rakastettaisi,
    rakastaisitte, rakastaisit, rakasteta, rakastettu, rakastatte,
    rakastaisivat, rakastaen, rakastakaamme, rakastaisimme,
    rakastivat, rakastit, rakasta, rakastat, rakastin, rakastamme,
    rakastetaan, rakastettiin, rakasti, rakastanut, rakastaisin,
    rakastakaa, rakastavat, rakastan, rakastaisi, rakastimme,
    rakastaa, rakastettaisiin
================
rakast{aØe} /v ;
================


roihuaa
    (1 ) << roihu halu-A/v >> roihuttiin, roihunnut, roihusivat,
    roihuta, roihusi, roihua, roihutessa, roihuten, roihuaa,
    roihuavat
    (2) << roihua{kØ}{aØe} /v >> roihuaa, roihuakin
================
roihu halu-A/v ;
================


rikkoontuivat
    (1) << rikkoon{tn}u /v >> rikkoontuessa, rikkoontua,
    rikkoontuivat, rikkoontuisi, rikkoontuu, rikkoontui,
    rikkoontunut, rikkoontunee, rikkoontuvat, rikkoonnu
=================
rikkoon{tn}u /v ;
=================


ryhtyvät
```

[11]The Downloadable Version of the Finnish Text Collection, "sktp-dl, ftc-dl", ID: http://urn.fi/urn:nbn:fi:lb-2016050206, The resource is available in FIN-CLARIN Kielipankki - the Language Bank of Finland at http://urn.fi/urn:nbn:fi:lb-2014052719

```
    (1) << ryhty /v >> ryhtyi, ryhtyne, ryhtykäämme, ryhtykööt,
ryhtyköön, ryhtyy, ryhtyen, ryhtyvät, ryhtyisivät, ryhtyisi,
ryhtykää, ryhtyisimme, ryhtynevät, ryhtynyt, ryhtynen,
ryhtyivät, ryhty, ryhtyessä, ryhtyisin, ryhtyä, ryhtynee
    (2) << ryh{td}y /v >> ryhtyi, ryhtyne, ryhtykäämme, ryhtykööt,
ryhtyköön, ryhtyy, ryhtyen, ryhtyvät, ryhdyimme, ryhdyttäne,
ryhdyttiin, ryhdyttäköön, ryhdyttäkö, ryhdymme, ryhdyn,
ryhtyisivät, ryhdyin, ryhtyisi, ryhtykää, ryhdyitte,
ryhtyisimme, ryhtynevät, ryhdy, ryhdyttäneen, ryhdytään,
ryhdyttäessä, ryhtynyt, ryhtynen, ryhtyivät, ryhdyttäisiin,
ryhdytte, ryhdytty, ryhtyessä, ryhtyisin, ryhtyä, ryhdytä,
ryhdyttäisi, ryhdyttävä, ryhdyit, ryhtynee, ryhdyt
    (3) << ryhtyv{ä∅e} /v >> ryhtyvän, ryhtyvää, ryhtyvät, ryhtyvä
=============
ryh{td}y /v ;
=============


repeäisi
    (1) << re{pv}e katke-A/v >> repeävät, revennyt, repesin,
repeän, repesi, revetessä, repeäisi, repeää, repee,
repeäisivät, repesivät, revetä, repeä
==================
re{pv}e katke-A/v ;
==================


rajasi
    (1) << rajas{e∅} /v >> rajasta, rajasivat, rajasi, rajasimme,
rajastaan
    (2) << raja sala-A/v >> rajaat, rajaavat, rajattu, rajaan,
rajattaneen, rajaten, rajatkaa, rajata, rajaamme, rajasivat,
rajaisimme, rajattiin, rajattaisi, rajaisivat, rajasimme,
rajattaisiin, rajasi, rajaisi, rajattaessa, rajattava, rajaisit,
rajaisin, rajannut, rajaa, rajataan
===============
raja sala-A/v ;
===============
```

# B    Test of guessing entries from a corpus

The evaluation of the method sketched in Section 8 was based on the same word form
list out of SKTP as in the Appendix A. Python scripts were written to implement the
method and the corpus of word form types beginning with *r* was processed. The
following is a list of a sample of 30 proposed lexicon entries out of that list. Not all
results proposed by the algorithm were taken because there was much noise in those
based on just a few word forms.[12] Thus only entries which covered at least eight
distinct word forms were considered here. They are taken out of a total list of some
350 proposed entries. through equal interval sampling. Seven out of the 30 appear to
be incorrect (marked with -), others are OK (marked with +).

1. + RAAPUSTAA raapust{a∅e} /v raapusti raapustin raapustivat raapustaa raapustaisi
   raapustaisin raapustan raapustanut raapustavat raapusteta raapustetaan raapustettava
   raapustettiin raapustettu

2. + RAATAA raa{td}{aoe} /v raada raadan raadat raadatte raadetaan raadettava raadet-
   tiin raadettu raadoin raataa raataen raataessa raataisi raataisivat raatanut raatavat raatoi

---

[12]The mapping proposes some entries for most word forms. Certain forms of nouns happen to be similar
to some verb forms and occasionally a couple of such misleading forms uniquely determine an entry.

raatoivat

3. + RAIKUA `rai{kØ}u  /v` raiu raikua raikuen raikuessa raikui raikuisi raikuisivat raikuivat raikukoot raikunut raikuu raikuvat

4. - (*RAKASTA as juosta) `rakas{eØ}  /v` rakasta *rakastaan* rakastaisi *rakastako* rakastaman rakastaneen rakastava *rakasten* rakastu

5. - (*RANKATA without gradation) `ranka  sala-A/v` rankaisi rankaisin rankaisivat *rankaa rankaan* rankannut *rankasi* rankata rankataan rankattava rankattiin rankattu

6. + RAPISTELLA `rapistel{eØ}  /v` rapisteli rapistelivat rapistella rapistellaan rapistellen rapistellessa rapistelee rapistelen rapistelevat

7. + RASKAUTTAA `raskaut{tØ}{aØe}  /v` raskauta raskauteta raskautettiin raskautettu raskautti raskauttaa raskauttaisi raskauttanut raskauttavat

8. - (*RATKAA as kaivaa) `ratk{aoe}  /v` ratkaisi ratkaisimme ratkaisin ratkaisivat ratketa ratketaan ratkettava ratkettiin ratkoi ratkoimme ratkoivat

9. + RAVATA `rava  sala-A/v` ravaisin ravaa ravaan ravaatte ravaavat ravannee ravannut ravasi ravasimme ravasivat ravata ravataan ravaten ravatessa ravattaisiin ravattava ravattiin ravattu

10. + REAGOIDA `reago  haravo-i/v` reagoi reagoimme reagoin reagoisi reagoisin reagoisit reagoisitte reagoisivat reagoit reagoivat reagoi reagoida reagoidaan reagoiden reagoidessa reagoimme reagoin reagoinevat reagoinut reagoit reagoitaisi reagoitaisiin reagoitava reagoitiin reagoitu reagoivat reagoinnut

11. + REKISTERÖITYÄ `rekisteröity  /v` rekisteröity rekisteröityi rekisteröityisi rekisteröityisivät rekisteröityivät rekisteröitynyt rekisteröityvät rekisteröityy rekisteröityä

12. - (*REPEÄ as kylpeä and without gradation) `rep{eiØ}  /v` repi REPIN repisi repisimme repisin repisivät repivät repee REPET repeä repien repiessä

13. + REVETÄ `re{pv}e  katke-A/v` repee repesi repesin repesivät repeä repeäisi repeäisivät repeän repeävät repeää revennyt revetessä revetä

14. + RIEPOTELLA `riepot{tØ}el{eØ}  /v` riepotella riepotellaan riepotellessa riepotellut riepoteltava riepoteltiin riepoteltu riepotteli riepottelisi riepottelivat riepottele riepottelee riepottelevat

15. + RIITAUTUA `riitau  antau-TU/v` riitauduin riitauduta riitauta riitauttaneen riitautua riitautui riitautuivat riitautunut riitautuu riitautuvat

16. + RIKKOONTUA `rikkoon{tn}u  /v` rikkoonnu rikkoontua rikkoontuessa rikkoontui rikkoontuisi rikkoontuivat rikkoontunee rikkoontunut rikkoontuu rikkoontuvat

17. - (*RISKIÄ as sallia) `risk{iØ}  /v` *riski riskimme riskin riskisi riskit riskien riskimme* RISKINE *riskinen riskiä*

18. - (*RIVIÄ as sallia) `riv{iØ}  /v` *rivi rivimme rivin rivisi rivit rivien* RIVIESSÄ *rivimme rivin rivinen rivit riviä*

19. + ROIHUTA `roihu  halu-A/v` roihua roihuaa roihuavat roihunnut roihusi roihusivat roihuta roihuten roihutessa roihuttiin

20. (*ROKOTAA as muistaa without gradation) - `rokot{aØe}  /v` rokotimme ROKOTIVAT rokota rokotamme rokoteta rokotetaan rokotettaessa rokotettaisi rokotettaisiin rokotettava rokotettiin rokotettu

21. + ROSKATA `roska  sala-A/v` roskaisivat roskaa roskaan roskaavat roskanne roskannut roskasi roskasivat roskata roskataan

22. + RUKSIA `ruks{iØ}  /v` ruksi ruksin ruksit ruksivat ruksi ruksia ruksien ruksii ruksin ruksit ruksitaan ruksittu ruksivat

23. + RUNTATA `runt{tØ}a  sala-A/v` runtannut runtata runtataan runtaten runtattava runtattiin runtattu runttaisi runttaa runttaavat runttasi runttasin runttasivat

24. + RUSTATA `rusta sala-A/v` rustaisi rustaa rustaamme rustaavat rustannut rustasi rustasin rustasivat rustata rustataan rustatessa rustattaessa rustattava rustattiin rustattu

25. + RYHMITTYÄ `ryhmit{t∅}y` /v ryhmity ryhmityin ryhmitymme ryhmityttiin ryhmittyen ryhmittyessä ryhmittyi ryhmittyisi ryhmittyisivät ryhmittyivät ryhmittynyt ryhmittyvät ryhmittyy ryhmittyä

26. + RYNNIÄ `rynn{i∅}` /v rynni rynnin rynnivät rynni rynnien rynniessä rynnii rynnin rynninyt rynnittiin rynnittävä rynnitä rynnitään rynnivät rynniä

27. + RYYDITTÄÄ `ryydit{t∅}{ä∅e}` /v ryyditettiin ryyditetty ryyditetään ryyditti ryydittivät ryydittäen ryydittäessä ryydittäisi ryydittänyt ryydittävät ryydittää

28. + RYÖVÄTÄ `ryövä sala-A/v` ryöväisi ryövännyt ryöväsi ryöväsivät ryövättiin ryövätty ryövätä ryövätään ryövää ryöväävät

29. + RÄKSYTTÄÄ `räksyt{t∅}{ä∅e}` /v räksytetty räksytetään räksytä räksytän räksytti räksyttivät räksyttäessä räksyttänyt räksyttävät räksyttää

30. + RÖKITTÄÄ `rökit{t∅}{ä∅e}` /v rökitimme rökitettiin rökitetty rökitettävä rökitämme rökitti rökittivät rökittäisi rökittänyt rökittävät rökittää

For results 4, 5, 8, 12 and 20 also a better solution is present in the list of all solutions. The incorrect entries passed the test because there happened to be some misspelled tokens (shown as SMALL CAPS) forms of other verbs (shown in san serif) or nominals (shown as *emphasized*) which fitted those entries but not to the correct ones. The false results 12 and 20 would have been avoided if there were no typos in the corpus. In the absence of the misspelled words, the fase entries would have failed because the correct one also generates the same set of word forms (plus many others). The list of word forms in false results 17 and 18 are almost exclusively nouns. The false results 4, 5 and 8 contain each a set of forms from two different common verbs. The data hints that one ought to have some method of weighing the goodness of competing candidate entries. If some entry convincingly accounts a word form, that word form could be excluded from the lists of other entries.

# Tracking Typological Traits of Uralic Languages in Distributed Language Representations


Johannes Bjerva
Department of Computer Science
University of Copenhagen
Denmark
bjerva@di.ku.dk

Isabelle Augenstein
Department of Computer Science
University of Copenhagen
Denmark
augenstein@di.ku.dk



## Abstract

Although linguistic typology has a long history, computational approaches have only recently gained popularity. The use of distributed representations in computational linguistics has also become increasingly popular. A recent development is to learn distributed representations of language, such that typologically similar languages are spatially close to one another. Although empirical successes have been shown for such language representations, they have not been subjected to much typological probing. In this paper, we first look at whether this type of language representations are empirically useful for model transfer between Uralic languages in deep neural networks. We then investigate which typological features are encoded in these representations by attempting to predict features in the *World Atlas of Language Structures*, at various stages of fine-tuning of the representations. We focus on Uralic languages, and find that some typological traits can be automatically inferred with accuracies well above a strong baseline.



## Tiivistelmä

Vaikka kielitypologialla on pitkä historia, siihen liittyvät laskennalliset menetelmät ovat vasta viime aikoina saavuttaneet suosiota. Myös hajautettujen representaatioiden käyttö laskennallisessa kielitieteessä on tullut yhä suositummaksi. Viimeaikainen kehitys alalla on oppia kielestä hajautettu representaatio, joka esittää samankaltaiset kielet lähellä toisiaan. Vaikka kyseiset representaatiot nauttivatkin empiiristä menestystä, ei niitä ole huomattavasti tutkittu typologisesti. Tässä artikkelissa tutkitaan, ovatko tällaiset kielirepresentaatiot empiirisesti käyttökelpoisia uralilaisten kielten välisissä mallimuunnoksissa syvissä neuroverkoissa. Pyrkimällä ennustamaan piirteitä *World Atlas of Language Structures*-tietokannassa tutkimme, mitä typologisia ominaisuuksia nämä representaatiot sisältävät. Keskityimme uralilaisiin kieliin ja huomasimme, että jotkin typologiset ominaisuudet voidaan automaattisesti päätellä tarkkuudella, joka ylittää selvästi vahvan perustason.







*Proceedings of the 4th International Workshop for Computational Linguistics for Uralic Languages (IWCLUL 2018)*, pages 78–88,
Helsinki, Finland, January 8–9, 2018. ©2018 Association for Computational Linguistics

# 1 Introduction

For more than two and a half centuries, linguistic typologists have studied languages with respect to their structural and functional properties, thereby implicitly classifying languages as being more or less similar to one another, by virtue of such properties (Haspelmath, 2001; Velupillai, 2012). Although typology has a long history (Herder, 1772; Gabelentz, 1891; Greenberg, 1960, 1974; Dahl, 1985; Comrie, 1989; Haspelmath, 2001; Croft, 2002), computational approaches have only recently gained popularity (Dunn et al., 2011; Wälchli, 2014; Östling, 2015; Bjerva and Börstell, 2016; Deri and Knight, 2016; Cotterell and Eisner, 2017; Peters et al., 2017; Asgari and Schütze, 2017; Malaviya et al., 2017). One part of traditional typological research can be seen as assigning sparse explicit feature vectors to languages, for instance manually encoded in databases such as the World Atlas of Language Structures (WALS, Dryer and Haspelmath, 2013). A recent development which can be seen as analogous to this, is the process of learning distributed language representations in the form of dense real-valued vectors, often referred to as *language embeddings* (Tsvetkov et al., 2016; Östling and Tiedemann, 2017; Malaviya et al., 2017). These language embeddings encode typological properties of language, reminiscent of the sparse features in WALS, or even of parameters in Chomsky's Principles and Parameters framework (Chomsky, 1993; Chomsky and Lasnik, 1993; Chomsky, 2014).

In this paper, we investigate the usefulness of explicitly modelling similarities between languages in deep neural networks using language embeddings. To do so, we view NLP tasks for multiple Uralic languages as different aspects of the same problem and model them in one model using multilingual transfer in a multi-task learning model. Multilingual models frequently follow a hard parameter sharing regime, where all hidden layers of a neural network are shared between languages, with the language either being implicitly coded in the input string (Johnson et al., 2017), given as a language ID in a one-hot encoding (Ammar et al., 2016), or as a language embedding (Östling and Tiedemann, 2017). In this paper, we both explore multilingual modelling of Uralic languages, and probe the language embeddings obtained from such modelling in order to gain novel insights about typological traits of Uralic languages. We aim to answer the following three research questions (RQs).

RQ 1 To what extent is model transfer between Uralic languages for PoS tagging mutually beneficial?

RQ 2 Are distributed language representations useful for model transfer between Uralic languages?

RQ 3 Can we observe any explicit typological properties encoded in these distributed language representations when considering Uralic languages?

# 2 Data

## 2.1 Distributed language representations

There are several methods for obtaining distributed language representations by training a recurrent neural language model (Mikolov et al., 2010) simultaneously for different languages (Tsvetkov et al., 2016; Östling and Tiedemann, 2017). In these recurrent multilingual language models with long short-term memory cells (LSTM, Hochreiter and Schmidhuber, 1997), languages are embedded into a $n$-dimensional space. In order for multilingual parameter sharing to be successful in this setting, the neural network is encouraged to use the language embeddings to encode features of language. Other work has explored learning language embeddings in the context of neural machine translation (Malaviya et al., 2017). In this work, we explore the embeddings trained by Östling and Tiedemann (2017), both in their original state, and by further tuning them for PoS tagging.

## 2.2 Part-of-speech tagging

We use PoS annotations from version 2 of the Universal Dependencies (Nivre et al., 2016). We focus on the four Uralic languages present in the UD, namely Finnish (based on the Turku Dependency Treebank, Pyysalo et al., 2015), Estonian (Muischnek et al., 2016), Hungarian (based on the Hungarian Dependency Treebank, Vincze et al., 2010), and North Sámi (Sheyanova and Tyers, 2017). As we are mainly interested in observing the language embeddings, we down-sample all training sets to 1500 sentences (approximate number of sentences in the Hungarian data), so as to minimise any size-based effects.

## 2.3 Typological data

In the experiments for RQ3, we attempt to predict typological features. We extract the features we aim to predict from WALS (Dryer and Haspelmath, 2013). We consider features which are encoded for all four Uralic languages in our sample.

# 3 Method and experiments

We approach the task of PoS tagging using a fairly standard bi-directional LSTM architecture, based on Plank et al. (2016). The system is implemented using DyNet (Neubig et al., 2017). We train using the Adam optimisation algorithm (Kingma and Ba, 2014) over a maximum of 10 epochs, using early stopping. We make two modifications to the bi-LSTM architecture of Plank et al. (2016). First of all, we do not use any atomic embedded word representations, but rather use only character-based word representations. This choice was made so as to encourage the model not to rely on language-specific vocabulary. Additionally, we concatenate a pre-trained language embedding to each word representation. That is to say, in the original bi-LSTM formulation of Plank et al. (2016), each word $w$ is represented as $\vec{w} + LSTM_c(w)$, where $\vec{w}$ is an embedded word representation, and $LSTM_c(w)$ is the final states of a character bi-LSTM running over the characters in a word. In our formulation, each word $w$ in language $l$ is represented as $LSTM_c(w) + \vec{l}$, where $LSTM_c(w)$ is defined as before, and $\vec{l}$ is an embedded language representation. We use a two-layer deep bi-LSTM, with 100 units in each layer. The character embeddings used also have 100 dimensions. We update the language representations, $\vec{l}$, during training. The language representations are 64-dimensional, and are initialised using the language embeddings from Östling and Tiedemann (2017). All PoS tagging results reported are the average of five runs, each with different initialisation seeds, so as to minimise random effects in our results.

## 3.1 Model transfer between Uralic languages

The aim of these experiments is to provide insight into **RQ 1** and **RQ 2**. We first train a monolingual model for each of the four Uralic languages. This model is then evaluated on all four languages, to investigate how successful model transfer between pairs of languages is. Results are shown in Figure 1. Comparing results within each language shows that transfer between Finnish and Estonian is the most successful. This can be expected considering that these are the two most closely related languages in the sample, as both are Finnic languages. Model transfer both to and from the more distantly related languages Hungarian and North Sámi is less successful. There is little-to-no difference in this monolingual condition with respect to whether or not language embeddings are used. As a baseline, we include transfer results when training on Spanish, which we consider a proxy of a distantly related languages. Transferring from Spanish is significantly worse ($p < 0.05$) than transferring from a Uralic language in all settings. Additionally, all transfer settings except for the Spanish setting are above a most frequent class baseline.

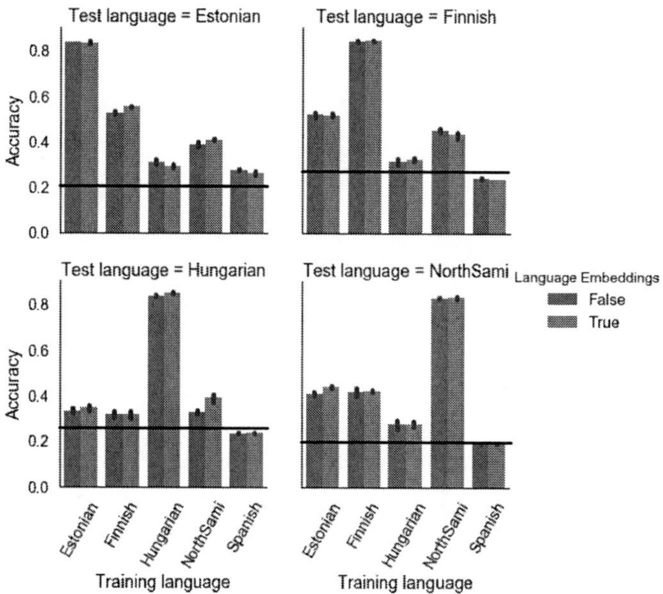


Figure 1: Monolingual PoS training. The x-axes denote the training languages, and the y-axes denote the PoS tagging accuracy on the test language at hand. The black line indicates the most frequent class baseline accuracy.

Next, we train a bilingual model for each Uralic language. Each model is trained on the target language in addition to one other Uralic language. Results are shown in Figure 2. Again, transfer between the two Finnic languages is the most successful. Here we can also observe a strong effect of whether or not language embeddings are incorporated in the neural architecture. Including language embeddings allows for both of the Finnic languages to benefit significantly ($p < 0.05$) from the transfer setting, as compared to the monolingual setting, indicated by the figure baseline. No significant differences are observed for other language pairs.

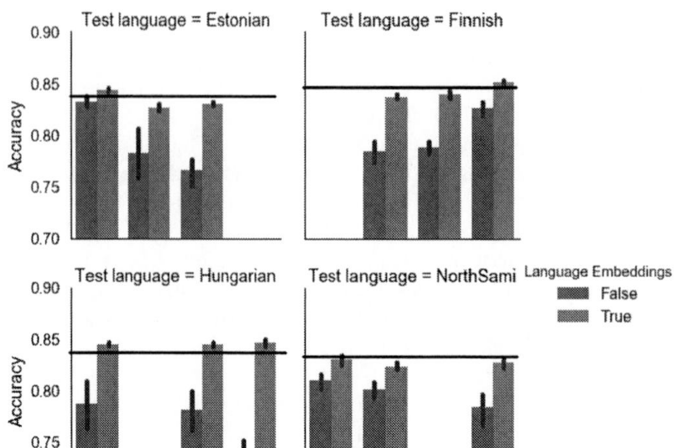

Figure 2: Bilingual PoS training. The x-axes denote the added training languages (in addition to the target language), and the y-axes denote the PoS tagging accuracy on the test language at hand. The black line indicates the monolingual baseline accuracy.


## 3.2  Predicting typological features with language embeddings

Having observed that language embeddings are beneficial for model transfer between Uralic languages, we turn to the typological experiments probing these embeddings. The aim of these experiments is to provide insight into **RQ 3**. We investigate typological features from WALS (Dryer and Haspelmath, 2013), focussing on those which have been encoded for the languages included in the UD.

We first train the same neural network architecture as for the previous experiments on all languages in UD version 2. Observing the language embeddings from various epochs of training permits tracking the typological traits encoded in the distributed language representations as they are fine-tuned. In order to answer the research question, we train a simple linear classifier to predict typological traits based on the embeddings. Concretely, we train a logistic regression model, which takes as input a language embedding $\vec{l}_e$ from a given epoch of training, $e$, and outputs the typological class a language belongs to (as coded in WALS). We train a single model for each typological trait and each training epoch. When $e$ is 0, this indicates the pre-trained language embeddings as obtained from Östling and Tiedemann (2017). Increasing $e$ indicates the number of epochs of PoS tagging during which the language embedding has been updated. All results are the mean of three-fold cross-validation. We are mainly interested in observing two things: i) Which typological traits do language embeddings encode?; ii) To what extent can we track the changes in these language embeddings over the course of fine-tuning for the task of PoS tagging?.

We train the neural network model over five epochs, and investigate differences of classification accuracies of typological properties as compared to pre-trained embeddings. A baseline reference is also included, which is defined as the most frequently occurring typological trait within each category. In these experiments, we disregard typological categories which are rare in the observed sample (i.e. of which we have one or zero examples). Looking at classification accuracy of WALS features, we can see four emerging patterns:

1. The feature is pre-encoded;
2. The feature is encoded by fine-tuning;
3. The feature is not pre-encoded;
4. The feature encoding is lost by fine-tuning.

One example per category is given in Figure 3. Two features based on word-ordering can be seen as belonging in the categories of features which are either pre-encoded or which become encoded during training. The fine-tuned embeddings do not encode the feature for whether pronominal subjects are expressed, or the feature for whether a predicate nominal has a zero copula.

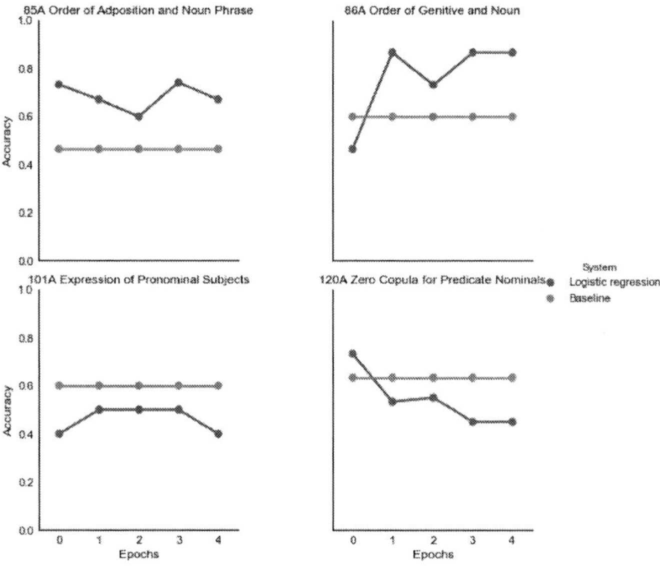


Figure 3: Predicting typological features in WALS. The x-axes denote number of epochs the language embeddings have been fine-tuned for. The y-axes denote classification accuracy for the typological feature at hand.

### 3.2.1 Predicting Uralic typological features

Finally, we attempt to predict typological features for the four Uralic languages included in our sample, as shown in Figure 4. Similarly to the larger language sample in Figure 3, the Uralic language embeddings also both gain typological information in some respects, and lose information in other respects. For instance, the pre-trained

embeddings are not able to predict ordering of adpositions and noun phrase in the
Uralic languages, whereas training on PoS tagging for two epochs adds this information.

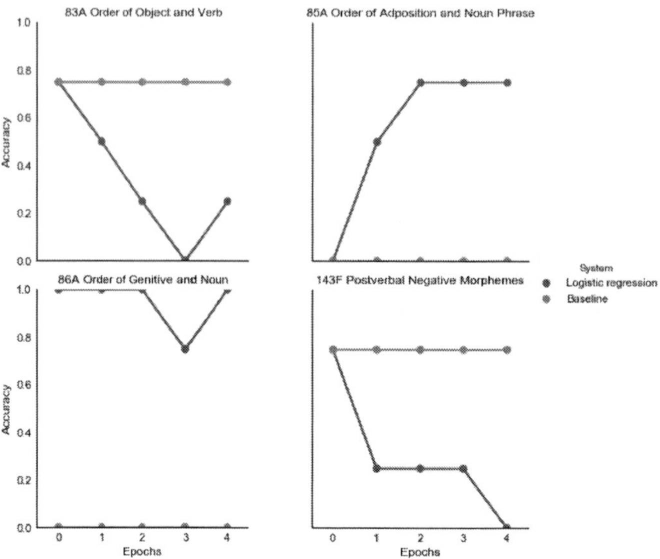



Figure 4: Predicting typological features in Uralic languages. The x-axes denote number of epochs the language embeddings have been fine-tuned for. The y-axes denote
classification accuracy for the typological feature at hand.

## 4  Discussion

### 4.1  Language embeddings for Uralic model transfer

In the monolingual transfer setting, we observed that transferring from more closely-
related languages was relatively beneficial. This is expected, as the more similar two
languages are, the easier it ought to be for the model to directly apply what it learns
from one language to the other. Concretely, we observed that transferring between
the two Finnic languages in our sample, Finnish and Estonian, worked relatively well.
We further observed that including language embeddings in this setting had little-to-
no effect on the results. This can be explained by the fact that the language embedding
used is the same throughout the training phase, as only one language is used, hence
the network likely uses this embedding to a very low extent.

In bilingual settings, omitting the language embeddings results in a severe drop
in tagging accuracy in most cases. This is likely because that treating our sample of
languages as being the same language introduces a large amount of confusion into the
model. This is further corroborated by the fact that treating the two Finnic languages
in this manner results in a relatively small drop in accuracy.

Including language embeddings allows for the model transfer setting to be beneficial for the more closely related languages. This bodes well for the low-resource case

of many Uralic languages in particular, and possibly for low-resource NLP in general. In the cases of the more distantly related language pairings, including language embeddings does not result in any significant drop in accuracy. This indicates that using language embeddings at least allows for learning a more compact model without any significant losses to performance.

### 4.2   Language embeddings for Uralic typology

Interestingly, the language embeddings are not only a manner for the neural network to identify which language it is dealing with, but are also used to encode language similarities and typological features. To contrast, the neural network could have learned something akin to a one-hot encoding of each language, in which case the languages could easily have been told apart, but classification of typological features would have been constantly at baseline level.

Another interesting finding is the fact that we can track the typological traits in the distributed language representations as they are fine-tuned for the task at hand. This has the potential to yield insight on two levels, of interest both to the more engineering-oriented NLP community, as well as the more linguistically oriented CL community. A more in-depth analysis of these embeddings can both show what a neural network is learning to model, in particular. Additionally, these embeddings can be used to glean novel insights and answer typological research questions for languages which, e.g., do not have certain features encoded in WALS.

In the specific case of Uralic languages, as considered in this paper, the typological insights we gained are, necessarily, ones that are already known for these languages. This is due to the fact that we simply evaluated our method on the features present for the Uralic languages in WALS. It is nonetheless encouraging for this line of research that we, e.g., could predict WALS feature 86A (*Order of Genitive and Noun*) based solely on these embeddings, and training a very simple classifier on a sample consisting exclusively of non-Uralic languages.

## 5   Conclusions and future work

We investigated model transfer between the four Uralic languages Finnish, Estonian, Hungarian and North Sámi, in PoS tagging, focussing on the effects of using language embeddings. We found that model transfer is successful between these languages, with the main benefits found between the two Finnic languages (Finnish and Estonian), when using language embeddings. We then turned to an investigation of the typological features encoded in the language embeddings, and found that certain features are encoded. Furthermore, we found that the typological features encoded change when fine-tuning the embeddings. In future work, we will look more closely at how the encoding of typological traits in distributed language representations changes depending on the task on which they are trained.

## Acknowledgements

The authors would like to thank Iina Alho and Anton Mallasto for help with translating the abstract to Finnish, Miryam de Lhoneux for feedback on an earlier version of this manuscript, and Robert Östling for giving us access to pre-trained language embeddings. We gratefully acknowledge the support of the NVIDIA Corporation with the donation of the Titan Xp GPU used for this research.

# References


Waleed Ammar, George Mulcaire, Miguel Ballesteros, Chris Dyer, and Noah Smith. 2016. Many languages, one parser. *Transactions of the Association of Computational Linguistics* 4:431–444.

Ehsaneddin Asgari and Hinrich Schütze. 2017. Past, present, future: A computational investigation of the typology of tense in 1000 languages. In *EMNLP*. Association for Computational Linguistics, pages 113–124.

Johannes Bjerva and Carl Börstell. 2016. Morphological Complexity Influences Verb-Object Order in Swedish Sign Language. In *Proceedings of the Workshop on Computational Linguistics for Linguistic Complexity (CL4LC)*. The COLING 2016 Organizing Committee, pages 137–141.

Noam Chomsky. 1993. *Lectures on government and binding: The Pisa lectures.* 9. Walter de Gruyter.

Noam Chomsky. 2014. *The minimalist program.* MIT press.

Noam Chomsky and Howard Lasnik. 1993. The theory of principles and parameters.

Bernard Comrie. 1989. *Language universals and linguistic typology: Syntax and morphology.* University of Chicago press.

Ryan Cotterell and Jason Eisner. 2017. Probabilistic typology: Deep generative models of vowel inventories. In *ACL*. Association for Computational Linguistics, pages 1182–1192.

William Croft. 2002. *Typology and universals.* Cambridge University Press.

Östen Dahl. 1985. *Tense and Aspect Systems.* Basil Blackwell Ltd., NewYork.

Aliya Deri and Kevin Knight. 2016. Grapheme-to-phoneme models for (almost) any language. In *ACL*. Association for Computational Linguistics, pages 399–408.

Matthew S. Dryer and Martin Haspelmath, editors. 2013. *WALS Online.* Max Planck Institute for Evolutionary Anthropology, Leipzig. http://wals.info/.

Michael Dunn, Simon J Greenhill, Stephen C Levinson, and Russell D Gray. 2011. Evolved structure of language shows lineage-specific trends in word-order universals. *Nature* 473(7345):79–82.

Georg von der Gabelentz. 1891. *Die Sprachwissenschaft, ihre Aufgaben, Methoden und bisherigen Ergebnisse.* Leipzig.

Joseph Greenberg. 1974. *Language typology: A historical and analytic overview,* volume 184. Walter de Gruyter.

Joseph H Greenberg. 1960. A quantitative approach to the morphological typology of language. *International journal of American linguistics* 26(3):178–194.

Martin Haspelmath. 2001. *Language typology and language universals: An international handbook,* volume 20. Walter de Gruyter.

J. Herder. 1772. *Abhandlung über den Ursprung der Sprache*. Berlin: Christian Friedrich Voß.

Sepp Hochreiter and Jürgen Schmidhuber. 1997. Long short-term memory. *Neural computation* 9(8):1735–1780.

Melvin Johnson, Mike Schuster, Quoc V. Le, Maxim Krikun, Yonghui Wu, Zhifeng Chen, Nikhil Thorat, Fernanda Viégas, Martin Wattenberg, Greg Corrado, Macduff Hughes, and Jeffrey Dean. 2017. Google's multilingual neural machine translation system: Enabling zero-shot translation. *Transactions of the Association of Computational Linguistics* 5:339–351.

Diederik Kingma and Jimmy Ba. 2014. Adam: A method for stochastic optimization. *arXiv preprint arXiv:1412.6980* .

Chaitanya Malaviya, Graham Neubig, and Patrick Littell. 2017. Learning language representations for typology prediction. In *EMNLP*. Association for Computational Linguistics, pages 2519–2525.

Tomas Mikolov, Martin Karafiát, Lukas Burget, Jan Cernockỳ, and Sanjeev Khudanpur. 2010. Recurrent neural network based language model. In *Interspeech*. volume 2, page 3.

Kadri Muischnek, Kaili Müürisep, and Tiina Puolakainen. 2016. Estonian dependency treebank: from constraint grammar tagset to universal dependencies. In *LREC*.

Graham Neubig, Chris Dyer, Yoav Goldberg, Austin Matthews, Waleed Ammar, Antonios Anastasopoulos, Miguel Ballesteros, David Chiang, Daniel Clothiaux, Trevor Cohn, et al. 2017. Dynet: The dynamic neural network toolkit. *arXiv preprint arXiv:1701.03980* .

Joakim Nivre, Marie-Catherine de Marneffe, Filip Ginter, Yoav Goldberg, Jan Hajic, Christopher D Manning, Ryan McDonald, Slav Petrov, Sampo Pyysalo, Natalia Silveira, et al. 2016. Universal dependencies v1: A multilingual treebank collection. In *Proceedings of the 10th International Conference on Language Resources and Evaluation (LREC 2016)*.

Robert Östling. 2015. Word order typology through multilingual word alignment. In *The 53rd Annual Meeting of the Association for Computational Linguistics and the 7th International Joint Conference on Natural Language Processing*. pages 205–211.

Robert Östling and Jörg Tiedemann. 2017. Continuous multilinguality with language vectors. In *EACL*. Association for Computational Linguistics, pages 644–649.

Ben Peters, Jon Dehdari, and Josef van Genabith. 2017. Massively multilingual neural grapheme-to-phoneme conversion. In *Proceedings of the First Workshop on Building Linguistically Generalizable NLP Systems*. pages 19–26.

Barbara Plank, Anders Søgaard, and Yoav Goldberg. 2016. Multilingual part-of-speech tagging with bidirectional long short-term memory models and auxiliary loss. In *ACL*. Association for Computational Linguistics, pages 412–418.

Sampo Pyysalo, Jenna Kanerva, Anna Missilä, Veronika Laippala, and Filip Ginter. 2015. Universal dependencies for finnish. In *NoDaLiDa*. Linköping University Electronic Press, 109, pages 163–172.

Mariya Sheyanova and Francis M. Tyers. 2017. Annotation schemes in north sámi dependency parsing. In *Proceedings of the 3rd International Workshop for Computational Linguistics of Uralic Languages*. pages 66–75.

Yulia Tsvetkov, Sunayana Sitaram, Manaal Faruqui, Guillaume Lample, Patrick Littell, David Mortensen, Alan W Black, Lori Levin, and Chris Dyer. 2016. Polyglot neural language models: A case study in cross-lingual phonetic representation learning. In *NAACL-HLT*. Association for Computational Linguistics, pages 1357–1366.

Viveka Velupillai. 2012. *An introduction to linguistic typology.* John Benjamins Publishing.

Veronika Vincze, Dóra Szauter, Attila Almási, György Móra, Zoltán Alexin, and János Csirik. 2010. Hungarian dependency treebank. In *LREC*.

Bernhard Wälchli. 2014. Algorithmic typology and going from known to similar unknown categories within and across languages. *Aggregating Dialectology, Typology, and Register Analysis: Linguistic Variation in Text and Speech* 28:355.

# New Baseline in Automatic Speech Recognition for Northern Sámi


Juho Leinonen
Aalto University
juho.leinonen@aalto.fi

Peter Smit
Aalto University
peter.smit@aalto.fi

Sami Virpioja
Utopia Analytics
Aalto University
sami.virpioja@aalto.fi

Mikko Kurimo
Aalto University
mikko.kurimo@aalto.fi



### Abstract

Automatic speech recognition has gone through many changes in recent years. Advances both in computer hardware and machine learning have made it possible to develop systems far more capable and complex than the previous state-of-the-art. However, almost all of these improvements have been tested in major well-resourced languages. In this paper, we show that these techniques are capable of yielding improvements even in a small data scenario. We experiment with different deep neural network architectures for acoustic modeling for Northern Sámi and report up to 50% relative error rate reductions. We also run experiments to compare the performance of subwords as language modeling units in Northern Sámi.

### Tiivistelmä

Automaattinen puheentunnistus on kehittynyt viime vuosina merkittävästi. Uudet innovaatiot sekä laitteistossa että koneoppimisessa ovat mahdollistaneet entistä paljon tehokkaammat ja monimutkaisemmat järjestelmät. Suurin osa näistä parannuksista on kuitenkin testattu vain valtakielillä, joiden kehittämiseen on tarjolla runsaasti aineistoja. Tässä paperissa näytämme että nämä tekniikat tuottavat parannuksia myös kielillä, joista aineistoa on vähän. Kokeilemme ja vertailemme erilaisia syviä neuroverkkoja pohjoissaamen akustisina malleina ja onnistumme vähentämään tunnistusvirheitä jopa 50%:lla. Tutkimme myös tapoja pilkkoa sanoja pienempiin osiin pohjoissaamen kielimalleissa.


## 1 Introduction

The field of automatic speech recognition (ASR) has advanced rapidly in the last couple of years, in large part thanks to deep neural networks (DNNs). For decades there






Proceedings of the 4th International Workshop for Computational Linguistics for Uralic Languages (IWCLUL 2018), pages 89–99,
Helsinki, Finland, January 8–9, 2018. ©2018 Association for Computational Linguistics

has been active research trying to replace Gaussian mixture models (GMM) with various neural network configurations. Yet, only after 2010 the full power of neural networks started to be noticed when multiple groups started reporting huge improvements in their implementations (Hinton et al., 2012). At the same time, the computational power of modern graphics processing units (GPU) has made it feasible to utilize very large DNNs with very large training data sets. For speech recognition, this has meant that the decades-old best practices are quickly being replaced by new and more powerful methods.

In this paper, we have documented our work to build a new baseline for Northern Sámi. Using DNNs for acoustic modeling has provided large improvements for well-resourced Uralic languages, but for under-resourced languages, the applicability has yet to be tested. For broadcast news data sets, the latest improvements for applying neural networks instead of GMM-based acoustic models have been in the range of 14% smaller relative word error rate (WER) for Finnish and 6% for Estonian (Smit et al., 2017b).

In languages with a rich morphological structure it is difficult to build statistical language models using words. If using $n$-gram word models, the vocabulary size becomes computationally challenging, and even worse, the growing lexicon decreases out-of-vocabulary (OOV) rate rather slowly. Furthermore, the lack of data for under-resourced languages makes building a large lexicon and $n$-gram difficult. For Finnish, Estonian, Arabic and Turkish it is common to use subword units such as morphs (Hirsimäki et al., 2006) or syllables (Choueiter et al., 2006) instead of words. In this work we follow this tradition and apply statistical morphs as subword units for Northern Sámi.

Because the pronunciation in Northern Sámi can be rather well covered by rules, a simple grapheme-to-phoneme conversion can be applied for our lexicon. This gives Northern Sámi and other such languages a significant advantage in ASR, since building a proper lexicon is one of the most arduous data preparation tasks for speech recognition.

We will use a popular open-source toolkit for speech recognition, Kaldi, and document the building of a speech recognizer. In addition to DNN-based acoustic modeling, we test new methods of subword modeling for morphologically rich languages, originally developed for Finnish. The main focus of the paper is to demonstrate these new techniques in building a new baseline for Northern Sámi for further research and comparison. We will compare our results to the previous Northern Sámi baseline results from Smit et al. (2016).


## 2   Methods


Our baseline system builds on the Northern Sámi recognizer by Smit et al. (2016), but with a few important changes. In acoustic modeling, we model triphones by hidden Markov models with Gaussian mixture model emission distributions (GMM-HMM) using mel frequency cepstral coefficients (MFCCs) as input features. The lexicon is based on subword units found by a data-driven method, and a long-context $n$-gram model is used for language modeling. However, while Smit et al. (2016) used the token-pass decoder of the AaltoASR toolkit (Pylkkönen, 2005; Hirsimäki et al., 2009), our system is based on the Kaldi toolkit (Povey et al., 2011) that has a decoder based on weighted finite-state transducers (WFST). Kaldi has also implemented quite a few improvements to the standard GMM-HMM methodology. To further improve the speech recognition accuracy in Northern Sámi we test recent developments on creating subword lexicon for Kaldi and acoustic modeling based on DNNs.

## 2.1 WFST-based speech recognition

Kaldi is an open source toolkit for speech recognition developed since the year 2009 by researchers from many different universities, lead by the John Hopkins University and Brno University of Technology (Povey et al., 2011). It is based on the use of weighted finite-state transducers (WFST) complimenting the work by Mohri et al. (2008). The advantage of WFST-based recognizers is that once the search network has been constructed and optimized effectively by the WFST methods, the decoding is very fast and accurate. Moreover, Kaldi's GMM-HMMs are improved by subspace Gaussians, word-position-dependent phones and advanced silence models.

## 2.2 Subword lexicon FSTs and language models

The small amount of training data and the morphological complexity of Northern Sámi make it problematic to build language models (LM) using words as the basic units. We applied the data-driven Morfessor Baseline method (Creutz and Lagus, 2002, 2007) to segment the words into subword units. Because all words in the language can be composed from these subword units, this approach provides an unlimited vocabulary for ASR (Hirsimäki et al., 2006). While Morfessor was developed to find units of language that resemble the surface forms of linguistic morphemes, the current implementation includes a parameter for adjusting the level of segmentation that the method produces (Virpioja et al., 2013). The optimal level of segmentation for ASR varies between languages, but a wide range of lexicon seems to produce near-optimal results (Smit et al., 2017b). We did not experiment with this parameter.

Recently, Smit et al. (2017b) implemented effective subword modeling in the WFST-based ASR framework. It modifies the basic lexicon FST by introducing different models for all four different positions where a subword can appear (as prefix, infix, suffix, or complete word) and provides the appropriate word-position-dependent phones. In Figure 1 a normal word lexicon is shown where $words is replaced by a linear FST of all pronunciations in the lexicon. In Figure 2 the same basic structure is shown for a subword lexicon.

When the ASR system uses a subword lexicon, the subword units in the output need to be joined back to construct complete word forms. This can be accomplished in different ways; popular approaches are using a separate word boundary units (e.g. Hirsimäki et al., 2009) or using a special character to indicate that there is no word boundary directly preceding the subword (e.g. Arisoy et al., 2009; Tarján et al., 2014). Smit et al. (2017b) experimented on different styles of subword markings and the conclusion was that the optimal boundary marking style might depend on the language. Other work by the same authors (Smit et al., 2017a) supports this hypothesis. Therefore, in this work, we also experiment on different boundary marking styles to select the one that fits best for Northern Sámi. In Table 1 the four possible styles of marking

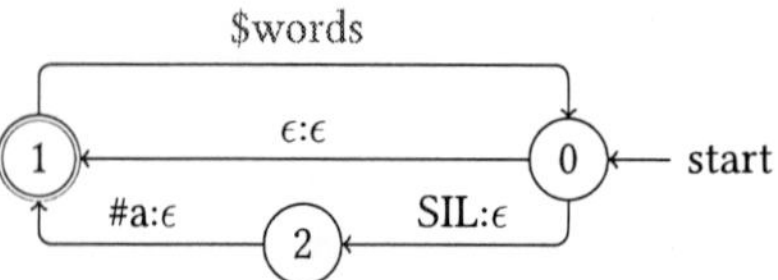


Figure 1: Prototype Lexicon FST for word-based lexicon. On each vertice in this graph is shown an input and output symbol. For example 'SIL:ε' indicates a SIL phone as input and a skip-token (ε) as output. The symbol #a is a disambiguation symbol which is required in Kaldi to make the FST determinizable. $words is a placeholder that is supposed to be replaced by a linear FST that maps all words to their appropriate word-position dependent phoneneme sequences.

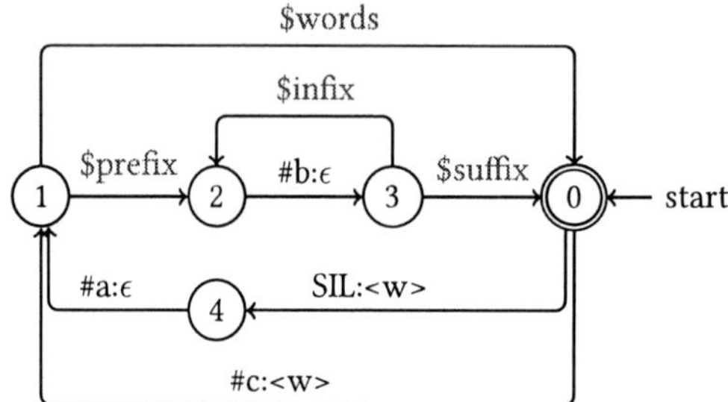


Figure 2: Prototype Lexicon FST for subword-based lexicon.

are shown. Note that the actual realization of the boundary character (here a +-sign) does not matter, but the locations of these markers do.

| Style (abbreviation) | Example |
| --- | --- |
| Boundary Tag(<w>) | <w> dan <w>rádje riikka t <w> |
| left-marked (+m) | dan rádje +riikka +t |
| right-marked (m+) | dan rádje+ riikka+ t |
| left+right-marked (+m+) | dan rádje+ +riikka+ +t |

Table 1: Four methods to mark the subword units in the sequence "dan rádjeriikkat"

As the $n$-gram language models are trained on the subword units, high-order $n$-grams are needed to provide a context of a reasonable length. We use the Kneser-Ney growing algorithm (Siivola et al., 2007) to train high-order Kneser-Ney smoothed varigram models.

## 2.3   Deep neural networks

We experiment with three different neural network architectures, all of which have demonstrated the ability to model speech well with large amounts of data.

A time delay neural network (TDNN, Peddinti et al., 2015) is a type of a feedforward network. The main benefit for speech recognition is modeling the changes in duration and varying boundaries of phonemes in the speech signal. It is constructed by having also a time delayed copy of the signal as an input. This helps the network to disregard varying start and end points of the pattern in its classification.

TDNN models can be improved by using different training criteria that match the task of speech recognition better. Regular TDNN models are trained on a frame-based cross-entropy criterion. This means that the recognizer optimizes for the recognition of phones in each separate frame. Although this sounds ideal and works well in practice, it can be further improved upon by using a criterion that actually looks to the power to predict a sequence of phones. In Povey et al. (2016) these models are introduced and named "Lattice-free maximum mutual information" or colloquially "chain models". During the training of the network, a window of frames is not only classified, but a simple forward-backward algorithm is run to estimate the sequence that will be predicted by the real speech recognizer.

Long short-term memory (LSTM) networks are a variant of recurrent neural networks (RNN). In basic RNNs the state of the hidden layer is fed back to the next step as one of the inputs, giving the network a memory of the previous inputs. However, having many hidden layers might lead to a vanishing gradient problem, where during training the gradient "vanishes" while it propagates back in the network. To correct for this, LSTMs use a so-called memory cell, to balance which information should be carried for multiple steps in the network in "long-term memory", and when to use this information in the calculations for the current state in "short term". For a bidirectional-LSTM (BLSTM), this is happening in both directions.


## 3    Experiments

We start by demonstrating the improvements obtained without DNNs by Kaldi and WFST-based decoding in relation to the AaltoASR and token-passing decoding. We continue by comparing different subword boundary markings and choose the overall best for the next experiments, where we compare different types of DNN architectures for acoustic modeling. Finally, we show the effects of increasing the size of the language model training data.


### 3.1    Data

We use the same data sets as Smit et al. (2016) to provide a fair comparison. The data includes audio data from the UIT-SME-TTS corpus with one female and male speaker. For both speakers we train a speaker-dependent recognizer using 2.5 hours of audio. Rest of the data is divided into development and evaluation sets 3:2, roughly 1–1.5 hours total. Our initial language models are based on 10 000 randomly selected sentences from the Northern Sámi Wikipedia dump in addition to the acoustic model training sentences (TRAIN+WIKI). Further tests with a larger corpus are based on "Den samiske textbanken" (BIG).

**Audio**

| | Speaker | Gender | Title | Amount |
|---|---|---|---|---|
| | SF1 | Female | UIT-SME-TTSF | 3.3 hours |
| | SM1 | Male | UIT-SME-TTSM | 4.6 hours |

**Text**

| | Source | # sentences | # word tokens | # word types |
|---|---|---|---|---|
| | Sami Wikipedia | 10k | 88k | 20k |
| | Den samiske textbanken | 990k | 12M | 475k |

Table 2: Language and acoustic modeling data for the speech recognizer training.

## 3.2  Setup

We started by first building a simple monophone-based model on MFCCs extracted from the training data and used this to better align our audio data to the transcript. After this step, we trained a traditional triphone GMM-HMM model on these improved alignments.

For our TDNN we iterate the previous step by again aligning our data with the GMM-HMM model and used these alignments together with speed and volume perturbated training data for higher dimensional MFCC features. As a result, we get a five layers deep TDNN. A similar process was used to train the BLSTM and Chain model to generate networks with seven and six layers respectively.

For a word-based system, we trained a Kneser-Ney smoothed 3-gram model with the SRILM toolkit (Stolcke, 2002). For subword language modeling, we first trained a Morfessor model based on the TRAIN+WIKI corpus. We used Morfessor 2.0 implementation (Virpioja et al., 2013) with token-based training and the corpus weight parameter as 1.5. The words in the corpus were segmented to subword units with the aforementioned model using each of the different subword boundary markings. The subword $n$-gram models were then trained on the corpora using the VariKN toolkit (Siivola et al., 2007) with maximum $n$-gram length as 10.

For the BIG corpus we trained both 3-gram and 10-gram models with the same tools. The smaller model was used for first pass scoring and 10-gram model used afterward to rescore the lattices. In TRAIN+WIKI all results are with a single-pass 10-gram model. Table 3 shows the size of the different language models (LM) and lexicons. The ASR lexicon size varies due to the different subword boundary markings even if the words are segmented with the same Morfessor model.

We report for all experiments both the word error rate (WER) as well as the letter error rate (LER). The former is more common in general speech recognition research, while the latter is more common in evaluating speech recognition for agglutinative languages, where minor mistakes such as selecting a wrong inflectional suffix or splitting a compound word have very strong effects on WER.

## 3.3  Results

Table 4 compares the error rates of the GMM-HMM baselines from AaltoASR and Kaldi. Since the data and language models are the same the difference is due to the

| Data | Units | Lexicon (#types) | | LM (#n-grams) | |
| | | SF1 | SM1 | SF1 | SM1 |
|---|---|---|---|---|---|
| TRAIN+WIKI | words | 23.5k | 23.1k | 103.9k | 102.4k |
| | subwords, <w> | 14.3k | 14.1k | 751.8k | 747.6k |
| | subwords, +m+ | 19.1k | 18.7k | 610.9k | 600.0k |
| | subwords, +m | 16.1k | 15.8k | 608.7k | 596.9k |
| | subwords, m+ | 17.2k | 17.0k | 607.5k | 596.4k |
| BIG | words | 474.9k | | 5.9M | |
| | subwords, <w> | 93.9k | | 51.6M | |
| | subwords, +m+ | 172.4k | | 64.6M | |
| | subwords, +m | 122.2k | | 65.0M | |
| | subwords, m+ | 137.8k | | 64.4M | |

Table 3: Lexicon and language model sizes for word models and subword models with different boundary marking styles.

| | SF1 | | SM1 | |
| Toolkit | WER | LER | WER | LER |
|---|---|---|---|---|
| AaltoASR | 37.5 | 8.5 | 39.5 | 9.4 |
| Kaldi | 32.3 | 6.9 | 34.9 | 7.4 |

Table 4: Comparison between AaltoASR (Smit et al., 2016) and Kaldi with 10-gram LM based on TRAIN+WIKI and 2.5h of audio for both speakers.

toolkits, the decoders, and the GMM-HMMs implementations.

Table 5 continues with the Kaldi system to compare the four subword boundary markings. The differences are small given the size of the test data, but the traditional word boundary tag <w> seems to be a good choice and was used in the further experiments. It has the smallest lexicon, but because the boundary tag consumes one position in each $n$-gram context longer $n$-grams are utilized than in the other models. However, because the subword LMs are trained with the VariKN toolkit, the increase in the LM size is minimal.

| | SF1 | | SM1 | |
| Language Model | WER | LER | WER | LER |
|---|---|---|---|---|
| word 3-gram | 43.9 | 9.2 | 49.7 | 10.4 |
| subword 10-gram, <w> | 32.3 | 6.9 | 34.9 | 7.4 |
| subword 10-gram, +m+ | 33.8 | 7.1 | 38.1 | 8.2 |
| subword 10-gram, +m | 32.5 | 6.9 | 36.2 | 7.5 |
| subword 10-gram, m+ | 36.5 | 7.0 | 38.9 | 7.4 |

Table 5: Error Rates for different subword boundary markings. All models were trained with the TRAIN+WIKI corpus and 2.5h of audio.

Table 6 presents the main result of this paper, which is the comparison of GMM-HMM to various DNN architectures when the training data resources are limited. The special advantage of DNNs is their remarkable effectiveness in modeling "deep"

| Speaker | Acoustic model | | TRAIN+WIKI | | BIG | |
| --- | --- | --- | --- | --- | --- | --- |
| | Type | #params | WER | LER | WER | LER |
| | AaltoASR | 600k | 37.5 | .8.5 | 23.7 | 5.5 |
| | HMM-GMM | 858k | 32.3 | 6.9 | 19.9 | 3.8 |
| SF1 | TDNN | 6.6M | 24.8 | 4.9 | 14.7 | 2.5 |
| | Chain Model | 5.8M | 25.6 | 6.0 | 17.0 | 3.5 |
| | BLSTM | 10.8M | 25.6 | 5.3 | 13.9 | 2.7 |
| | AaltoASR | 600k | 39.5 | 9.4 | 20.9 | 4.9 |
| | HMM-GMM | 858k | 34.9 | 7.4 | 18.0 | 3.6 |
| SM1 | TDNN | 6.6M | 29.2 | 5.7 | 12.5 | 2.1 |
| | Chain Model | 5.8M | 29.8 | 6.0 | 15.2 | 2.8 |
| | BLSTM | 10.8M | 28.5 | 5.8 | 12.8 | 2.4 |

Table 6: Error Rates between TRAIN+WIKI and the BIG language model. Same acoustic data was used in all models. AaltoASR results are from Smit et al. (2016).

structures in data that the previous frameworks could not take into account. In speech recognition, this has been taken to mean that DNNs require large amounts of training data. However, it is possible that in limited applications such as speaker-dependent systems, DNNs may be able to find useful structures even from small amounts of data. Table 6 shows clear improvements in every DNN architecture compared to the GMM-HMM method. At the point of writing, our simplest network TDNN is at least as good or better than the more complex Chain model and BLSTM, but given more time to study optimal hyperparameters for small data settings, we might be able to train models surpassing the now new baseline.

Finally, Table 7 shows that the relative differences between different subword boundary markings do not change much even when the language models are trained using the larger corpus. As in Table 5, the relative differences are small given the size of the test data, but the traditional word boundary tag <w> is still unbeaten and all subword models are better than the word-based model.

| | SF1 | | SM1 | |
| --- | --- | --- | --- | --- |
| Language Model | WER | LER | WER | LER |
| word 3-gram | 17.6 | 3.1 | 17.0 | 2.8 |
| subword 10-gram, <w> | 14.7 | 2.5 | 12.5 | 2.1 |
| subword 10-gram, +m+ | 14.9 | 2.8 | 13.4 | 2.3 |
| subword 10-gram, +m | 14.6 | 2.7 | 14.6 | 2.4 |
| subword 10-gram, m+ | 16.3 | 2.6 | 13.7 | 2.3 |

Table 7: Error Rates between different boundary marking styles using the BIG language model. TDNN was used in all recognizers.

## 4  Conclusions

In this paper, we applied the state-of-the-art ASR framework based on Kaldi and DNN acoustic models to get a new baseline for Northern Sámi. The results were quite impressive with up to 50% relative error rate reduction. The only drawback in WFST-based speech recognition with large LMs is the size of the WFST search graph, which makes the memory consumption of the single pass decoding sometimes prohibitive. However, in most cases this can be compensated by a two-pass recognition where the second pass is used to rescore the existing search graph with the large LM. The single pass approach does also provide reasonable results already with a low order $n$-gram models. In addition, the modeling of position-dependent phones and other advanced acoustic modeling developments implemented in Kaldi was a clear benefit. Considering these it is recommended to apply Kaldi for the following research.

The results show clearly that at least in speaker-dependent systems, even with relatively small amounts of audio data, the DNNs were capable of finding structures in data that made them superior to the old state-of-the-art GMM-HMM models. DNNs are also very complex, and their techniques and methods are continuously advancing, so we expect to still achieve further significant improvements in near future. Also, even with the current techniques we should be able to improve the results further by more thoroughly optimizing the layer sizes and hyperparameters of the neural networks. For example, Mansikkaniemi et al. (2017) was able to improve the state-of-the art results for Finnish broadcast news results by 3% relative with such optimizations.

For the different types of subword boundary markings, our experiments resulted only small differences for Northern Sámi. Although the traditional word boundary tags gave slightly better results than the other marking styles more studies should be performed on how much the results depends on the language, data, and the length of the subword units.

The next step for improving the LMs in Northern Sámi is to apply recurrent neural networks. For RNNLMs, the whole word units have further disadvantages in morphologically rich languages, because the large vocabulary increases the dimensions of the input and output layers. For Finnish, using RNN language models with subword units has lowered the WER by 11% with a large training corpus (Smit et al., 2017a). Reducing the corpus size from 160 million tokens to 16 million tokens, which is close to our BIG data set for Northern Sámi, reduced the improvement only slightly to 9%. Smit et al. (2017a) show also promising results for Finnish and Arabic with purely character-based models.

For under-resourced languages specifically, an interesting future direction is to develop methods to better take advantage of a well-resourced related language. Even simple methods such as data pooling, acoustic model adaptation or bootstrapping with large amounts of unlabeled data have been popular. For Northern Sámi we could, for example, try to apply the data and expertise available in Finnish and Estonian. Regardless of the approach taken to improve the ASR, the system build in this paper provides a good baseline for further experiments.

## Acknowledgements

We thank the University of Tromsø for the access to their Northern Sámi datasets and acknowledge the computational resources provided by the Aalto Science-IT project.

This work was financially supported by the Tekes Challenge Finland project TELLme, Academy of Finland under the grant number 251170, and Kone foundation.

# References

Ebru Arisoy, Dogan Can, Siddika Parlak, Hasim Sak, and Murat Saraclar. 2009. Turkish broadcast news transcription and retrieval. *IEEE Transactions on Audio, Speech, and Language Processing* 17(5):874–883. https://doi.org/10.1109/TASL.2008.2012313.

Ghinwa Choueiter, Daniel Povey, Stanley F. Chen, and Geoffrey Zweig. 2006. Morpheme-based language modeling for Arabic LVCSR. In *ICASSP 2006 – IEEE International Conference on Acoustics, Speech and Signal Processing*. pages 1053–1056. https://doi.org/10.1109/ICASSP.2006.1660205.

Mathias Creutz and Krista Lagus. 2002. Unsupervised discovery of morphemes. In *Proceedings of the ACL 2002 Workshop on Morphological and Phonological Learning*. Association for Computational Linguistics, Stroudsburg, PA, USA, volume 6 of *MPL '02*, pages 21–30. https://doi.org/10.3115/1118647.1118650.

Mathias Creutz and Krista Lagus. 2007. Unsupervised models for morpheme segmentation and morphology learning. *ACM Transactions on Speech and Language Processing (TSLP)* 4(1):3.

Geoffrey Hinton, Li Deng, Dong Yu, Goerge E. Dahl, Abdel-rahman Mohamed, Navdeep Jaitly, Andrew Senior, Vincent Vanhoucke, Patrick Nguyen, Tara N. Sainath, and Brian Kingsbury. 2012. Deep neural networks for acoustic modeling in speech recognition: The shared views of four research groups. *IEEE Signal Processing Magazine* 29(6):82–97. https://doi.org/10.1109/MSP.2012.2205597.

Teemu Hirsimäki, Mathias Creutz, Vesa Siivola, Mikko Kurimo, Sami Virpioja, and Janne Pylkkönen. 2006. Unlimited vocabulary speech recognition with morph language models applied to Finnish. *Computer Speech & Language* 20(4):515–541.

Teemu Hirsimäki, Janne Pylkkönen, and Mikko Kurimo. 2009. Importance of high-order n-gram models in morph-based speech recognition. *IEEE Transactions on Audio, Speech, and Language Processing* 17(4):724–732. https://doi.org/10.1109/TASL.2008.2012323.

André Mansikkaniemi, Peter Smit, and Mikko Kurimo. 2017. Automatic construction of the Finnish Parliament Speech Corpus. In *INTERSPEECH 2017 – 18th Annual Conference of the International Speech Communication Association*. Stockholm, Sweden.

Mehryar Mohri, Fernando Pereira, and Michael Riley. 2008. Speech recognition with weighted finite-state transducers. In *Springer Handbook of Speech Processing*, Springer, pages 559–584.

Vijayaditya Peddinti, Daniel Povey, and Sanjeev Khudanpur. 2015. A time delay neural network architecture for efficient modeling of long temporal contexts. In *INTERSPEECH 2015 – 16th Annual Conference of the International Speech Communication Association*. Dresden, Germany, pages 3214–3218.

Daniel Povey, Arnab Ghoshal, Gilles Boulianne, Lukas Burget, Ondrej Glembek, Nagendra Goel, Mirko Hannemann, Petr Motlicek, Yanmin Qian, Petr Schwarz, Jan

Silovsky, Georg Stemmer, and Karel Vesely. 2011. The Kaldi speech recognition toolkit. In *ASRU 2011 – IEEE Workshop on Automatic Speech Recognition & Understanding*.

Daniel Povey, Vijayaditya Peddinti, Daniel Galvez, Pegah Ghahremani, Vimal Manohar, Xingyu Na, Yiming Wang, and Sanjeev Khudanpur. 2016. Purely sequence-trained neural networks for ASR based on lattice-free MMI. In *INTERSPEECH 2016 – 17ᵗʰ Annual Conference of the International Speech Communication Association*. San Francisco, pages 2751–2755. https://doi.org/10.21437/Interspeech.2016-595.

Janne Pylkkönen. 2005. An efficient one-pass decoder for Finnish large vocabulary continuous speech recognition. In *Proceedings of The 2nd Baltic Conference on Human Language Technologies*. pages 167–172.

Vesa Siivola, Teemu Hirsimaki, and Sami Virpioja. 2007. On growing and pruning Kneser–Ney smoothed-gram models. *Audio, Speech, and Language Processing, IEEE Transactions on* 15(5):1617–1624.

Peter Smit, Siva Reddy Gangireddy, Seppo Enarvi, Sami Virpioja, and Mikko Kurimo. 2017a. Character-based units for unlimited vocabulary continuous speech recognition. In *ASRU 2017 – IEEE Workshop on Automatic Speech Recognition & Understanding*.

Peter Smit, Juho Leinonen, Kristiina Jokinen, and Mikko Kurimo. 2016. Automatic speech recognition for Northern Sámi with comparison to other Uralic languages. In *Proceedings of the Second International Workshop on Computational Linguistics for Uralic Languages*. pages 80–91.

Peter Smit, Sami Virpioja, and Mikko Kurimo. 2017b. Improved subword modeling for WFST-based speech recognition. In *INTERSPEECH 2017 – 18ᵗʰ Annual Conference of the International Speech Communication Association*. Stockholm, Sweden.

Andreas Stolcke. 2002. SRILM — an extensible language modeling toolkit. In *Proceedings of the 7th International Conference on Spoken Language Processing (ICSLP-2002)*. pages 901–904.

Balázs Tarján, Tibor Fegyó, and Péter Mihajlik. 2014. A bilingual study on the prediction of morph-based improvement. In *Fourth International Workshop on Spoken Language Technologies for Under-Resourced Languages (SLTU-2014)*. pages 131–138.

Sami Virpioja, Peter Smit, Stig-Arne Grönroos, and Mikko Kurimo. 2013. Morfessor 2.0: Python implementation and extensions for Morfessor Baseline. Report 25/2013 in Aalto University publication series SCIENCE + TECHNOLOGY, Department of Signal Processing and Acoustics, Aalto University, Helsinki, Finland.

# Initial Experiments in Data-Driven Morphological Analysis for Finnish

Miikka Silfverberg
University of Colorado Boulder
Department of Linguistics
`miikka.silfverberg@colorado.edu`

Mans Hulden
University of Colorado Boulder
Department of Linguistics
`mans.hulden@colorado.edu`

### Abstract

This paper presents initial experiments in data-driven morphological analysis for Finnish using deep learning methods. Our system uses a character based bidirectional LSTM and pretrained word embeddings to predict a set of morphological analyses for an input word form. We present experiments on morphological analysis for Finnish. We learn to mimic the output of the OMorFi analyzer on the Finnish portion of the Universal Dependency treebank collection. The results of the experiments are encouraging and show that the current approach has potential to serve as an extension to existing rule-based analyzers.

### Tiivistelmä

Esittelemme kokeita aineistolähtöisellä syväoppimismenetelmiin perustuvalla suomen kielen morfologisella analysaattorilla. Esittelemämme järjestelmä perustuu merkkipohjaisiin LSTM-malleihin ja esiopetettuihin sanaupotuksiin. Järjestelmämme oppii matkimaan OMorFi-jäsennintä, joka on suomen kielen morfologinen analysaattori. Teemme kokeita Universal Dependency -puupankkikokoelman suomenkielisellä osuudella. Kokeemme osoittavat, että koneoppimismenetelmät tarjoavat lupaavan lähestymistavan suomen kielen morfologiseen analyysiin.

## 1  Introduction

The task of morphological analysis consists of providing a word form with the complete set of morphological readings it can attain (see Figure 1). It is a cornerstone in the development of natural language processing (NLP) utilities for morphologically complex languages such as the Uralic languages. It is a necessary preprocessing task because of the high type-to-token ratio, which is prevalent in morphologically complex languages. Additionally, phenomena like compounding and derivation, which frequently produce previously unseen lexemes, necessitate the use of morphological analyzers.



*Proceedings of the 4th International Workshop for Computational Linguistics for Uralic Languages (IWCLUL 2018)*, pages 100–107,
Helsinki, Finland, January 8–9, 2018. ©2018 Association for Computational Linguistics

```
tunne   tunne    Noun+Sg+Nom
        tuntea   Verb+Act+Impv+Sg2
        tuntea   Verb+Act+Indv+Pres+Con
```

Figure 1: A complete set of morphological readings for the Finnish word *tunne*.

Hand-crafted analyzers (Koskenniemi, 1983) are the gold standard for morphological analysis. Creation of such analyzers is, however, a labor intensive process and requires expertise in linguistics, the target language and the rule formalisms used to create these analyzers. Moreover, analyzers need to be continuously updated with new lexemes in order to maintain high coverage on running text.

In this paper, we investigate an alternative to hand-crafted analyzers, namely, data-driven morphological analyzers which are learned from annotated training data. In our case, the training data consists of words and complete sets of analyses. During test time, the system takes a Finnish word such as *kisaan* ('into the competition' or 'I am competing') as input and gives a set of analyses

$$\{\texttt{Noun+Sg+Ill, Verb+Act+Indv+Pres+Sg1}\}$$

as output.

We present experiments in data-driven morphological analysis of Finnish. We learn to mimic the OMorFi analyzer (Pirinen et al., 2017) on the Finnish portion of the Universal Dependency treebank collection (Pyysalo et al., 2015). The data sets and OMorFi analyzer are further discussed in Section 3. We use a deep learning model encompassing a character-level recurrent model, which maps words onto sets of analyses as explained in Section 4. Our results, described in Section 5, show that this line of research is encouraging. We present related work in Section 2 and present concluding remarks in Section 6.

## 2   Related Work

The task of data-driven morphological analysis has received far less attention than morphological tagging and disambiguation which aim at producing exactly one analysis, which is correct in a given sentence context. Because hand-crafted morphological analyzers have been shown to improve the performance of neural taggers (Sagot and Martínez Alonso, 2017), the task of data-driven morphological analysis is, nevertheless, important.

The task explored in this paper is closely related to the construction of morphological guessers (Lindén, 2009), where the aim is to guess the inflectional type of a word. To the best of our knowledge deep learning methods have, however, not been applied to this task. In contrast, there is a growing body of work on deep learning for word form generation (Cotterell et al., 2017, 2016). In word form generation, or morphological reinflection, the aim is to generate word forms given lemmas and morphological analyses. Therefore, it can be seen as a natural counterpart to morphological analysis. Our work is inspired by the encoder-decoder models commonly applied in morphological reinflection (for example Kann and Schütze (2017)) but the task at hand is naturally quite different.

Several approaches have been explored for returning one analysis, or a small set of possible analyses, for a word form in context. For example, Kudo et al. (2004) apply

Conditional Random Fields for morphological analysis of Japanese but their system only returns one tokenization for a sentence and one analysis per token. This is not the same task as the one we are exploring, where the objective is to return the complete set of possible analyses. Similar in spirit is the work on Kazakh morphological analysis by Makhambetov et al. (2015). Their system, based on Hidden Markov Models, returns a subset of the analyses of a token which could plausibly occur in a given context. Sequence models are a natural choice when the aim is to generate one analysis for each word form but they are not suitable for our needs because we want to generate complete sets of analyses.

## 3    Data and Resources

We conduct experiments on the Finnish part of the Universal Dependency treebank collection (UD_Finnish) (Pyysalo et al., 2015). We analyze corpus tokens using the OMorFi[1] morphological analyzer (Pirinen et al., 2017) which is a high coverage Finnish open-source morphological analyzer capable of analyzing compounds and derivations.

Because we are learning to mimic the output of the OMorFi analyzer, we have to filter out tokens which are not recognized by OMorFi from the training, development and test set (approximately 3% of tokens in UD_Finnish are not recognized by OMorFi).

We slightly transform the analyses provided by OMorFi by removing lemma information since this paper does not investigate lemmatization.[2] Consequently, we conflate analyses which only differ with regard to the lemma.

Table 1 describes the Finnish UD treebank analyzed by OMorFi. The partition into training, development and test set follows the standard split provided by version 2.0 of the UD_Finnish treebank.

Table 1: Description of data sets used in experiments. Average ambiguity refers to the average count of distinct analyses for tokens recognized by OMorFi.

|        | Tokens  | Tokens recognized by OMorFi | Avg. Ambiguity |
|--------|---------|-----------------------------|----------------|
| Train  | 162,827 | 157,317 (96.6%)             | 1.82           |
| Devel. | 18,311  | 17,762 (97.0%)              | 1.76           |
| Test   | 21,070  | 20,447 (97.0%)              | 1.84           |

As explained in Section 4, we use pretrained word vectors to initialize word embeddings. These were trained using the word2vec implementation in the gensim toolkit (Řehůřek and Sojka, 2010) on approximately 71M words of Finnish newsgroup data from the Suomi24 corpus[3]. The corpus contains texts available from the discussion forums of the Suomi24 online social networking website between years 2001 and 2015.

---

[1] https://github.com/flammie/omorfi/releases/tag/20170515
[2] We did not investigate lemmatization because it can easily be treated as a reinflection task using existing methods.
[3] Aller Media ltd. (2014). The Suomi 24 Corpus (2015H1) (text corpus). Kielipankki. Retrieved from http://urn.fi/urn:nbn:fi:lb-201412171

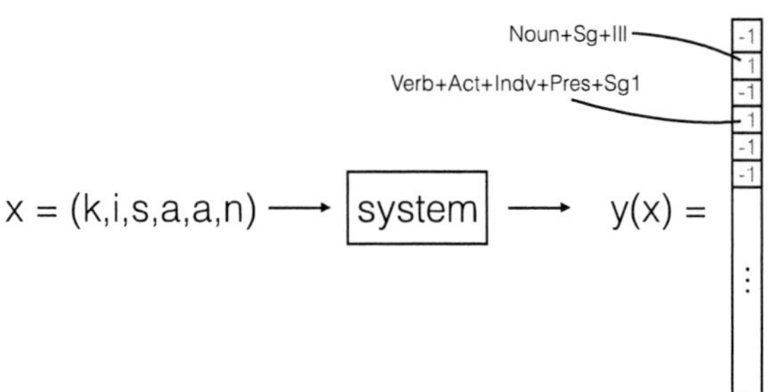


Figure 2: The system gets a Finnish word, *kisaan* ('I am competing' or 'into the competition'), as input. It then outputs the set of valid morphological analyses for the input word. For example, *kisaan* has two valid morphological analyses Noun+Sg+Ill and Verb+Act+Indv+Pres+Sg1. The input word is fed to the system as a sequence of letters $x = (k, i, s, a, a, n)$. The output $y(x)$ is a vector in $\{-1, 1\}^N$, where each index corresponds to a morphological analysis. The entry at index $i$ is 1, iff $i$ corresponds to a valid morphological analysis for the input word. Otherwise, it is $-1$.

## 4   Model

Morphological analysis can be formulated as a multi-label classification task, that is, the objective is to return a set of analyses for each input. We accomplish this by predicting an output vector for each input example. The vector contains one element for each morphological analysis type (for example Noun+Sg+Nom) and its values encode which of the analyses are active for a given input example (see Figure 2).[4] We structure the task in the following way. Each input token $x = x_1...x_n \in \Sigma^*$ (where $\Sigma$ is the Finnish alphabet) is mapped into a vector $\mathbf{y}(x) \in \{-1, 1\}^{|A|} \subset \mathbb{R}^{|A|}$, where $A$ is the set of morphological analyses found in the training data. The value $\mathbf{y}(x)_i = 1$ if the analysis corresponding to index $i$ is a valid analysis for token $x$. Otherwise, $\mathbf{y}(\mathbf{x})_i = -1$.

Our system is based on word embeddings $\mathbf{e}(x)$ and character-based embeddings $\mathbf{B}(x_1, ..., x_n)$ using a bidirectional LSTM network (Hochreiter and Schmidhuber, 1997; Schuster and Paliwal, 1997). We use the final cell state of the bidirectional LSTM as our character-based embedding (that is, we do not employ an attention mechanism). The word embedding $\mathbf{e}(x)$ and the character-based embedding $\mathbf{B}(x_1, ..., x_n)$ are summed and fed into a single-layer linear perceptron network whose output is the vector $\mathbf{y}(x)$.[5]

We initialize word embeddings using pretrained word vectors as explained in Section 5. For OOV tokens, which are not found in the training set and which additionally are not present in the pretrained word embedding, we use a special unknown word embedding. During training time we randomly replace the embeddings of training words with the unknown word embedding in order to train it.

When training the system, we optimize the L1-loss of the prediction vector $\mathbf{y}(x)$ given the gold standard analysis vector $\mathbf{y} \in \{-1, 1\}^{|A|}$ as shown in Equation 1. It is

---

[4]In the case of Finnish, this leads to a high dimensional vector because there are thousands of possible morphological analysis types.

[5]In addition to summing the character-based embedding and pretrained word embedding vector, we also experimented with concatenating the vectors. Unfortunately, this did not improve the accuracy of the system. However, it did increase training time. Therefore, we opted for summing vectors.

easily seen that the loss is minimized when the predicted vector exactly equals $\mathbf{y}$.

$$\mathcal{L}(\mathbf{y}(x), \mathbf{y}) = \sum_{i=0}^{|A|} |\mathbf{y}(x)_i - \mathbf{y}_i| \tag{1}$$

In order to analyze a token $x$, we first generate the vector $\mathbf{y}(x)$ and then return all analyses corresponding to indices $i$ for which $\mathbf{y}(x)_i > 0$. For words in the test set, which are present in the training set, we give the set of analyses found in the training set. This substantially improves performance of the system in the early stages of training but has little effect after the system is fully trained.

## 5  Experiments and Results

We perform experiments on the UD_Finnish treebank as explained above. We train the system on the training data and report performance on the held-out test set.

The system was implemented using the Dynet toolkit (Neubig et al., 2017). We set all hyper-parameters using the development set and optimize the network using Adam (Kingma and Ba, 2014) with learning rate 0.0001 and beta values $\beta_1 = 0.9; \beta_2 = 0.999$. We train the system for 50 epochs.

We use word embeddings and character-based embeddings of dimension 200. Character-based embeddings are computed in the following way: We set the hidden state dimension of the character-based LSTM to 100 and use a single layer bidirectional LSTM network. We concatenate the final 100 dimensional cell states of the forward and backward component of the bidirectional LSTM. This gives us one 200 dimensional character-based embedding vector for the input word. As explained in Section 4, the word embedding and character-based embedding are then summed.

During training, we employ 50% dropout on recurrent connections in the character-based LSTM networks. We use pretrained word vectors to initialize word embeddings. These were trained using the word2vec (Mikolov et al., 2013) implementation in the gensim toolkit (Řehůřek and Sojka, 2010). In order to train the unknown word embedding discussed in Section 4, we randomly replace word embeddings during training with the unknown word embedding with probability 2%.

The system is evaluated with regard to accuracy for full analysis sets as well as recall, precision and f-score of analyses. Full analysis accuracy defined as $C/A$, where $C$ is the number of test set tokens, which received exactly the correct set of analyses, and $A$ is the count of all tokens in the test set. Recall is defined $r = TP/T$, where $TP$ is the amount of correct analyses that the system recovered and $T$ is the total amount of correct analyses in the gold standard test set. Similarly, precision is defined as $p = TP/P$, where $P$ is the total amount of analyses returned by the system. As familiar, f-score is defined as $2pr/(p + r)$.

Results of experiments are shown in Table 2. We present results separately for all tokens in the test set and OOV tokens, which were not present in the training set.

## 6  Discussion and Conclusions

All in all the results seem encouraging when taking into account that the proposed system is very straightforward. It is clear that performance drops drastically when the system is applied on words not occurring in the training set, however, almost half of OOV words still get the correct morphological analysis set from the system.

Table 2: Results of experiments.

|            | Accuracy | Recall | Precision | F-Score |
|------------|----------|--------|-----------|---------|
| All words  | 87.24    | 89.66  | 94.03     | 91.79   |
| OOV words  | 44.18    | 43.56  | 58.37     | 49.89   |

Roughly 27% of errors involve mix-ups between proper nouns and common nouns. At first glance, this might seem weird because Finnish proper nouns almost always start with an upper-case letter whereas common nouns do not. However, words in sentence initial position also start with an upper-case letter. Because the current system does not employ any contextual information, it can therefore not rely on capitalization when determining the distinction between common and proper nouns. It is noteworthy, that many of these erroneous analyses only differ from the gold standard with regard to part-of-speech (Noun versus Proper). The additional inflectional information, such as case and number, are frequently correct.

Another problem, which complicates the analysis of proper nouns, is that they are often missing from the pretrained word embedding which might otherwise provide good clues toward a proper noun interpretation. Word embeddings utilizing sub-word information such as fastText embeddings (Bojanowski et al., 2016) might improve accuracy for proper nouns. Incorporating sub-word information to pretrained embeddings remains future work at the present time.

Other common errors include assigning noun or adjective analyses to participles. For example, OMorFi gives *taitava* (skillful) both a participle and an adjective reading but it does not give an adjective reading to *sanova* (a participle form of 'to say'). The distinction is mainly a matter of convention and cannot be reliably determined from the orthography or distribution of the word. In addition to these common error types, there are a substantial amount of less frequent errors but a more thorough error analysis is required to interpret these and to offer a solutions for them.

It is clear that the precision of the system is greater than its recall. When applying an analyzer to a task such as morphological disambiguation or morphological tagging, this may be problematic because the disambiguation system cannot find the correct analysis in a given context if the morphological analyzer does not suggest it. It may, however, be possible to improve the recall of the system while reducing precision. As explained in Section 4, the analyzer outputs a label corresponding to index $i$ if $\mathbf{y}(x)_i > 0$, where $\mathbf{y}(x)$ is the output vector for example $x$. By replacing this formulation with $\mathbf{y}(x)_i > TH$, where $TH$ is an adjustable hyperparameter, it is possible to create a trade-off between precision and recall. This remains future work at the current time.

We proposed a simple system for data-driven morphological analysis. The system is based on a character-based bidirectional LSTM network and utilizes pretrained word embeddings. The system is directly optimized to produce complete sets of morphological analyses. We presented experiments on the Finnish Universal Dependency treebank. The experiments show that the system is clearly capable of learning to analyze unseen word forms but there is still room for substantial improvement.

## Acknowledgments

We want to thank the anonymous reviewers for their valuable comments.

# References


Piotr Bojanowski, Edouard Grave, Armand Joulin, and Tomas Mikolov. 2016. Enriching word vectors with subword information. *CoRR* abs/1607.04606. http://arxiv.org/abs/1607.04606.

Ryan Cotterell, Christo Kirov, John Sylak-Glassman, Géraldine Walther, Ekaterina Vylomova, Patrick Xia, Manaal Faruqui, Sandra Kübler, David Yarowsky, Jason Eisner, et al. 2017. CoNLL-SIGMORPHON 2017 shared task: Universal morphological reinflection in 52 languages. *arXiv preprint arXiv:1706.09031* .

Ryan Cotterell, Christo Kirov, John Sylak-Glassman, David Yarowsky, Jason Eisner, and Mans Hulden. 2016. The SIGMORPHON 2016 shared task—morphological reinflection. In *Proceedings of the 14th SIGMORPHON Workshop on Computational Research in Phonetics, Phonology, and Morphology*. pages 10–22.

Sepp Hochreiter and Jürgen Schmidhuber. 1997. Long short-term memory. *Neural Comput.* 9(8):1735–1780. https://doi.org/10.1162/neco.1997.9.8.1735.

Katharina Kann and Hinrich Schütze. 2017. The LMU system for the CoNLL-SIGMORPHON 2017 shared task on universal morphological reinflection. In *CoNLL Shared Task*.

Diederik P. Kingma and Jimmy Ba. 2014. Adam: A method for stochastic optimization. *CoRR* abs/1412.6980. http://arxiv.org/abs/1412.6980.

Kimmo Koskenniemi. 1983. Two-level model for morphological analysis. In *IJCAI*. volume 83, pages 683–685.

Taku Kudo, Kaoru Yamamoto, and Yuji Matsumoto. 2004. Applying Conditional Random Fields to Japanese Morphological Analysis. In Dekang Lin and Dekai Wu, editors, *Proceedings of EMNLP 2004*. Association for Computational Linguistics, Barcelona, Spain, pages 230–237.

Krister Lindén. 2009. Guessers for finite-state transducer lexicons. *Computational Linguistics and Intelligent Text Processing* pages 158–169.

Olzhas Makhambetov, Aibek Makazhanov, Islam Sabyrgaliyev, and Zhandos Yessenbayev. 2015. *Data-Driven Morphological Analysis and Disambiguation for Kazakh*, Springer International Publishing, Cham, pages 151–163.

Tomas Mikolov, Ilya Sutskever, Kai Chen, Greg S Corrado, and Jeff Dean. 2013. Distributed representations of words and phrases and their compositionality. In *Advances in neural information processing systems*. pages 3111–3119.

Graham Neubig, Chris Dyer, Yoav Goldberg, Austin Matthews, Waleed Ammar, Antonios Anastasopoulos, Miguel Ballesteros, David Chiang, Daniel Clothiaux, Trevor Cohn, Kevin Duh, Manaal Faruqui, Cynthia Gan, Dan Garrette, Yangfeng Ji, Lingpeng Kong, Adhiguna Kuncoro, Gaurav Kumar, Chaitanya Malaviya, Paul Michel, Yusuke Oda, Matthew Richardson, Naomi Saphra, Swabha Swayamdipta, and Pengcheng Yin. 2017. Dynet: The dynamic neural network toolkit. *arXiv preprint arXiv:1701.03980* .

Tommi A Pirinen, Inari Listenmaa, Ryan Johnson, Francis M. Tyers, and Juha Kuokkala. 2017. Open morphology of finnish. LINDAT/CLARIN digital library at the Institute of Formal and Applied Linguistics, Charles University. http://hdl.handle.net/11372/LRT-1992.

Sampo Pyysalo, Jenna Kanerva, Anna Missilä, Veronika Laippala, and Filip Ginter. 2015. Universal dependencies for finnish. In *NODALIDA*.

Radim Řehůřek and Petr Sojka. 2010. Software Framework for Topic Modelling with Large Corpora. In *Proceedings of the LREC 2010 Workshop on New Challenges for NLP Frameworks*. ELRA, Valletta, Malta, pages 45–50. `http://is.muni.cz/publication/884893/en`.

Benoît Sagot and Héctor Martínez Alonso. 2017. Improving neural tagging with lexical information. In *Proceedings of the 15th International Conference on Parsing Technologies*. Association for Computational Linguistics, Pisa, Italy, pages 25–31. http://www.aclweb.org/anthology/W17-63 4.

Mike Schuster and Kuldip K Paliwal. 1997. Bidirectional recurrent neural networks. *IEEE Transactions on Signal Processing* 45(11):2673–2681.

# Towards an open-source universal-dependency treebank for Erzya


Jack Rueter
University of Helsinki
Department of Modern Languages
Helsinki
jack.rueter@helsinki.fi

Francis Tyers
НИУ ВШЭ
School of Linguistics
Moscow
ftyers@hse.ru



### Abstract

This article describes the first steps towards a open-source dependency treebank for Erzya based on universal dependency (UD) annotation standards. The treebank contains 610 sentences with 6661 tokens and is based on texts from a range of open-source and public domain original Erzya sources. This ensures its free availability and extensibility. Texts in the treebank are first morphologically analyzed and disambiguated after which they are annotated manually for dependency structure. In the article we present some issues in dependency syntax for Erzya and how they are analyzed in the universal-dependency framework. Preliminary statistics are given for dependency parsing of Erzya, along with points of interest for future research.



### Tiivistelmä

Tässä artikkelissa kerrotaan ersän kielen avoimen puupankin ensimmäisistä askeleista, joissa sovelletaan universaaliriippuvuus-annotaatiota (UD). Puupankki sisältää 610 virkettä joissa on yhteensä 6661 tokenia ja se perustuu avoimeen ersänkieliseen originaalikirjoituksiin. Tällä tavalla varmistetaan puupankin saatavuutta ja laajennettavuutta. Puupankin tekstit on ensin analysoitu morfologisella jäsentimellä ja disambiguoitu, minkä jälkeen suoritetaan loppuyksiselitteistäminen käsin ja lisätään riippuvuussuhteet. Artikkelissa esitetään joitakin kysymyksiä, jotka esiintyvät ersän lauseoppia sovellettaessa universaaliriippuvuus-kehyksiin. Annetaan alkutilastoja ersän jäsennyksestä sekä ajatuksia tulevan tutkimuksen näkemyksistä.



### Abstract

Те статиясонть сёрмадтано эрзянь келень од ресурсадо, конась весеменень панжадо, чувтокс валрисьмень пурнавксто, чувтонь банкто, ды юртонзо путомадо. Валрисьмень анализэнь теемстэ нолдави тевс масторлангонь вейсэнь аннотация, конаньсэ невтеви валрисьме пелькстнэнь вейкест-вейкест эйстэ чувтокс аштема лувост (Universal Dependency UD). Статиянть сёрмадомсто чувтонь банкось ашти 610 валрисьмеде, косо весемезэ 6661 токент (валт-лоткосема тешкст), материалосьашти весеменень панжадо эрзякс сёрмадозь литературанть эйстэ. Истя чувтонь банкось саеви-келейгавтови кинень мелезэ – ресурсась ванстсы оляксчинзэ. Вася пурнавксонь валрисьметненень тееви морфологиянь анализ, конась мейле седе вадрялгавтови синтаксисэнь анализсэ.







*Proceedings of the 4th International Workshop for Computational Linguistics for Uralic Languages (IWCLUL 2018)*, pages 108–120, Helsinki, Finland, January 8–9, 2018. ©2018 Association for Computational Linguistics

Мейле келень ванкшныцясь сонсь невти кона пелькстнэ конатнень эйстэ аштить. Статиясонть макстано зярыя кевкстемат, конат чачить эрзянь кель UD марто вастневемстэ. Макстано эрзянь келень анализдэ васнянь статистика ды арсемат-мельть келень ванкшномань сыця ёнкстнэде-тевтнеде.

# 1   Introduction

This article describes work towards the development of a Universal Dependencies-based dependency treebank for Erzya, a Uralic language traditionally spoken in the Volga Region. Little if any computational-linguistic research has been published on syntactic parsing for Erzya. A valuable resource in the study and development of syntactic parsing is a treebank—a corpus of parsed texts containing gold-standard syntactic annotation.

Freely available treebanks exist for many languages, one particularly interesting set is the group of over 60 languages represented in Universal Dependencies (UD), where Erzya is now one of the smaller "upcoming languages"[1]. This mutual presentation makes it possible to understand and utilize language-independent dependency tagging with direct analogy from other Uralic languages, such as Finnish, Estonian, North Sami and Hungarian, as well as languages sharing other morphosyntactic characteristics with Erzya. The UD environment also makes direct reference to terminology definition resources, such as those offered by SIL[2], and research in the World Atlas of Language Structures (WALS)[3].

To our knowledge, however, no previous treebank exists for either of the Mordvinic languages, although there are closed annotated corpora, such as MORMULA at the University of Turku[4], quantlang-uhlcs[5] in Helsinki, and the semi-limited ERME[6].

In building our treebank we take advantage of previous work done by Rueter in Helsinki Finite-State Transducer Technology (HFST) morphological analysis and part-of-speech tagging for Erzya on the Giellatekno infrastructure, as well as ongoing disambiguation work with Constraint Grammar (VISLCG).

The remainder of the paper is organized as follows. Section 2 gives some background linguistic information on Erzya, and outlines some special challenges in parsing Erzya. In Section 3 we describe the corpus that we annotated and the methodology used in annotating it. Section 4 gives a sketch of some decisions we have made with respect to annotation guidelines, referring back to the discussion in Section 2. For reasons of space and time, these guidelines are by no means complete, but they do present a subset of guidelines which are of particular interest.

# 2   Background

## 2.1   Erzya

*Erzya* is one of the two Mordvinic languages traditionally spoken in scattered villages throughout the Volga Region and former Russian Empire by well over a million in the

---

[1] http://universaldependencies.org/

[2] http://www.glossary.sil.org/

[3] http://wals.info/

[4] http://www.helsinki.fi/~kopotev/finnish_corpora_eng.pdf

[5] Quantifiers and Quantification in Finnish and Languages Spoken in the Central Volgakama Region – UHLCS http://urn.fi/urn:nbn:fi:lb-2016012202

[6] Erme – Erzya and Moksha Extended Corpora http://urn.fi/urn:nbn:fi:lb-201407306

| Case | Definite | Form | Function |
|---|---|---|---|
| Nom | Def | /ś/ /t́ńe/ | def subject, predicative<br>topic marker |
| Nom | Indef | - | ind subject, predicative<br>ind attribute, object<br>ind Adp complement |
| Nom | PxSg3 | /Ozo/ | subject, predicative |
| Gen | Indef | /Oń/ | Ind genitive attribute<br>Ind object, Adp complement<br>embedded subject, object |
| Gen | Def | /Ońt́/ | def object<br>def adp complement |
| Ine | Indef | /sO/ | locative, instrumental<br>object |

Table 1: Some cases and functions. *Note that with the exception of the third person singular possessive suffix, there is generally no distinctions made for number or genitive/nominative marking in the possessive declension.*

beginning of the 20th century and down to approximately half a million in the 2010 census[7]. For some, however, Erzya is only a part of the conglomerate Mordvin index, a population with the status of most numerous among the Uralic languages in Russia. Since there is no Mordvin language, as it were, but rather the closely related (adjacent yet not contiguous) Erzya and Moksha languages with their literary representation, research in syntax has often attempted to encompass the two.

Erzya, like many Uralic languages, is agglutinative with extensive morphology, agreement and constituent ordering phenomena that present a challenge to any syntactic description of the language. The most prominent of these challenges apparent from the start are case marking, definiteness, ellipsis, numerals, and copula variation between dependent and independent morphology. An open-source finite-state morphological analyzer constructed for Erzya[8] provides ample tagging for the annotation, but there is still plenty of work to be done with disambiguation. Erzya, much like other Ural-Altaic languages (Tyers and Washington, 2015), assigns more than one function to its cases. It also attests to intricate constituent ordering and minimal conjunction/subjunction marking, which will be one topic future research.

As indicated in Table 1, the definite nominative singular might be attested with the dependency relation, *nsubj, root* (in certain equative predications[9], example (1)), and to indicate a postposed topic (see example (5.b)).

---

[7] https://efo.revues.org/1829
[8] http://giellatekno.uit.no/cgi/index.myv.eng.html
[9] Bryzhinski: chapID2:paragID5:sentID5 line 6.

(1)

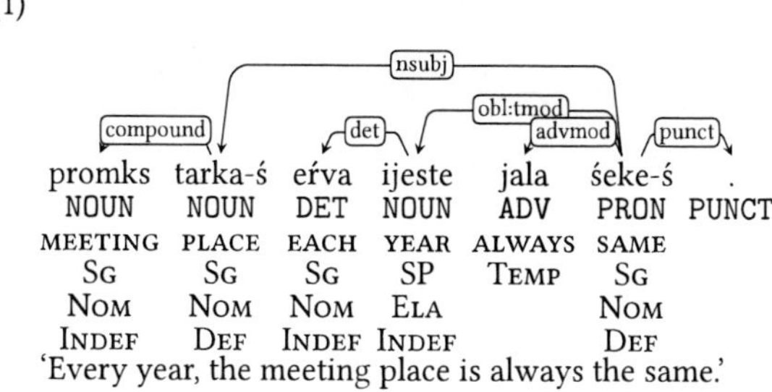



| promks | tarka-ś | eŕva | ijeste | jala | śeke-ś | . |
|--------|---------|------|--------|------|--------|---|
| NOUN | NOUN | DET | NOUN | ADV | PRON | PUNCT |
| MEETING | PLACE | EACH | YEAR | ALWAYS | SAME | |
| SG | SG | SG | SP | TEMP | SG | |
| NOM | NOM | NOM | ELA | | NOM | |
| INDEF | DEF | INDEF | INDEF | | DEF | |

'Every year, the meeting place is always the same.'

## 3 Methodology

### 3.1 Corpus

To form a corpus, we were able to utilize materials by Erzya authors previously secured for language research purposes while in the Republic of Mordovia. The number of sources utilized is extremely limited, due to the elementary state of the developing treebank.

| Document | Description | Sentences | Tokens | Av. length |
|----------|-------------|-----------|--------|------------|
| Valskeń gudok | short story by Anoshkin, V. | 4 | 36 | 9 |
| Kirdažt | Novel manuscript by Bryzhinski, M.I. | 270 | 3487 | 12.9 |
| Veĺeń vajgeĺt | Miniatures by Chetvergov, E. | 105 | 957 | 9.1 |
| Pićipalakst | Foreword; Dunyashin, A. | 75 | 633 | 8.4 |
| Lažnića Sura | Novel by Kutorkin, A.D. | 155 | 1534 | 9.9 |
| Separate | Individual phrases | 1 | 11 | 11 |
| | | 610 | 6661 | 10.9 |

Table 2: Statistics on the composition of the corpus

The initial materials are representitive of original Erzya-language materials from the late 1920s to the turn of the new millennium. The Separate Individual phrases file will serve for documenting cited materials from scientific publications, such as the most recent Erzya syntax Агафонова et al. (2011).

The figures in Table 3 are incomplete, but do provide an initial ball park figure. It was noted that subsequent work will need to be done with extended dependency relations, as a small number of the cases returned included the values *appos* and *conj*. Also, the high number of genitive occurrences with the *obl* relation would indicate the presence of adpositions. Although the inessive had been indicated earlier as an object case, there was not a single instance where it occurred as a dependent case. The distinction of the dependency relations *nmod* versus *nmod:poss* in the statistics has been taken in following with usage in the Finnish UD projects; in subsequent contemplation, this may, in fact, be unnecessary since the genitive case already indicates a possessive relation in contrast to the inessive case with a spatial meaning as a noun modifier.

## 4 Annotation guidelines

When entering a group, such as UD, it is nearly imperative that all tagging conform with practices attested in the group. As such, it has been easy to compromise and

|  | obl | nmod | nmod:poss | obj | root | nsubj |
|---|---|---|---|---|---|---|
| `Case=Nom\|Definite=Def` | 1 | _ | _ | _ | 6 | 170 |
| `Case=Nom\|Definite=Ind` | 37 | 10 | _ | 99 | 52 | 154 |
| `Case=Nom\|Number[psor]=Sing\|Person[psor]=3` | _ | _ | _ | _ | 1 | 41 |
| `Case=Gen\|Definite=Ind` | 23 | 6 | 106 | 53 | 2 | 3 |
| `Case=Gen\|Definite=Def` | 65 | 2 | 24 | 80 | _ | _ |
| `Case=Dat\|Definite=Ind` | 10 | _ | _ | _ | 1 | _ |
| `Case=Dat\|Definite=Def` | 33 | _ | _ | _ | _ | _ |
| `Case=Ine\|Definite=Ind` | 45 | _ | _ | _ | 1 | _ |

Table 3: Syntactic functions associated with different combinations of case, possession and definiteness.

relabel/learn values for various features in order to arrive at the group norm, on the one hand, and present new features, on the other. Work centered around indication for features (number, person), relations (aux, compound) as well as the handling of ellipsis and numerals. Certain phenomena clearly require additional time for thought and development. Work has been facilitated by the use of UD ANNOTATRIX (Tyers et al., 2018), a tool for annotating treebanks in UD.

## 4.1 Number

The Erzya language like its closely related sibling Moksha has what is often called the object or definite conjugation. Unlike Hungarian, Nenets, Khanty and Mansi, however, the object conjugation of the Mordvinic languages morphologically indicates 1st, 2nd and 3rd person as well as singular and plural for some of the object and subject referents (Keresztes (1999); Trosterud (2006) 246–303). This means that a separates set of number and person features must be present to distinguish them from the already existent Number, Person, Number[psor] and Person[psor] features. Fortunately there were already Number[obj] and Person[obj], so only Number[subj] and Person[subj] were required as new features.

(2)

    ńej-iźe
see-IND.PRT1.ScSG3.OcSG3
'he/she/it saw him/her/it'

In examples (2) and (3) there is an actual non-ambiguous morphological distinction for third person singular subject in combination with third person singular object in (2) and third person plural object in (3).

(3)

    ńej-ińźe
see-IND.PRT1.ScSG3.OcPL3
'he/she/it saw them'

Example (4) is also unambiguous, as both arguments are singular in value. Neither argument need be present, but both are allowed.

(4)

> ńej-imik
> see-Ind.Prt1.ScSg2.OcSg1
> 'you[sg] saw me'

Although it is possible to use personal pronouns in subject and direct object position, their presence is not the normal situation. Context awareness is required that transcends conventional sentence boundaries, hence there is person and number disambiguation present that is not discernible from the morphology but rather the larger context.

## 4.2 Copula and polarity

Erzya attests to varied non-verbal predication Turunen (2010) and negation Hamari (2007) strategies. The copula is divided into locative and non-locative usage, and this dichotomy can readily be observed in the morphology of the negative copulas, i.e., where the negative locative copula is represented by /araś-/ (which is conjugated with the help of a morphologically dependent copula), whereas the presentation of equative or class membership negation is shown with the non-flective word form /avoĺ/. Further negation is manifest in the converbal negation element /apak/ (which can also be conjugated), first preterite /eź-/, conjunctional /avoĺ-/, optative and prohibitive /iĺa-/, and the negative particle /a/. All of these can trigger the dependency relation **aux:neg**, which in the case of the polarity markers /a/ and /avoĺ/ to all parts of speech.

| Proh/Opt | Ind.Prt1 | Cnd | Prc.Neg | Part.Neg | Part.Neg.Emp |
|----------|----------|-----|---------|----------|--------------|
| /iĺa-/ | /eź-/ | /avoĺ-/ | /apak/ | /a/ | /avoĺ/ |

Table 4: Negation

The six polarity markers in Table 4. can be divided into two categories. The prohibitive/optative, indicative first preterite and conditional stems along with the polarity marker for participles and converb (elsewhere gerund) constructions are all limited to use with verbal forms.

Whereas the negative particle /a/ can occur with many parts of speech, it is the non-flective word form /avoĺ/ or emphatic negative that is used in clausal negation. Clausal negation in combination with the imperative mood evokes a contrast in the prohibitive strategy in /iĺa-/. The clausal negation particle /avoĺ/ in combination with the second person imperative produces a contrastive negative imperative, whereas the prohibitive /iĺa-/ (**Mood=Proh**) is combined in the modern literary norm with a connegative form. This has not been attested in WALS van der Auwera et al. (2013).

## 4.3 Dependent copula morphology

Copula morphology is dependent and independent in Erzya. While many grammarians of the past century have referred to dependent copula morphology as noun conjugation, earlier presentations, such as Wiedemann (1864) (§77), refer to it as a suffixed copula. Judging from the fact that the dependent morphology can be attached to nouns in various declensional forms, as well as adjectives, numerals, adverbs, adpostions and non-finite verb forms, the phenomenon might more readily be referred to as a clitic.

| Tense | Sg1 | Sg2 | Sg3 | Pl1 | Pl2 | Pl3 |
|---|---|---|---|---|---|---|
| Nonpast | /mon odan/ | /ton odat/ | /son od/ | /miń odtano/ | /tiń odtado/ | /siń odt/ |
| Prt2 | /mon odoĺiń/ | /ton odoĺit́/ | /son odoĺ/ | /miń odoĺińek/ | /tiń odoĺid́e/ | /siń odoĺt́/ |

Table 5: Dependent copula morphology ('young or new')

Thus we have independent copula in /uĺń-/ (prt1) and /uĺ-/ (prs), on the one hand, and dependent copula morphology in -/Oĺ/-, etc.), on the other. Both the *nonpast* and *prt2* conjugation are virtually identical to their verbal subject conjugation counterparts; essentially the *prt2* in verbs is a combination of the short *nomen agentis* + the *prt2* used for copula function beyond the scope of finite verbs.

The dependent and independent morphologies present a challenging problem for dependency analysis in Erzya, whereas both can be in equative, class member, assertive, locative vs existential, and possessive vs belong-to predication. A dichotomy, however, is introduced where the Universal Dependency guidelines stating that the copula should be the dependent of the lexical predicate are applied only to independent copula.

The copula as dependent morphology attaches to what some scholars have considered the subject, but some scholars working with Moksha have approached this from a discourse point of view Kholodilova (2016). Instead of splitting the copula off as a separate leaf node, we have annotated the instances with dependent morphology as the head of the structure. Here constituent ordering might be an underlying factor to be considered in future work with the Erzya UD treebank.

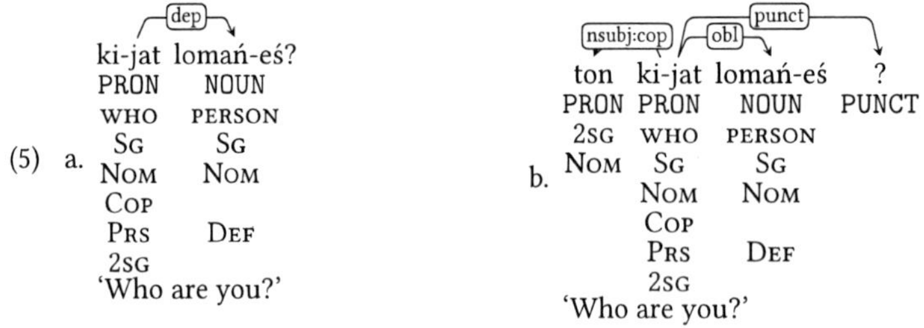

In both sentences with and without the second person singular personal pronoun, it is obvious that the word /lomań-eś/ can only be interpreted as an extra element; more than likely a topic marker. The interrogative pronoun /ki-jat/ in the predicative takes the subject second person singular, whereas the third person singular topic marker would not have triggered second person singular agreement.

## 4.4  Further auxiliaries

In addition to the copula and negation, the definition of additional auxiliaries in Erzya take us to necessitives. Necessitives in Erzya have parallels in Finnish, Komi-Zyrian and partially in Skolt Sami, in that a non-nominative case is used to indicate the actor, which might be construed as a subject when aligned with other European, accusative languages. In Erzya, it is the Dative that is used as in *mońeń* in example (3).

114

(6)

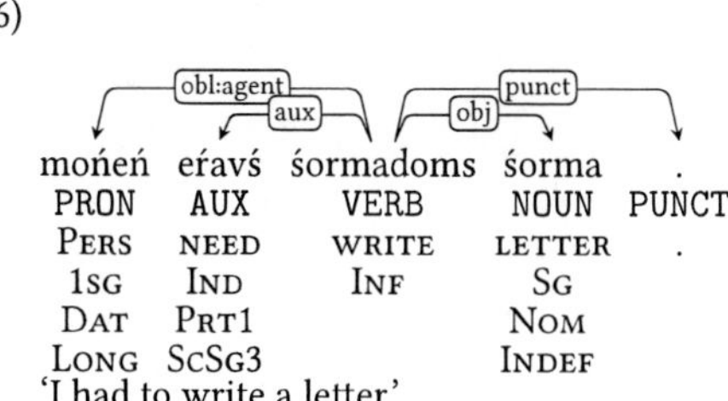



| mońeń | eŕavś | śormadoms | śorma | . |
|-------|-------|-----------|-------|---|
| PRON | AUX | VERB | NOUN | PUNCT |
| PERS | NEED | WRITE | LETTER | . |
| 1SG | IND | INF | SG | |
| DAT | PRT1 | | NOM | |
| LONG | ScSG3 | | INDEF | |

'I had to write a letter.'

Discussion with Erzya and Komi native scholars has also introduced the idea of adding verbs indicating future to the list of auxiliaries, this, however, would be problematic, due to the second meaning involved, namely, inchoative/inceptive albeit an aspect marker. In this initial Erzya treebank, auxiliaries have been limited to copulas, negation and necessitives.

## 4.5   Compound nouns

The most recent orthographic word list of the Erzya language Бузакова et al. (2012) prescribes a mathematical strategy to compounding, i.e. if the first element is a nominative singular indefinite form (also called absolute form) with no evident derivation (sometimes a rather gray definition) two nouns are written as a single unit. This solution is not entirely related to the writing practices of the last century, and there do prove to be certain problems. The most evident problems are ensemble nouns containing mensural classifiers (for definition see Lyons (1977): p.463; cf. Rueter (2013): p.108).

(7) a.

| keľme | veď | vedra |
|-------|-----|-------|
| ADJ | NOUN | NOUN |
| COLD | WATER | BUCKET |
| SG | SG | SG |
| NOM | NOM | NOM |
| INDEF | INDEF | INDEF |

'bucket of cold water'

b.

| pokš | vedra | veď |
|------|-------|-----|
| ADJ | NOUN | NOUN |
| BIG | BUCKET | WATER |
| SG | SG | SG |
| NOM | NOM | NOM |
| INDEF | INDEF | INDEF |

'big bucket of water'

In both instance we are talking about a measurement of water, whereas the idea of a bucket especially intended for water would be constructed in the telic noun /veď vedra/.

## 4.6   Noun head ellipsis

An analogy of symmetric negation as described in Miestamo (2013) can be applied to the description of the Erzya nominal phrase declension. In symmetric negation the structure of the negative is identical to the structure of the affirmative, except for the presence of the negative marker(s).

In a similar way, it is the final word of the Erzya noun phrase that is symmetrically declined while modifiers (with the exception of some determinatives) appear in what is termed the absolute form. Determinatives such as /iśťamo/ 'like this/that' can agree in number with the head noun. (NB. some descriptions Bartens (1999) maintain that regular adjectives might agree for number as well, but this type of apparent agreement, seems to be limited to parts of the northwestern dialect)

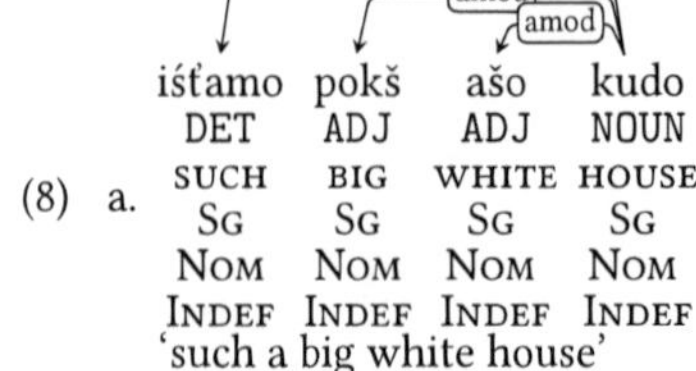

(8) a.
|  | išťamo | pokš | ašo | kudo |
|---|---|---|---|---|
|  | DET | ADJ | ADJ | NOUN |
|  | SUCH | BIG | WHITE | HOUSE |
|  | Sɢ | Sɢ | Sɢ | Sɢ |
|  | Nᴏᴍ | Nᴏᴍ | Nᴏᴍ | Nᴏᴍ |
|  | Iɴᴅᴇꜰ | Iɴᴅᴇꜰ | Iɴᴅᴇꜰ | Iɴᴅᴇꜰ |

'such a big white house'

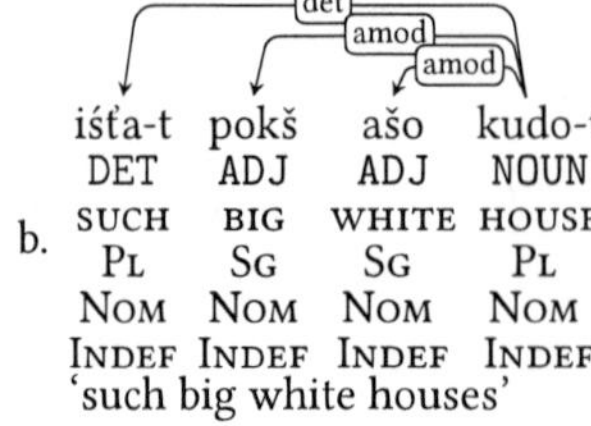

b.
|  | išťa-t | pokš | ašo | kudo-t |
|---|---|---|---|---|
|  | DET | ADJ | ADJ | NOUN |
|  | SUCH | BIG | WHITE | HOUSE |
|  | Pʟ | Sɢ | Sɢ | Pʟ |
|  | Nᴏᴍ | Nᴏᴍ | Nᴏᴍ | Nᴏᴍ |
|  | Iɴᴅᴇꜰ | Iɴᴅᴇꜰ | Iɴᴅᴇꜰ | Iɴᴅᴇꜰ |

'such big white houses'

(9)

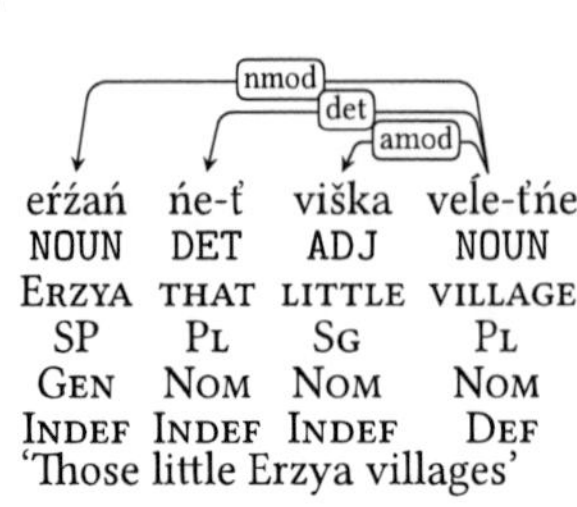

| eŕźań | ńe-ť | viška | veľe-ťńe |
|---|---|---|---|
| NOUN | DET | ADJ | NOUN |
| Eʀᴢʏᴀ | THAT | LITTLE | VILLAGE |
| SP | Pʟ | Sɢ | Pʟ |
| Gᴇɴ | Nᴏᴍ | Nᴏᴍ | Nᴏᴍ |
| Iɴᴅᴇꜰ | Iɴᴅᴇꜰ | Iɴᴅᴇꜰ | Dᴇꜰ |

'Those little Erzya villages'

In an elliptical construction, where the noun head is recoverable or inferable from the context[10], the case ending is merely joined to the final modifier of the noun phrase. In practice, the final modifier can be an adjective (such as color, size, shape, etc.), a participle or converb, a determinatives (ordinal, demonstratives, collective numerals), non-core case-form nouns (including: Ine, Abe, Cmpr, Tra, Prl, etc.). If the modifiers are genitive in form, however, they generally require an additional /śe/ element, i.e. a demonstrative type element. Finally, it should be noted that this kind of construction usually takes either definite or possessive access marking, see Rueter (2010).

(10)

> piže-ťńe
> green-N.SP.Gᴇɴ.Iɴᴅᴇꜰ-Pʟ.Nᴏᴍ.Dᴇꜰ
> 'the green ones'

(11)

> ruzoń-śe-ťńe
> Russian-N.SP.Gᴇɴ.Iɴᴅᴇꜰ-Dᴇᴛ.Dᴇᴍ.Sɢ-Pʟ.Nᴏᴍ.Dᴇꜰ
> 'the Russian ones'

Less frequent, perhaps due to contextual presuppositions, comes the vowel-final modifier with the additional determinative. This more complex construction presupposes a contrastive context.

(12)

> ašo-śe-ťńe
> white-A.Sɢ.Nᴏᴍ.Iɴᴅᴇꜰ-Dᴇᴛ.Dᴇᴍ.Sɢ-Pʟ.Nᴏᴍ.Dᴇꜰ
> 'those white ones'

In elliptical constructions of the nominal phrase, the part-of-speech has been retained in column 4, whereas column 6 bares witness to a deluge of ordered zero-derivation, and column eight indicates the actual dependency relation of the noun phrase head.

---

[10] http://www.glossary.sil.org/term/elliptical-construction

## 4.7  Numerals

The Erzya language has several types of regular counting, cardinal, collective, distributive, multiplicative. There is no problem with counting nouns, such as singular concrete items, pairs or sets (such as socks, batches, broods); these numerals can be readily connected with the *nummod* dependency relation to the noun they modify. Problematic are the missing dependency relations which might better be characterized as iterative numerals; they also count entities, i.e. iterations of a predication (similar to once, twice, but not twofold, double or the second time).

Associative collectives have also been an initial problem, but by following ongoing discussions involving the use of French *tout* the relevant dependency relations would be, perhaps, *advcl* and *acl*, even *det*. Associative collectives, such as 'both of you' are regular for numerals far beyond ten.

(13)

    pand-śť           kolmokśť
    pay-IND.PRT1.ScPL3  three-NUM.ITER
    'they payed three times'

(14)

    pand-śť           kolmońkirda
    pay-IND.PRT1.ScPL3  three-NUM.MULT
    'they payed triple/threefold'

(15)

    pand-śť           kolmoń-kolmoń        jeuro
    pay-IND.PRT1.ScPL3  three-NUM.DISTR Euro-N.SG.NOM.INDEF
    'they payed three Euros each'

(16)

    pand-śť           kolmoćeďe
    pay-IND.PRT1.ScPL3  three-NUM.ORD.PAR
    'they payed for the third time'

# 5  Future work

Since treebank work with Erzya is barely off the ground, there is still plenty of work to do with guidelines for further and consistent annotation. In the time since this paper was originally submitted much experience has been obtained with regard to consistent annotation. One primary undertaking in the guidelines, however, is to render them workable for the closely related Moksha language. When more treebanks have been added, there should be more opportunity to apply the Erzya model since the morphological analyzers for both languages have been designed using parallel tagging strategies where ever possible. The automation of dependency relation assignment will require further work in constituency ordering documentation, as Erzya is a so called pro-drop language attesting to low frequency for conjunctions and other syntactic structural markers.

# 6  In conclusion

This has been a description of the first steps to building Erzya treebanks in accordance with Universal Dependencies. Much space has been dedicated to extensive morphological contemplation, where the matters requiring in-depth consideration are actually the minimalized set of dependency relations in tandem with morphological information, i.e., minimal use of language-dependent subfeatures. Hopefully, this work will provide a means for pivoting and sharing in what has been achieved for larger languages.

# Acknowledgements

We would like to extend our appreciation to Anssi Yli-Jyrä as Research Fellow from the Academy of Finland (dec. No 270354 - A Usable Finite-State Model for Adequate Syntactic Complexity), who has made it possible to work with Erzya UD for three months.

We are also appreciative of work done by anonymous reviewers, whose comments have definitely helped improved our approach to the work.

Our gratitude has no end when it comes to all the painstaking work done by Erzyan writers in the documentation of their language.

# References


Raija Bartens. 1999. *Mordvalaiskielten rakenne ja kehitys*, volume 232 of *Suomalais-Ugrilaisen Seuran Toimituksia*. Suomalais-Ugrilainen Seura, Helsinki.

Arja Hamari. 2007. *The negation of stative relation clauses in the Mordvin languages*, volume 254 of *Suomalais-Ugrilaisen Seuran Toimituksia*. Suomalais-Ugrilainen Seura, Helsinki.

László Keresztes. 1999. *Development of Mordvin Definite Conjugation*, volume 233 of *Suomalais-Ugrilaisen Seuran Toimituksia*. Suomalais-Ugrilainen Seura, Helsinki.

Maria Kholodilova. 2016. *Moksha non-verbal predication*, Printon, Tallinn, pages 229–259. Uralica Helsingiensia 10.

John Lyons. 1977. *Semantics 2*. Cambridge University Press.

Matti Miestamo. 2013. *Symmetric and Asymmetric Standard Negation*, Max Planck Institute for Evolutionary Anthropology, Leipzig, chapter 113. http://wals.info/chapter/113.

Jack Rueter. 2010. *Adnominal Person in the Morphological System of Erzya*, volume 261 of *Suomalais-Ugrilaisen Seuran Toimituksia*. Suomalais-Ugrilainen Seura, Helsinki.

Jack Rueter. 2013. *On quantification in the Erzya language*, LINCOM, Muenchen, pages 99–118.

Trond Trosterud. 2006. *Homonymy in the Uralic Two-Argument Agreement Paradigms*, volume 251 of *Suomalais-Ugrilaisen Seuran Toimituksia*. Suomalais-Ugrilainen Seura, Helsinki.

Rigina Turunen. 2010. *Nonverbal Predication in Erzya*. A. S. Pakett, Tallinn.

Francis M. Tyers, Mariya Sheyanova, and Jonathan North Washington. 2018. UD Annotatrix: An annotation tool for Universal Dependencies. In *Proceedings of the 16th International Workshop on Treebanks and Linguistic Theories*. page [to appear].

Francis M. Tyers and Jonathan N. Washington. 2015. Towards a free/open-source Universal-dependency treebank for Kazakh. In *3rd International Conference on Turkic Languages Processing, (TurkLang 2015)*. pages 276–289.

Johan van der Auwera, Ludo Lejeune, and Valentin Goussev. 2013. *The Prohibitive*, Max Planck Institute for Evolutionary Anthropology, Leipzig. http://wals.info/chapter/71.

F. J. Wiedemann. 1864. *GRAMMATIK DER ERSAMORDWINISCHEN SPRACHE*. MÉMOIRES DE L'ACADEMIE IMPERIALE DES SCIENCES DE ST.-PETERSBOURG. Buchdruckerei der Kaiserlichen Akademie der Wissenschaften., St. Petersburg–Riga–Leipzig.

Н.А. Агафонова, Р.А. Алёшкина, Г.Ф. Беспаова, Водясова Л.П., Клементьева Е.Ф., И.Н. Рябов, Г.В. Рябова, А.М. Харитонова, and В.П. Цыпкайкина, editors. 2011. *Эрзянь кель. Синтаксис: тонавтнемапель*. Издательство мордовского университета, Саранск.

Р.Н. Бузакова, Е.Н. Лисина, М.В. Мосин, and В.П. Цыпкайкина, editors. 2012. *Эрзянь келень орфографиянь валкс.* «Красный Октябрь» типографиясь, Саранск.

# Utilization of Nganasan digital resources:
# a statistical approach to vowel harmony


Fejes, László
Hungarian Academy of Sciences
Research Institute for Linguistics
fejes@nytud.hu


## Abstract


According to the wide-spread belief, although Nganasan has vowel harmony, the harmonic class of a given stem is unpredictable, completely lexicalized. The research made on two different digital sources of Nganasan (a lexicon of a morphological analyzer with harmonic class of the stems tagged and a morphologically annotated corpus) shows that in most of the cases the harmonic class of stems is well predictable based on the vowels in it. Nganasan vowels belong to two harmonic classes except for one neutral vowel.


## Kivonat


A széles körben elterjedt felfogás szerint a nganaszanban ugyan van magánhangzó-harmónia, de a tövek harmóniaosztálya megjósolhatatlan, teljes mértékben lexikalizálódott. Két különböző nganaszan digitális forráson (egy morfológiai elemző tőtárán, illetve egy morfológiailag annotált korpuszon) elvégzett elemzés azonban azt mutatja, hogy hogy az esetek többségében a tövek harmóniaosztálya megbízhatóan megjósolható a tőben szereplő magánhangzók alapján. A nganaszan magánhangzók – egy semleges magánhangzó kivételével – két harmóniaosztályba sorolhatóak.


In the past decade, we have observed an intensive growth of computational linguistic projects on Uralic languages. Some researchers build annotated corpora for their own research, some others develop morphological analyzers for practical tasks (spellchecking etc.). Since these instruments (analyzers, annotated corpora) give a

---






*Proceedings of the 4th International Workshop for Computational Linguistics for Uralic Languages (IWCLUL 2018)*, pages 121–140,
Helsinki, Finland, January 8–9, 2018. ©2018 Association for Computational Linguistics

basic analysis of linguistic structure, even linguists who are not experts of the given language are able to do research based on the annotation. However, although many of these sources are open or at least accessible in some way, it is very rare that someone makes use of the sources built by others for their own research.

I would like to present how I utilized two different Nganasan digital resources to solve a problem of Nganasan vowel harmony. Neither of these projects had been intended to analyze phenomena connected to Nganasan vowel harmony. Furthermore, I am not an expert on Nganasan. However, thanks to digital resources, I could discover regularities of Nganasan morphophonology unknown even for experts.

# 1 Nganasan vowel harmony: completely lexicalized harmonic class?

The Nganasan vowel inventory contains eight vowels and two diphthongs (see Table 1, based on Helimski 1998, 483 and Várnai 2002, 33).

|  | Palatal | | Velar | |
|---|---|---|---|---|
|  | illabial | labial | illabial | labial |
| high | *i* | *ü* | *ɪ*[1] | *u* |
| mid | *e* |  | *ə* | *o* |
| low |  |  | *a* |  |
| diphthongs | *ⁱa* |  |  | *ᵘa* |

Table 1: The vowel system of Nganasan

Nganasan has two kinds of vowel harmony ( Helimski 1998, 492-493; Várnai 2002, 55-60). One of these is a palatovelar harmony with alternating pairs *i : ɪ* and *ü : u*. The palatal variant is used when we find high palatal vowels (*i* or *ü*) in the preceding syllable, the velar variant is used in any other case. Since palatovelar harmony works only in cases when the other kind of vowel harmony (see below) also works, there is always an *i : ɪ : ü : u* alternation. Palatovelar harmony is very regular; therefore, it is not interesting for us.

The other kind of harmony is much more complex. The alternating pairs we find in this kind of harmony are presented in Table 2 (the variants given in parentheses are the results of palatovelar harmony described above).

---

[1] This vowel is represented in different ways in different publications: *ï* ( Helimski 1998), *i̯* ( Várnai 2002; Wagner-Nagy 2002a), *i* ( Brykina et al.) etc.

| after U stems | after I stems |
|:---:|:---:|
| *u (ü)* | *ι (i)* |
| a | *ι (i)* |
| *a* | *ⁱa* |

Table 2: Suffix internal vowel alternation according to vowel harmony

In this alternation, the alternating pairs differ in a different property in each of the three subtypes. In the first case, it seems to be a roundness harmony. In the second case, the main difference is in vowel height. In the third case, the first component of the diphthong differs in height and palatality from the alternating vowel, while the second component is exactly the same. In the following, I call this type of harmony U/I harmony, while I call the first type of harmony discussed above palatovelar harmony.

Whereas palatovelar harmony in Nganasan is obviously a new phenomenon, U/I harmony is a relict of the Uralic palatovelar harmony. Helimski ( Helimski 1998, 490) states that as a result of changes in the vowel system, the patterns of vowel harmony have also changed. Following Helimski ( Helimski 1998, 490–491), literature on Nganasan morphophonology states that today it is unpredictable whether a given stem belongs to U stems or I stems ( Várnai 2002, 56, Várnai and Wagner-Nagy 2003, 322, Katzschmann 2008, 333–334).

Nonetheless, I supposed that the vowels of the stem may determine which harmonic class a specific stem belongs to. I decided to check this hypothesis in digital resources by statistical methods, using simple Perl scripts to see whether there is a connection between the quality of the vowels and the harmonic class of the stem.

## 2 Vowel statistics based on a lexicon

The first resource I used for my research was the lexicon of the Nganasan morphological analyzer (`http://www.morphologic.hu/urali/`). This program was developed between 2001 and 2009 by Beáta Wagner-Nagy, Zsuzsa Várnai, Sándor Szeverényi and Attila Novák. Although the development of the analyzer also served as a test field of the morphophonological rules described earlier, U/I harmony was not involved. The lexicon was based on *Chrestomathia Nganasanica* ( Wagner-Nagy 2002b) and on a Russian–Nganasan–Russian dictionary ( Kosterkina et al. 2001).

Attila Novák was kind to send me the lexicon file, so I was able to compare the vowel skeleton of the stems to their harmonic class. In the lexicon file, verbs are listed in their infinitive forms. Since the suffix of the infinitive alternates according to U/I harmony, it was easy to determinate which harmonic class the given verb stem belongs to. About the 7% of the 3359 suffixable (verb, noun, adjective and numeral) stems were not tagged to belong to any of the harmonic classes, 19 stems were tagged I/U or U/I, both meaning that the stem can be suffixed with suffixes belonging both to the U and the I class: all these 19 stems were ignored. In the case of nouns, adjectives and numerals, most of the stems were explicitly tagged as U stems or I stems. Some stems belonging to some other parts of speech (adverbs, postpositions etc.) were also suffixable and tagged as belonging to one of the harmonic classes. All stems assigned to a certain harmonic class were taken into account, independently of the fact to which part of speech they belonged to.

## 2.1   Method

For statistics, I wrote a Perl script. First of all, I took the lexical items, I removed unnecessary information, so that only the stem form, the stem type and the meaning remained. I also modified transcription to make it more readable, but here I will not go into the details. The only thing I note is that I used å instead of $^u a$ and ä instead of $^i a$ to make pattern matching easier.

For every lexical item I generated a type, which contained only the harmonic class of the stem and the vowel skeleton (consonants were removed from the word form). I used two hashes, and the generated type served as a key in both of them. In the first one, the value was always a string, which contained the stems belonging to the given type. In the second one, the value was a number, and it contained the number of the lexical items belonging to the given type.

For example, the lexicon contained the word *kiriba* 'bread' in the form presented in Figure 1.

```
kiribaU[N:kenyér];en:;
```

Figure 1: Example line from the lexicon of the morphological analyzer

In this row, `kiriba` is the stem form, `U` indicates that this is a U stem, `N` is for noun, kenyér is the meaning in Hungarian, *en:* should stand for the meaning in English, but in most of the cases it is missing. The type of `kiriba` was `U: iia` indicating this is a U stem and it contains three vowels in the given order. There were two more words among U words with the same vowel skeleton: *kirbiśa(n-)* 'knife, scissors, razor' and *t́iid́a-* 'to hide'. Therefore, the value associated with the key `U: iia` in the first hash was what is presented in Figure 2 below and 3 in the second hash.

```
kirbibśa 'kés,| olló,| borotva'
kiriba 'kenyér'
t̆iiďa- 'elrejt'
```

Figure 2: Value associated with U: iia in the first hash

When I needed the number of stems matching a given pattern, I took all the keys from the second hash, and the sum of the values associated to the keys matching the required pattern was the number I needed. E.g. when I needed U stems with an *a* in the last syllable, I used the regular expression `/^U: .*a$/`. However, if I needed specific examples, I used the first hash, and listed the values associated with the keys matching the pattern.

## 2.2 Results

First of all, I took all the monosyllabic stems. If vowel quality is connected to the stem class in any way, it is supposed to be clear when there is only one vowel in the stem. The results presented in Table 3 showed that most of the monosyllabic stems containing a rounded vowel, *a* or the diphthong *ᵘa* belong to U stems.

|  | U stems | I stems |
|---|---|---|
| *o* | 5 | 2 |
| *ü* | 7 | 1 |
| *a* | 12 | 0 |
| *ᵘa* | 2 | 0 |

Table 3: Vowels tending to occur in U stems in monosyllabic words

The only rounded vowel that did not fit in this picture was *u*: although 5 monosyllabic stems with *u* belong to U stems and only 4 to I stems, the difference was not enough to prove connection between *u* and the U class. However, it seemed to be clear that most of the unrounded vowels are connected to the I class, as it is demonstrated in Table 4.

Nonetheless, monosyllabic stems with *ə* showed no significant difference:[2] 3 of them belonged to the U class and 5 of them to the I class.

---

[2] As a rough approach, I considered that data are significant if one of the two options has at least a two-thirds majority.

|   | U stems | I stems |
|---|---------|---------|
| *i* | 1 | 13 |
| *e* | 0 | 4 |
| *ı* | 2 | 6 |
| *ⁱa* | 0 | 3 |

Table 4: Vowels tending to occur in I stems in monosyllabic words

As a next step, I also examined polysyllabic stems containing the same vowel. The picture did not radically change: the results showed that rounded vowels (including the diphthong *ᵘa*) and *a* are connected to U stems, and unrounded vowels are connected to I stems: even stems with *u* showed the preference of U stems. The monosyllabic and polysyllabic stems together show a clear preference in the cases presented in Table 5.

|   | U stems | I stems |
|---|---------|---------|
| *u* | 41 | 6 |
| *ü* | 53 | 2 |
| *a* | 54 | 1 |
| *i* | 4 | 75 |
| *ı* | 2 | 23 |

Table 5: Vowels tending to occur in U or I stems in mono- and polysyllabic words

Since non-first syllable *e* and *o* are rare, usually occurring in fresh loanwords, I could not find any polysyllabic words with just *e*. However, there was one (native) word with two *o*s: *d̓oot* 'ember, firebrand', and it was an I stem. Despite that fact I considered *o* to be connected to U stems: maybe it is not the best solution, but data show that non-first syllable *o* occurs mostly in U stems, irrespective of other vowels in the stem: *rabot̓ij* 'worker', *kresto* 'cross', *t̓emodanə* 'suitcase', *kilogrammə* 'kilogram', *kilomətra* 'kilometer', *honu'o* 'plait, braid' etc. Non-first syllable diphthongs are not so rare as non-first syllable *e* or *o*, but I could find just one stem containing more than one diphthong: *mⁱaið̓ⁱa-* 'to be married, to have a husband' (an I stem, as we expect).

However, it seemed that *ə* is not connected to any of the stem types: I found altogether 49 mono- and polysyllabic U stems containing no other vowel but *ə*, while 38 such stems were I stems. My conclusion was that Nganasan U/I harmony is basically a roundness harmony. I found two exceptions: the vowel *a*, although phonetically unrounded, occurred in U-stems almost without exceptions. Therefore I decided to take it as a phonologically rounded vowel. So, in the following when I write "rounded vowel", the set also includes *a* and diphthong *ᵘa*. The vowel *ə* was ambiguous, it did not trigger either of the stem classes. All other unrounded vowels were connected with I stems.

If we have a look at Table 2 again, we can see that after U stems we find vowels which occur mostly in U stems, while after I stems we find vowels which usually occur in I stems. That is exactly what we are expecting when speaking about vowel harmony. Nonetheless, we expect that it will work even with stems containing different vowels. I distinguished the following types of stems:

- U: containing exclusively rounded vowels (*u, o, ü, a* or diphthong *ᵘa*);

- Ux: containing exclusively rounded vowels (*u, o, ü, a* or diphthong *ᵘa*) and neutral *ə*;

- I: containing exclusively unrounded vowels (*i, e, ı* or diphthong *ⁱa*);

- Ix: containing exclusively unrounded vowels (*i, e, ı* or diphthong *ⁱa*) and neutral *ə*;

- UI: containing both rounded (*u, o, ü, a* or diphthong *ᵘa*) and unrounded vowels (*i, e, ı* or diphthong *ⁱa*), but not neutral *ə*;

- UIx: containing both rounded (*u, o, ü, a* or diphthong *ᵘa*) and unrounded vowels (*i, e, ı* or diphthong *ⁱa*) and also *ə*;

The results justified my supposition (Table 6).

|  | U stems | I stems |
|---|---|---|
| **U** | 562 (96%) | 24 (4%) |
| **Ux** | 895 (90%) | 94 (10%) |
| **I** | 12 (5%) | 230 (95%) |
| **Ix** | 81 (16%) | 417 (84%) |
| **UI** | 276 (52%) | 252 (48%) |
| **UIx** | 213 (48%) | 228 (52%) |

Table 6: Correlations between the vowel skeleton and harmonic class of stems

These numbers show that if a stem contains exclusively rounded or exclusively unrounded vowels, the stem type is highly predictable: just every twentieth bet will be wrong. However, the presence of a neutral vowel will spoil our chances. If the stem contains rounded and neutral vowels, every tenth bet will be wrong; if it contains unrounded and neutral vowels, we loose every sixth bet. Nonetheless, even these chances can be considered very good; it shows a high predictability of stem type based on the vowels the stem contains. Moreover, when the stem contains both rounded and unrounded (and possibly neutral) vowels, it seems to be completely unpredictable whether the stem belongs to the U class or the I class.

If we look at the composition of the stems, we can see that 2315 stems (70%) are (internally) harmonic (that is they belong to the U, Ux, I or Ix category), and just 969 stems (30%) are disharmonic. (The 87 stems containing just ə are ignored here.re.) That shows that also inside stems, rounded vowels prefer to occur with other rounded vowels and unrounded vowels with other unrounded vowels.

Bisyllabic words with both rounded and unrounded vowels showed that the stem type is more closely related to the last than to the first syllable (Table 7, first two rows).

| bisyllabic stems | U stems | I stems |
|---|---|---|
| $\{u, o, a, ü, {}^{u}a\} + \{i, e, ı, {}^{i}a\}$ | 43 (31%) | 94 (69%) |
| $\{i, e, ı, {}^{i}a\} + \{u, o, a, ü, {}^{u}a\}$ | 66 (79%) | 18 (21%) |
| $\{u, o, a, ü, {}^{u}a\} + ə$ | 93 (87%) | 14 (13%) |
| $ə + \{u, o, a, ü, {}^{u}a\}$ | 70 (85%) | 12 (15%) |
| $\{i, e, ı, {}^{i}a\} + ə$ | 13 (18%) | 59 (82%) |
| $ə + \{i, e, ı, {}^{i}a\}$ | 12 (25%) | 36 (75%) |

Table 7: Harmonic classes of bisyllabic disharmonic stems

Although in polysyllabic words (words of three or more syllables) overall statistics did not show any evident correlation with the first, penultimate or last syllable, it became clear that the final syllables have a key role in deciding the stem type. If we examine bisyllabic stems with a rounded vowel and a neutral vowel, we find no striking difference between the penultimate and last position (Table 7, third and fourth rows). However, when we find an unrounded and a neutral vowel in a bisyllabic word, the penultimate syllable seems to be more relevant (Table 7, last two rows).

In polysyllabic disharmonic stems, when the final two vowels are both rounded or both unrounded, the stem type is highly predictable. Nonetheless, if we find a rounded and an unrounded vowel in the final two syllables, their order does not help to predict the stem type (Table 8).

When we find a neutral and a round vowel in the last two syllables of a polysyllabic disharmonic stem, it helps to predict the stem type, especially when the rounded vowel is in the last syllable. However, when we find a neutral and an unrounded vowel in the last two syllables of a polysyllabic disharmonic stem, although it helps

| two final syllables | U stems | I stems |
|---|---|---|
| {*u, o, a, ü, ᵘa*} | 91 (91%) | 9 (9%) |
| {*i, e, ɪ, ⁱa*} | 14 (16%) | 71 (84%) |
| {*u, o, a, ü, ᵘa*} + {*i, e, ɪ, ⁱa*} | 39 (53%) | 35 (47%) |
| {*i, e, ɪ, ⁱa*} + {*u, o, a, ü, ᵘa*} | 72 (48%) | 77 (52%) |

Table 8: Harmonic classes of polysyllabic stems with harmonic and disharmonic vowels in the last syllables

to predict the stem type, our prediction will be wrong more often than in the case of rounded vowels. Moreover, the stem type is more predictable if the unrounded vowel is in the penultimate syllable than when it is in the last one (Table 9).

| two final syllables | U stems | I stems |
|---|---|---|
| {*u, o, a, ü, ᵘa*} + *ə* | 78 (66%) | 41 (34%) |
| *ə* + {*u, o, a, ü, ᵘa*} | 21 (87%) | 3 (13%) |
| {*i, e, ɪ, ⁱa*} + *ə* | 24 (27%) | 66 (73%) |
| *ə* + {*i, e, ɪ, ⁱa*} | 35 (38%) | 56 (62%) |

Table 9: Harmonic classes of polysyllabic stems with a harmonic and a neutral vowel in the last syllables

It seems that the roundedness of the vowels in the first part of the word counts even when the last two vowels are neutral. The order of the rounded and unrounded vowels makes a difference even when the two last syllables are neutral. Note, however, that the number of examples is very low here. Therefore, the reliability of statistics is disputable (Table 10).

| two neutral final syllables | U stems | I stems |
|---|---|---|
| {*u, o, a, ü, ᵘa*} ...+ *ə* + *ə* | 125 (79%) | 34 (21%) |
| {*i, e, ɪ, ⁱa*} ...+ *ə* + *ə* | 33 (35%) | 61 (64%) |
| {*u, o, a, ü, ᵘa*} + {*i, e, ɪ, ⁱa*} ... + *ə* + *ə* | 2 (20%) | 8 (80%) |
| {*i, e, ɪ, ⁱa*} + {*u, o, a, ü, ᵘa*} ... + *ə* + *ə* | 4 (57%) | 3 (43%) |

Table 10: Harmonic classes of polysyllabic stems with a rounded and a neutral vowel in the last syllables

We can conclude that in Nganasan we have two harmonic classes of vowels and a neutral vowel. The vowels in the stem play a great role in the decision which variant of an alternating suffix will be attached to the stem: the variant which contains the vowel belonging to the same harmonic class as the vowels of the stem. When the stem contains vowels belonging to both classes, vowels closer to the suffix (i.e. closer to the end of the stem) play a more significant role. In most of the cases the stem category is well predictable, in other cases (when it contains exclusively neutral vowels or vowels belonging to both harmonic classes) we can predict that the stem category is unpredictable.

It is clear that Nganasan vowel harmony works in a very different way from Finnish or Hungarian vowel harmony, or vowel harmony known from any other Uralic (or Turkic) language.[3] However, since the main principle of the examined phenomenon is that the vowels of the suffix must belong to the same group as the vowels of the stem, it must be considered a type of vowel harmony.

## 3  Vowel statistics based on a corpus

When I started to spread news on my findings, Beáta Wagner-Nagy suggested checking my results against different sources on Nganasan, namely on the Nganasan Spoken Language Corpus or NLSC (Brykina et al.). While the Nganasan Morphological Analyzer was tested on a text collection of one fieldworker from one informant ( or NLSCLabanauskas 2001), NSLC contains texts collected by different fieldworkers, from different informants at different times.

### 3.1  Method

I downloaded 54 xml files, each containing an annotated text. First, using a Perl script, I removed xml tags and other irrelevant information. I got a file which contained different annotation tiers in different lines. With the help of another Perl script, I merged every word in one line with its annotation. In the new files, every line contained a word segmented to morphs, then a tab character followed by the meaning of the stem in English and Russian, separated by a pipe (vertical line) from each other, and separated by a hash mark form the morpheme tags following it. Annotation was followed by a tab character and the reference number in parentheses. (Reference numbers were kept to help debugging.) Consequently, the example above was converted to the string presented in Figure 3.

The hashtag was necessary since sometimes the gloss for meaning also contained a hyphen like in Figure 4.

---

[3]The analysis of these differences are out of scope of the current study.

kontu-gu-mə      take.away|увезти#-IMP-1SG.O     (694)

Figure 3: Word form and analysis put in one line

Abamu-nu      Ust'-avam|Усть-Авам#-GEN.1PL

Figure 4: Hyphen in meaning


In some marginal cases, the glosses in Russian and in English were different or
the annotation was missing. I gave a feedback on these cases to the developers of the
corpus, and I ignored these instances. It was not a considerable loss, because most of
the ignored word forms did not contain any suffixes.

My next step was merging all the word forms occurring in the text into one text
file. In this file, word forms were presented similarly to the previous one, but reference numbers were omitted and the frequency of the form (e.g. the total number of
occurrences in the 54 texts) stood at the end of the line. Since our example word form
occurred only once, the line containing it will look like in Figure 5.

kontu-gu-mə      take.away|увезти#-IMP-1SG.O     1

Figure 5: Word form and analysis with its frequency


In this file word forms were listed in a quasi-alphabetic order. It makes it easy to
notice that the same stems are sometimes glossed in a different way. For example,
above the line presented in Figure 5, we find the line presented in Figure 6

kontu-gu-mə      carry|отнести#-IMP-1SG.O     1

Figure 6: Word form and analysis with its frequency


We can also find the stem *kontu-* glossed with the meaning 'lead/отвести' nearby.
We can also find the stem *kondu-*, most of the times glossed as 'take.away/увезти',
but as 'kill/убить', too. This is important because the next step was the identification
of the stems. Every stem allomorph with a given meaning was considered to be a
separate stem. Therefore, although both *kontu-* and *kondu-* in all of their meanings
belong to the same verb, they counted as five different stems (see Figure 7; numbers
at the end of the lines indicate the number of word forms in which the given stem
allomorph occurs with the given meaning – it is ignored how many times the given
word forms occur).

This is important because this method inavoidably modifies the results of statistics.

```
kondu  'kill|убить'         3
kondu  'take.away|увезти'        7
kontu  'carry|отнести'      1
kontu  'lead|отвести'       1
kontu  'take.away|увезти'       22
```

Figure 7: Word form and analysis with its frequency

However, the probability that a stem which proves our expectations will be overrepresented is the same that a stem which contradicts our hypothesis will be overrepresented. Therefore, we can hope this result will reflect roughly the same as a more precise approach, namely, if we tried to associate all the allomorphs of a lexeme with all glossed meanings to a single stem.

To get the stems organized as presented above, I used another Perl script. This segmented the word forms and made two files: the list of stems (as presented above) and a list of suffixes (as presented in Figure 8).

From this file, I generated another list in which allomorphs are ordered according to their functions (Figure 9).[4]

The next step was to define which morphs undergo vowel harmony and which harmonic class they belong to. Since Nganasan morphophonology is very complex, I categorized allomorphs manually. Allomorphs containing no vowels undergoing harmony (such as [1SG.O] or [IMP] *ŋəə*) were simply left out of the list. Only those allomorphs were taken as undergoing harmony which had at least one pair belonging to the other harmonic class. For example, *-gu-, -gü-, -ku-* and *-kü-* undergo palatal harmony, and according to the literature (e.g. Helimski 1998, 493, Várnai 2002, 57–59) this happens only when it also undergoes rounding harmony. However, (despite the relatively high number of the above mentioned allomorphs, especially with *u*), none of the allomorphs *-gɪ-, -gi-, -kɪ-* or *-ki-* were attested, I took *-gu-, -gü-, -ku-* and *-kü-* as allomorphs not undergoing rounding harmony. Because of the same reason, *-ŋəi-* was also taken as a suffix not undergoing vowel harmony. However, other allomorphs beginning with *ŋ* were regarded as belonging to one or other harmonic class (see Figure 10).[5]

---

[4]The Nganasan Spoken Language Corpus uses the character *i* to indicate velar illabial high vowel. For technical reasons, these are substituted by *ï* in the presented codes. For the same reason, *ʔ* is replaced by ? and *'* is replaced by a vertical straight apostrophe.

[5]In fact, not all these allomorphs are the allomorphs of the same morpheme. The allomorphs beginning with *k* or *g* are always used in first person forms, therefore a tag something like [1IMP] or [IMP1] would be more appropriate for them. The allomorph *-ŋəə-* is used for third persons in the subjective and

```
[...]
gu [DRV] 1
gu [DUR] 2
gu [IMP] 33
[...]
gü [IMP] 8
[...]
mə [1SG.O] 66
mə [1SG] 2
mə [ACC.1SG] 28
mə [ACC.SG.1SG] 46
mə [DRV] 1
mə [EXCL.[NOM.SG]] 3
mə [EXCL] 4
mə [MOM] 3
mə [NOM.1SG] 8
mə [NOM.SG.1SG] 93
mə [SG.1SG] 3
[...]
```

Figure 8: List of suffixes (segments)

Allomorphs tagged in a slightly different way but clearly belonging to the same morpheme were also included in the list (see Figure 11).

Allomorphs clearly belonging together but containing different zero allomorphs were also taken into account, see Figure 12.

Allomorphs undergoing alternation but containing vowels belonging to different harmonic classes were indicated with an exclamation mark (see Figure 13). Later these allomorphs were not taken into account, but they were collected to another list for further studies. They may be a result of an annotation mistake, a slip of the tongue, signs of disintegration of vowel harmony (maybe not independently of language loss) etc.

objective conjugation, -ŋəi- occurs in third person reflexive conjugation: these are two distinct morphemes again. The allomorphs -ŋu- and -ŋü- are used in second person subjective and objective conjugation, -ŋa- in second person reflexive conjugation, while -ŋi- and -ŋı- occur in second person forms of all the three conjugations: two additional morphemes with some overlapping allomorphs again. So we have to speak about six different morphemes, tagged in different ways (c.f. Helimski 1998, 505, Wagner-Nagy 2002a, 110). Nonetheless, this problem does not influence my statistics.

```
[1SG.O] mə 66
[1SG.O] n'ə 1
[...]
[IMP] gu 35
[IMP] gü 8
[IMP] ku 51
[IMP] kü 5
[IMP] ŋa 5
[IMP] ŋi 2
[IMP] ŋu 21
[IMP] ŋü 3
[IMP] ŋəi 5
[IMP] ŋəə 25
[IMP] ŋï 24
[IMP…] ŋu 1
```

Figure 9: List of suffixes ordered by tags (segments)

```
U[IMP] ŋa 5
I[IMP] ŋi 2
I[IMP] ŋu 21
U[IMP] ŋü 3
I[IMP] ŋï 24
```

Figure 10: Suffixes having allomorphs with vowels belonging to both harmonic
classes were taken as morphemes undergoing vowel harmony

```
U[IMP…] ŋu 1
```

Figure 11: Harmonizing suffix with a uniquely formed tag with its harmony class
tagged

```
U[LOCN.[ACC.SG]] rəmu 1
I[LOCN.[GEN.SG]] d'əmï 1
U[LOCN.[NOM.SG]] rəmu 1
```

Figure 12: List of suffixes with zero allomorphs with their harmony class tagged

```
I[LOC.PL] tini 28
![LOC.PL] tinü 1
U[LOC.PL] tünü 1
```

Figure 13: List of suffixes with their harmony class tagged and a non-categorizable allomorph among them

Based on this definition of harmonic classes of suffixes, all the suffixes were replaced by their harmonic classes in our file. E.g. our example in Figure 5 was first reassigned into a form presented in the first line of Figure 14 and then the suffixes were changed into their harmonic classes, as it is presented in the second line. NB, although at first sight *-gu-* may seem to belong to the U harmonic class, it is neutral (see above). However, the form presented in the third line contains two harmonic suffixes, therefore it is changed into the form presented in the fourth line of the same figure.

```
kontu[take.away|увезти]-gu[IMP]-mə[1SG.O]
kontu[carry|отнести]-N-N
kontu-ra-?a take.away|увезти#-PASS-PF.[3SG.S]
kontu[take.away|увезти]-U-U
```

Figure 14: Annotations realigned to the morphs they belong to and changed to their harmonic classes

Interestingly, I have found about 200 word forms in which I could identify suffixes belonging to both of the harmonic classes, e.g. see Figure 15. In this case, my classification contradicts the literature (e.g. Wagner-Nagy 2002a, 78), according to which the plural lative suffix always contains *i*, therefore it is not a harmonic suffix. However, I took it as an alternating suffix because I could find forms *-tü-* and *-ntü-* as in the word forms shown in Figure 16.

```
ma-ti-tü tent|чум#-LAT.PL-3SG
ma[tent|чум]-I-U
```

Figure 15: Stem with two suffixes belonging to different harmonic classes

It is worth noting that the word form meaning 'to his tents' has two different forms here: *matitü* and *matütu* and the suffix is never attested with vowels *ı* or *u*. A similar case is attested with the coaffix of perfect verbs, which should also contain *i* all the

```
ma[tent|чум]-tü[LAT.PL]-tu[OBL:3SG]
ku[which|какой]-ni[LOCPRON]-ə[ADJZ]-ntü[LAT.PL]-ndü [OBL.2PL]
ŋabtə[hair|волосы]-tü[LAT.PL]-tü[OBL.3SG]
```

Figure 16: Plural lative suffixes with *ü*

time ( Wagner-Nagy 2002a, 101). But it also occurs with *a*, *ü* and *ı* and several kinds of diphthongs (see below) in the annotated corpus.

In any case, I ignored word forms with suffixes (seemingly) belonging to different harmonic classes and used just the forms in which all the suffixes belonged to the same harmonic class (or were neutral).

## 3.2 Results

I made two kinds of statistics on these forms. The first shows the composition (vowel skeleton) of the stems before the suffixes of the two harmonic classes. I used harmonic categories based on the previous study. However, the corpus contained two diphthongs, unknown by the literature ( Helimski 1998, 483, Várnai 2002, 33) and not used by the morphological analyzer: $^i a$ and $^{ü}a$ (for pattern matching, substituted by ı̧ and ű, respectively). As a hypothesis, I treated $^i a$ as unrounded (as $^i a$ is) and $^{ü}a$ as rounded (as $^{ü}a$ is). The distribution shown by the statistics is presented in Table 11.

|        | U class    | I class    |
|--------|------------|------------|
| U      | 395 (87%)  | 59 (13%)   |
| Ux     | 305 (78%)  | 85 (22%)   |
| I      | 26 (11%)   | 205 (89%)  |
| Ix     | 52 (25%)   | 153 (75%)  |
| UI     | 148 (51%)  | 142 (49%)  |
| UIx    | 42 (49%)   | 44 (51%)   |
| only ə | 39 (59%)   | 27 (41%)   |

Table 11: Number of stems with a given vowels skeleton type before suffixes belonging to different harmonic classes

The results show again that harmonizing suffixes with rounded vowels tend to occur after stems with rounded vowels and harmonizing suffixes with unrounded vowels tend to occur after stems with unrounded vowels. The presence of a neutral vowel weakens this tendency. After stems containing vowels belonging to both or none of the harmonic classes the harmonic class of the suffix is unpredictable.

To check whether the categorization of each vowel is proper, I also made statistics for the separate vowels. I counted how many times they occur in stems suffixed by the rounded and unrounded variants of harmonizing suffixes. (If the same vowel occurs twice or three times in the same stem, it is counted as two or three occurrences, respectively.)

|  | **U class** | **I class** |
|---|---|---|
| *u* | 360 (73%) | 135 (27%) |
| *o* | 204 (76%) | 64 (24%) |
| *a* | 570 (80%) | 135 (20%) |
| *ü* | 314 (82%) | 71 (18%) |
| $^u a$ | 53 (91%) | 5 (9%) |
| $^ü a$ | 6 (86%) | 1 (14%) |
| *i* | 218 (33%) | 417 (67%) |
| *e* | 42 (24%) | 135 (76%) |
| *ı* | 44 (17%) | 222 (83%) |
| $^i a$ | 28 (35%) | 51 (65%) |
| $^ı a$ | – | 2 (100%) |
| *ə* | 540 (58%) | 383 (42%) |

Table 12: Number of different vowels before suffixes belonging to different harmonic classes

The data presented in Table 12 show that at least two thirds of any vowel occurs in stems before a suffix belonging to the same harmonic class as I classified them. Although neutral *ə* also occurs more times before U class suffixes, the range here is considerably lower than the lowest value for vowels classified as belonging to a harmonic class (seven twelfth instead of eight).

## 3.3   Some problems

There were almost 250 stems which occurred with suffixes belonging to both of the harmonic classes. In the statistics above, they were presented as two different stems belonging to different harmonic classes. E.g. the word *basa* 'iron, money' was tagged as an U stem in the morphonological analyzer. In the corpus, in most of the cases it is followed by suffixes belonging to the U class (or neutral), but in some cases it is followed by the I class variant of the destinitive suffix (Figure 17).

However, similarly to the case of the plural lative suffix and the perfect coaffix seen above, the destinitive suffix is attested only with vowels *i, ü* and *ı*, therefore it is

```
basa-ði-n'i? iron|железо#-DST-ACC.PL.1PL
basa[iron|железо]-I-I
basa-ði-n'ü? money|деньги#-DST-ACC.PL.1PL
basa[money|деньги]-I-U
basa-ði-t'ü iron|железо#-DST-ACC.PL.3SG
basa[iron|железо]-I-U
```

Figure 17: Suffixed forms of *basa* 'iron, money'

disputable whether it is a harmonizing suffix. Moreover, the (nominative-accusative-genitive) plural form with a first person plural possessor (PL1.PL) also occurs with vowels *i* and *ü* only. If we removed all these suffixes from the list of the harmonizing suffixes, rounding harmony would seem more regular.

Nonetheless, there are cases which are more complicated. Sometimes we find suffixes of different harmonic classes a certain stem, see Figure 18.

```
ŋad'a-ðu younger.sibling|младший.брат/сестра#-NOM.SG.3SG
ŋad'a-ði younger.sibling|младший.брат/сестра#-NOM.SG.3SG
```

Figure 18: The same form with suffixes belonging to different harmonic classes

In this case, the suffix occurs with all the four harmonizing vowels and I have found no explanation for the lack of vowel harmony in the second case. All such cases need a detailed analysis.

Moreover, to evaluate the results, it will be necessary to check the distribution of seemingly irregular forms among the different informants. If we find that many of these forms come from a smaller group of informants, we have to suggest that they are further on the way of language loss (cf. Helimski 1998, 493) and therefore data from them are not reliable for researching Nganasan vowel harmony in its intact form. However, data from these people are a useful source for the research of language loss.

# 4 Conclusion

Contrary to what we find in the literature on Nganasan morphophonology, Nganasan U/I vowel harmony proved to be quite well predictable by a statistical analysis of Nganasan data. It is basically a rounding harmony, although phonetically unrounded *a* belongs to rounded vowels and *ə* does not belong to either of the classes. The two very different digital sources of Nganasan show basically the same tendency: stems containing rounded vowels tend to be suffixed with harmonizing suffixes containing rounded vowels and stems containing unrounded vowels tend to be suffixed with harmonizing suffixes containing unrounded vowels.

## Acknowledgments

The research was financed by the NKFI 119863 Experimental and theoretical investigation of vowel harmony patterns. I would like to thank Attila Novák and Beáta Wagner-Nagy for providing material for my research and Péter Rebrus and Miklós Törkenczy for their support of my work. I am particularly grateful for the assistance given by Nóra Wenszky. My special thanks are extended to György Soros for his help of founding the Department of Theoretical Linguistics of the Eötvös Loránd University.

## References

Maria Brykina, Valentin Gusev, Sándor Szeverényi, and Beáta Wagner-Nagy. ????
Nganasan Spoken Language Corpus (NSLC). Archived in Hamburger Zentrum für Sprachkorpora. Version 0.1. http://hdl.handle.net/11022/0000-0001-B36C-C. Accessed 2017-06-16, published2016-12-23.

Eugene Helimski. 1998. *The Uralic Languages*, Routledge, London and New York, chapter Nganasan, pages 480–515.

Michael Katzschmann. 2008. *Chrestiomathia Nganasanica*. Norderstedt, Hamburg.

N. T. Kosterkina, A. Č. Momde, and T. Ju. Ždanova. 2001. *Slovar' nganasansko-russkij i russko-nganasanskij*. Prosvesčenije, Sankt-Petersburg.

Kazys Labanauskas. 2001. *Nganasanskaja fol'klornaja hrestomatija*. Number 6 in Fol'klor narodov Tajmyra. Tajmyrskij okružnyj centr narodnogo tvorčestva, Dudinka.

Zsuzsa Várnai. 2002. *Chrestomathia nganasanica*, SZTE Finnugor Tanszék – MTA Nyelvtudományi Intézet, Szeged – Budapest, chapter Hangtan, pages 33–69.

Zsuzsa Várnai and Beáta Wagner-Nagy. 2003. Magánhangzó-harmónia a nganaszanban. *Nyelvtudományi Közlemények* 100:321–337.

Beáta Wagner-Nagy. 2002a. *Chrestomathia nganasanica*, SZTE Finnugor Tanszék – MTA Nyelvtudományi Intézet, Szeged – Budapest, chapter Alaktan, pages 71–126.

Beáta Wagner-Nagy. 2002b. *Chrestomathia nganasanica*, SZTE Finnugor Tanszék – MTA Nyelvtudományi Intézet, Szeged – Budapest, chapter Szójegyzék, pages 274–291.

# Parallel Forms in Estonian Finite State Morphology


Heiki-Jaan Kaalep
University of Tartu
Department of Language Technology

`Heiki-Jaan.Kaalep@ut.ee`



## Abstract

Parallel forms are two or more synonymous forms that convey an identical set of morpho-syntactic categories in a paradigm cell of a word. They deserve attention from a theoretical linguistic, as well as from a computational point of view. How do humans know which form to choose, and how should this preference be modelled computationally? The paper gives an overview of parallel forms in Estonian and discusses reasons for surface form variation. A considerable part of the article is dedicated to a simplified, but still technically detailed example of handling parallel plural partitive forms, one of which is more common, and the other a rarer form. An example is used to explicate the proposed method of handling parallel forms in finite state morphology, coupled with considerations of their preferencial choice. The method involves using a combination of two-level rules as a way of controlling the combinatorial explosion of continuation lexicons. The design has been implemented to fully cover the inflectional morphology of Estonian.



## Kokkuvõte

Rööpvormid on ühe sõna erinevad muutevormid, millel on sama grammatiline tähendus. Nad väärivad tähelepanu nii teoreetilise kui ka arvutilingvistika poolt. Kuidas teavad inimesed, millist vormi valida, ja kuidas seda teadmist modelleerida? Artikkel annab ülevaate rööpvormidest eesti keeles ja arutleb nende olemasolu põhjuste üle. Suur osa artiklist on pühendatud lihtsustatud, kuid siiski







*Proceedings of the 4th International Workshop for Computational Linguistics for Uralic Languages (IWCLUL 2018)*, pages 141–155,
Helsinki, Finland, January 8–9, 2018. ©2018 Association for Computational Linguistics

tehniliselt detailsele näitele, kuidas käsitleda mitmuse osastava rööpvorme, millest seejuures üks on tavaline ja teine haruldane. Näite abil selgitatakse, kuidas rööpvorme ja nende valikueelistusi saaks lõplike muundurite morfoloogias käsitleda. Pakutav meetod, mida on kasutatud kogu eesti keele sõnamuutuse modelleerimiseks, hõlmab kahetasemeliste reeglite kasutamist, millega piiratakse jätkuleksikonide kombinatoorset plahvatust.

# 1   Introduction

It is possible that a word paradigm cell is filled by two or more synonymous forms that realise the same set of morpho-syntactic categories. These alternative realizations are called *doublets* in the German linguistic tradition (Mörth and Dressler, 2014), *parallel forms* (Raadik, 2013) in the Estonian tradition (which will be followed in the current paper), and *overabundant forms* (Thornton, 2012).

Computationally, parallel forms pose no problem for analysis, as different surface forms are mapped to the same bundle of morpho-syntactic categories. However, per synthesis the situation is reversed, as one must decide which form to generate, and how does one choose in the case of one-to-many mapping? Traditionally, analysis has been the main application, be it in the context of spell-checking or information retrieval, thus instances when one surface form maps to several lemmas and/or morpho-syntactic categories have received much attention as the problem of ambiguity. This tradition may explain why parallel forms have received less attention, despite them posing a challenge in terms of explaining human language and the generation of rule-based machine translation.

# 2   Reasons for surface form variation

Parallel forms may occur due to different dialects than the written norm is based upon, or due to language change that is currently happening

The first scenario implies that some speakers have different intuitions regarding word inflection, because they have different dialectal backgrounds, e.g. the Standard German *Park-s* and the Swiss-German *Pärke* (parks). The parallel forms are the result of defining the norm in a liberal manner, thus allowing the inflectional systems of different dialects to co-exist under a common normative umbrella.

The second scenario implies that the speakers have different intuitions regarding word inflections, because although they all share a language variety (dialect), it changes over time. The existence of parallel forms in this case is at odds with the principles of communication: the speaker can only choose one of the parallel forms at a given time, and one would expect the other forms to eventually fall into disuse. The existence of parallel forms in this scenario would indicate that the language has not finished its particular process of change.

It is not easy to decide which scenario is applicable to a given language: co-existence of dialects or language change. The question may be answered by investigating how new and rare words are inflected.

In the case of vigorous dialects, when speakers see a new word, they will first designate it to several inflectional classes (based on their dialect-specific intuition), and later, after mutual communication, may arrive at an agreement on a single acceptable, norm-adhering inflectional class.

In the case of language change, the speakers' initial intuitions about inflecting a new word are uniform. It is also expected that speakers abandon the previous inflectional classes of old words so that they join new ones.

In Estonia, the influence of dialects on morphology has become marginal.

When confronted with a rare or previously unseen word, speakers of Estonian immediately exhibit a remarkable consensus about what is the generally accepted (i.e. normal, correct) way of forming its inflectional forms. Their lack of disagreement is noteworthy, because in terms of an unseen word, the speakers could not have discussed its inflectional class beforehand.

Moreover, instances of actual negotiations about the inflectional class of a rare or new word (e.g. a foreign name) are virtually absent in everyday communication.

Evidence from a 270 million token corpus collected in 2013 from the internet called etTenTen [1] shows that there is actually no need for such negotiations: there is almost no variety in the choice of the inflectional class of a new word; typing errors account for a much larger amount of variation in word forms than misclassifications into alternative inflectional classes.

The vocabulary used in the corpus comprises 7.5 million wordforms. An Estonian morphological analyser [2], relying only on its lexicon and algorithm of productive derivation and compounding (thus using no guessing) classified 2.7 million of these wordforms as unknown. Manual check of 2,700 (0.1%) of the unknowns revealed that only 10 wordforms were inflected incorrectly (resulting from inflectional misclassification by the writer), while 300 contained a typing error. The rest of the unknown words were actually instances of incorrect punctuation (typically resulting in concatenating several words), proper names, foreign language words, and true neologisms, not showing variation in inflectional classes.

---

[1] `http://downloads.sketchengine.co.uk/ettenten13.processed.prevert.xz`, searchable at `http://www.keeleveeb.ee`
[2] `https://github.com/Filosoft/vabamorf`

However, at closer inspection one may observe a few telling instances when Estonians do have problems in deciding what the correct inflectional class of a word is. Those instances fall into two scenarios. In the first scenario, the choice is between an exceptional, old, unproductive inflectional class versus a regular, productive one, and involves cases when an old word has become rare and thus its exceptional inflectional behaviour cannot be remembered by everyone, or when an Estonian family name coincides with a common noun belonging to an exceptional inflectional class (e.g. in English the plural of the family name *Foreman* is *Foremans*, not *Foremen*). In the second scenario, the choice is between two productive classes, and happens when a new word or proper noun has extra-morphological properties that belong to orthogonal categories (e.g. phonetic properties and wordiness) that incidentally predict different productive class memberships. For example, *Breivik* is a foreign name that appeared in Estonian texts only in 2011. Being disyllabic and ending in *-ik*, it should phonetically belong to the class of *u*-ending singular genitives (*Breiviku*). Being a new and foreign word, it is an out-of-vocabulary word w.r.t. conventional Estonian, and thus should belong to the class of *i*-ending singular genitives (*Breiviki*). According to et-TenTen, 75% of the 400 mentions are *Breiviki*, and 25% *Breiviku*. The other possible stem vowels, *a* and *e*, are never used.

## 3   Parallel forms and finite state morphology

(Beesley and Karttunen, 2003, p. 300–310) used English plurals as a convenient example of parallel forms and showed elegant ways of dealing with them. They differentiated *overriding plurals*, i.e. situations when an irregular form substitutes the regular one, and *extra plurals*, i.e. situations when the regular forms also remain in use, without attempting to differentiate the forms according to their usage preference. Indeed, adding an extra lexical tag (e.g. *Use/Rare*) to the lexical string via an appropriate continuation lexicon would be very simple. The sole formal issue would be the multiplication of continuation lexicons, as this extra tag would effectively make otherwise similar inflectional classes formally different.

In the case of many continuation lexicons (each embodying an inflectional class), and some slots in the paradigm having multiple realisations, independent of the inflectional class, the number of lexicons explodes, as noted by (Beesley and Karttunen, 2003, p. 302–304).

Nevertheless, it is this approach that has been adopted when describing Finnish and Sami [3], in both cases it was assumed that parallel forms are due to dialects. In each language, non-preferred forms are marked with +Use/NG ("no generation"). The

---

[3]See /fin and /sme in `https://victorio.uit.no/langtech/trunk/langs/`

motivation came from rule-based machine translation, where one needs to synthesise only one wordform per one paradigm cell of a word (Antonsen et al., 2016).

By default, an inflectional type (represented via a cascade of continuation lexicons) is such that every paradigm slot has exactly one surface realisation. If a slot has possibly two realisations, then this inflectional type bifurcates: in addition to the old one with a unique realisation, there will be a new one with one parallel form. Upon adding preference information, this new inflectional type will bifurcate again: one version will be with form A preferred, the other with form B preferred. One inflectional type became three. If there happens to be one more paradigm cell that can have two realisations, then each of the previous inflectional types will have three more variants: thus a single inflectional type has become nine.

This attempt to make the description more informative has resulted in an inflated and less general description, and this is not a desirable result.

An alternative method would be to use a filtering mechanism that first defines a separate list of individual word forms and then use *Priority union*, following (Beesley and Karttunen, 2003, p. 306-309), or (Pruulmann-Vengerfeldt, 2010) for Estonian. The downside of this is that some surface forms of a word become decoupled from the dictionary headword in the stem lexicon, which in turn creates description difficulties when the headwords are homographs with different inflection patterns; there are more than 400 homographic words of this type in the Estonian lexicon in the Giellatekno repository [4].

## 4 Estonian

Estonian is a Fenno-Ugric language. It is closely related to Finnish, although a speaker of only Estonian and one of only Finnish are unlikely to understand each other. Finnish has retained its original nature more than Estonian, which has lost vowel harmony and moved from an agglutinative language towards a flective one. A specific regular difference is that Estonian has lost the last phone from many words it shares with Finnish, which has resulted in it losing some of the regularities of the Finnish inflectional system, and in the adding of innovations as a substitute.

Estonian has 14 cases, both in the singular and plural. Table 1 lists the possible affix variants and stem vowels that must be concatenated to a consonant-ending stem of the declinable word paradigm (stem gradation patterns are not presented). Note that the vowels *a*, *e*, *i*, and *u* are traditionally classified as theme vowels, associated with the stem, and thus not counted as affixes.

---

[4] https://victorio.uit.no/langtech/trunk/experiment-langs/est/

|  | singular | plural |
|---|---|---|
| grammatical cases |  |  |
| nominative | ∅ | [∅ a e i u] d |
| genitive | ∅, a, e, i, u | e, [∅ a e i u] te, [∅ a e i u] de |
| partitive | ∅, d, [∅ a e i u] t | id, [∅ a e i u] sid, e, i, u |
| semantic cases |  |  |
| illative | ∅, a, e, i, u, de, [∅ a e i u] sse | [te de e i u] sse |
| inessive | [∅ a e i u] s | [te de e i u] s |
| elative | [∅ a e i u] st | [te de e i u] st |
| allative | [∅ a e i u] le | [te de e i u] le |
| adessive | [∅ a e i u] l | [te de e i u] l |
| ablative | [∅ a e i u] lt | [te de e i u] lt |
| translative | [∅ a e i u] ks | [te de e i u] ks |
| terminative | [∅ a e i u] ni | [te de e i u] ni |
| essive | [∅ a e i u] na | [te de e i u] na |
| abessive | [∅ a e i u] ta | [te de e i u] ta |
| comitative | [∅ a e i u] ga | [te de e i u] ga |

Table 1: Declinable word affixes and added stem vowels

There are two general implicational patterns (or rules of referral) in the paradigm. The singular genitive stem serves as the base for forming singular semantic cases (except illative ending in ∅ or *-de*), plus the plural nominative; and the plural genitive stem serves as the base for all plural semantic cases (this even applies to otherwise very exceptional words).

## 5   Parallel forms in Estonian

Normative Estonian linguists favour parallel forms, accepting various realisations of the number and case category in declinable words. According to a normative dictionary (Raadik, 2013) that categorizes all declinations into 26 inflectional types, there is not a single type that does not contain words with several possible realisations per some categories, with two paradigm slots especially likely to have two parallel forms: the singular illative (Sg Ill) and plural partitive (Pl Par). Thirteen types exhibit type-internal parallelism per all plural semantic cases, and seven types exhibit the same parallelism per some words. Eight inflectional types have parallel forms per Pl Par, seven types exhibit total and exhaustive parallelism per Sg Ill, and twelve types exhibit the same parallelism per at least some of their words. Two more types have parallel haplology forms per Sg Ill. In addition, a word may simultaneously belong to more than one inflectional class, which results in another set of slots with parallel forms. Of the 26, only seven inflectional types (six of them, with a total of 300 words, may be characterized as unproductive inflectional classes) contain no words that also belong to some other inflectional type.

Thus, the language norm assumes that it is very common for a word to have multiple ways of forming a surface form per some morpho-syntactic category bundle.

Usage-wise, the distribution of such forms is very skewed, though. For example, consider the frequency counts of words and their Pl Par forms in etTenTen per *taim* (plant), *luu* (bone) and *kamp* (gang): *taim* 42665, Pl Par *taimi/taimesid* 6868/9, *luu* 7060, Pl Par *luid/luusid* 699/13, *kamp* 6271, Pl Par *kampu/kampasid* 7/22. This example shows a universal trend in languages: if a case form is infrequent, its forming tends to be regular (*kampasid* in this example).

At a very rough approximation, Finnish could be regarded as a previous form of Estonian: some morphological features of Finnish have disappeared from Estonian. There are many words that are similar in both languages (save for the final lost phones in Estonian), and some of these are partly inflected in a way that resembles Finnish. For example, consider the Estonian *taim* (Finnish *taimi* (plant)). The Finnish Pl Par is *taimia*, while the Estonian irregular form is *taimi* (the regular form being *taimesid*). Or consider *luu* (Finnish *luu* (bone)). The Finnish Pl Par is *luita*, while the Estonian irregular form is *luid* (the regular form being *luusid*). Both these words have rather frequent Pl Par forms, which are lagging behind in their journey from the past, not yet caught up by the change. It is these types of words — otherwise regular, but having some exceptional frequent form that is a remnant from the past — that the following treatment addresses.

## 6 Parallel forms in Estonian FSM

When a word form is analysed or generated, usage info is written out with the grammatical categories of an inflectional form (Figure 1).

Conceptually, usage information is unrelated to the morphological description (morphotactics and morphonology). However, if one wishes to encode it in the lexicon, then — being a characteristic of individual words — it should be attached to the stem entries, and must be propagated from the stem entry to the final wordform.

For inflectional classes where alternative affixes are common, but still applicable only to a subset of individual words, one needs rules for selecting:

1. the inflectional affix (the traditional task of morphology)
2. a tag that indicates whether the word form is rare or common (not a traditional

```
taim+N+Pl+Par             taimi
taim+N+Pl+Par+Use/Rare    taimesid
kamp+N+Pl+Par             kampasid
kamp+N+Pl+Par+Use/Rare    kampu
```

Figure 1: Lexical and surface sides of Pl Par of *taim* (plant) and *kamp* (gang)

task of morphology, but similar to adding usage notes such as *archaic* or *colloquial* to forms in a paradigm table or traditional dictionary)

The affixes concerned are:

1. Per Pl Par: 1.1. *-sid* or $\emptyset$ with stem vowel change; 1.2. *-sid* or *-id*

2. Per Sg Ill: *-sse* or $\emptyset$ with stem grade strengthening.

The task is to generate forms. We know that per Pl Par, *-sid* is always possible, and per Sg Ill, *-sse* is always possible, and that the alternative form is possible only if a tag indicates so in the stem lexicon. If an alternative form exists, it is also the more common one, unless it has some tag in the stem lexicon indicating otherwise.

The full implementation covering Estonian inflection is available in the Giellatekno repository [5].

In the Giellatekno infrastructure, the standard way of building a transducer begins with modelling morphotactics by concatenating stems and continuation lexicons. The next step is modelling morphophonology by applying two-level rules (Koskenniemi, 1983) to the output of the previous transducer. This step substitutes and removes some symbols, typically abstract phonemes and functional symbols that were previously introduced to provide meaningful context to the rules.

Incidentally, a two-level rule can be used as a filter to prune some paths from a transducer. Every two-level rule says what output side symbol corresponds to which input side symbol, given a certain context. Imagine that the input symbol has only one potential corresponding output symbol. Now if the context does not match, then it is impossible to have this symbol correspondence in the path, and a path cannot be built. In a similar vein, one can define pruning contexts for input symbols that have more than one corresponding output symbol.

The following sections show how lexicons and two-level rules interact to arrive at the results on Figure 1. The exemplary alternation of *-sid* vs $\emptyset$ per Pl Par is used to explain the process.

---

[5] `https://victorio.uit.no/langtech/trunk/experiment-langs/est/`

```
LEXICON NOUNS
          taim+N:taim%>%{pl.i%} EIT ;                ! plant
          kamp+N:kamp%>%{pl.u%}%{rare%} PIIM ;    ! gang

LEXICON EIT         ! 1C with stem vowel e
              :%{sg.e%} 1C ;

LEXICON PIIM        ! 1C with stem vowel a
              :%{sg.a%} 1C ;

LEXICON 1C            ! monosyllabic consonant-ending word
              :%>%{s%}%{i%}%{d%} PL_PAR_VARIANT ;

LEXICON PL_PAR_VARIANT    ! pl partitive may have parallel forms
   +Use/Rare:%{rare%} PL_PARTITIVE ;     ! less used form
            : PL_PARTITIVE ;                 ! default form

LEXICON PL_PARTITIVE
          +Pl: PARTITIVE ;

LEXICON PARTITIVE
          +Par: # ;
```

Figure 2: Relevant extracts from `lexc`-lexicons to build pre-`twol` representations per Pl Par of *taim* and *kamp*

```
taim+N           +Pl+Par:taim >{pl.i}       {sg.e}>{s}{i}{d}
taim+N+Use/Rare+Pl+Par:taim >{pl.i}       {sg.e}>{s}{i}{d}{rare}
kamp+N           +Pl+Par:kamp >{pl.u}{rare}{sg.a}>{s}{i}{d}
kamp+N+Use/Rare+Pl+Par:kamp >{pl.u}{rare}{sg.a}>{s}{i}{d}{rare}
```

Figure 3: Pre-`twol` representations per the plural partitive of *taim* and *kamp*

# 7 Lexicons for parallel forms

Figure 2 gives `lexc` examples per *taim* and *kamp*.

The final desired lexical and surface strings per the parallel forms of these words would be as in Figure 1; the outcome from the `lexc` lexicons are on Figure 3.

If a word has an exceptional $\emptyset$-ending short form in addition to the default *sid*-ending Pl Par, i.e. one that is formed by substituting the stem vowel with a different one, then the vowel is explicitly given at the stem entry as {pl.i} or {pl.u} (see Figure 2).

The symbol > denotes a morpheme border; {s}{i}{d} constitute *-sid* and the $\emptyset$ alternation (see Figure 4 ).

A speaker of Estonian knows that they can often choose between alternative ways of generating a Pl Par wordform. This knowledge is expressed by the continuation lexicon PL_PAR_VARIANT with two entries: one is the default, and the other the less used form. Which is which, depends on the word and is marked in the stem lexicon: if the parallel form is actually less used that the default one, then the lexicon entry contains the tag {rare}. Note that the less used form has +Use/Rare on the lexical side, and a corresponding tag {rare} (which will not be visible in the final form) on the surface side.

The lexical and surface sides of the transducer path of a single wordform are assembled piece-wise when compiling the lexicon, starting from a stem lexicon and proceeding via a cascade of continuation classes. PL_PAR_VARIANT bifurcates the path, one of them containing {rare}. If this path contains {rare} somewhere upstream (originating from the stem lexicon), then this is the less preferred wordform and thus should contain +Use/Rare on its lexical side. In essence, one should check for the parity of {rare} tags.

# 8 Two-level rules for affixes

Figure 3 shows the input side of the two-level rules[6]. The strings are underspecified and redundant at the same time, so the rules must specify the output symbols, as well as prune some paths.

The input symbols with curly braces have the following possible output (surface) realisations: {s}:s {s}:0 {i}:i {i}:0 {d}:d {d}:0 {rare}:0, Pl Par stem vowels {pl.i}:i {pl.i}:0 {pl.u}:u {pl.u}:0, stem vowels {sg.e}:e {sg.e}:0 {sg.a}:a {sg.a}:0. PlSV per two-level rules is a set of plural stem vowels {pl.i} {pl.u}, and stemV stands for all stem vowels a e i u. Notice singular and plural stem vowels

---

[6]The formalism is described in `https://web.stanford.edu/~laurik/.book2software/twolc.pdf`

```
%{i%}:i <=>   :s _ :d ;   ! sid

%{d%}:d <=>   :s :i _ ;   ! sid

%{s%}:s  =>   _ :i :d ;   ! sid
```

Figure 4: Rules for alternating -*sid* with $\emptyset$

```
%{s%}:0 =>  P1SV:stemV   :* _ %{i%}:0 %{d%}:0;

Vx:0   <=>  %> P1SV:stemV :0* _ :0* %{s%}:0 ;
    where Vx in ( %{sg.a%} %{sg.e%} %{sg.u%} %{sg.i%} );

Vx:Vy  <=>  :Consonant :0* %> _ :0+ %{s%}:0 ;
    where Vx in ( %{pl.e%} %{pl.i%} %{pl.u%} )
          Vy in (      e        i        u    )
    matched ;
```

Figure 5: Rules per affixes -*sid* and $\emptyset$

have been defined in a way that makes it possible to allow them to surface only in certain contexts.

Conceptually, it is not only individual symbols that may be underspecified at this stage, but whole multi-character units such as -*sid* vs $\emptyset$. One may view these parallel affixes as different values of a single variable that depend on some context factors, and one can also treat an affix as a trigger to filter some context; in reality, it is enough to use only {s} (which happens to occur in all the relevant contexts) as a trigger. The affixes -*sid* and $\emptyset$ must be described symbol-by-symbol via the rules on Figure 4.

The first rule on Figure 5 states that the $\emptyset$-affix form may occur only if there is an appropriate tag in the stem lexicon entry.

The second rule says that a singular stem vowel cannot surface (i.e. it must be realized as 0), if there is already a plural stem vowel and a $\emptyset$-affix .

The third rule says that a plural stem vowel must surface, if the form has a $\emptyset$-affix.

# 9 Two-level rules for usage tags

Two-level formalism is (mis)used to prune spurious paths that emerge from continuation lexicons. The key is to remember that an allowed path may contain either zero or two {rare} tags: the first {rare} originates from the stem lexicon, the second from a continuation class lexicon. Remember also that the path contains the surface symbols that define the alternative forms and which can also be used as context conditions.

The first rule on Figure 6 (with multiple contexts) defines all the contexts where the {rare} tag may occur. First, it may occur immediately after the parallel form tag in the stem lexicon ({pl.i} or {pl.u}); this is where the lexicon writer has put it. Second, it may occur immediately after an inflectional ending, but only in a certain context (if it gets there via the continuation lexicon that pairs the lexical side +Use/Rare with the surface side {rare}). Note that although the parallel form tag indicates that the word has an alternative form, its existence in this pre-final surface form alone is not sufficient to determine the final form. The correct way of reading the rule contexts should be backwards from the end: a rare Pl Par form ends with $\emptyset$, if the path contains {rare} after the plural stem vowel {pl.i} or {pl.u}, which gets realised as the surface vowel (defined here via sets P1SV and stemV); a rare Pl Par ends with *-sid*, if there is no {rare} after the plural stem vowel (P1SV). Notice that in this context this vowel must surface as $\emptyset$, because it is the singular stem vowel that goes with *-sid*; this choice of the correct vowel is achieved by the two-level rules on Figure 5.

The first rule on Figure 6 connects {rare} with lexicon tags and spelled-out inflectional affixes. The affixes, in turn, should also be connected to the {rare} and lexicon tags (embodied by the set {P1SV}). This is what the second and third rules do. Notice that {s} is used as the crucial symbol to define the rest of the affix, thus these rules really relate affixes to context, not just the symbol itself.

The second rule states that the Pl Par surface form with *-sid* cannot be common (i.e. not rare, \{rare}) if the word already has a common short Pl Par form.

The third rule on Figure 6 states that a short Pl Par cannot be common if the lexicon tag says it is rare.

Figure 7 shows the result of pruning two-level strings of the Pl Par forms *taimi / taimesid* (plant), where *taimesid* is the less-used form. Pairing the non-failed surface side strings with the lexical side from Figure 3, and removing the morpheme border symbol >, will yield the desired result of Figure 1.

```
%{rare%}:0 => P1SV: _ ;
            P1SV:stemV %{rare%}: :* %{s%}:0 %{i%}:0 %{d%}:0 _ ;
            P1SV:0    \%{rare%}: :* %{s%}:s %{i%}:i %{d%}:d _ ;

%{s%}:s /<= P1SV:0    \%{rare%}: :* _ %{i%}:i %{d%}:d \%{rare%}: ;

%{s%}:0 /<= P1SV:stemV %{rare%}: :* _ %{i%}:0 %{d%}:0 \%{rare%}: ;
```

Figure 6: Rules to prune paths with the tag {rare}

```
lexical: t a i m > {pl.i} {sg.e} > {s} {i} {d} .#.
surface: t a i m >   i      0    > 0   0   0       OK
surface: t a i m >   0      e    > s   i   d       FAIL

lexical: t a i m > {pl.i} {sg.e} > {s} {i} {d} {rare}
surface: t a i m >   i      0    > 0   0   0   0 FAIL
surface: t a i m >   0      e    > s   i   d   0 OK
```

Figure 7: Surface strings after applying the two-level rules

# Conclusion

Parallel forms, i.e. two or more synonymous forms that realise the same set of morpho-syntactic categories in a paradigm cell of a word, deserve attention from a linguistic theory, as well as from a computational point of view. The paper presented examples of technical solutions for handling parallel forms in Estonian. The proposed method involves using two-level rules as a way of controlling the combinatorial explosion of continuation lexicons. The simplified, but still technically detailed example consisted of only one paradigm slot and a single usage tag. In a full description of a language, there are likely more paradigm slots with parallel forms and/or more usage tags. Currently, the full treatment of Estonian also includes Sg Ill and +Use/NotNorm per word forms that are "incorrect" according to normative dictionaries.

# Acknowledgments

This work has been supported by the Estonian Ministry of Education and Research grant IUT 20-56 "Eesti keele arvutimudelid (Computational Models for Estonian)", by the Norwegian-Estonian Research Cooperation Programme grant EMP160 "SAMEST — Sami-Estonian language technology cooperation — similar languages, same technologies", and by the European Union through the European Regional Development Fund (Centre of Excellence in Estonian Studies).

# References

Lene Antonsen, Trond Trosterud, and Francis M. Tyers. 2016. A north saami to south saami machine translation prototype. *North European Journal of Language Technology* 4:11–27. http://www.nejlt.ep.liu.se/2016/v4/a02/.

Kenneth R. Beesley and Lauri Karttunen. 2003. *Finite State Morphology*. CSLI Studies in Computational Linguistics. CSLI Publications.

Kimmo Koskenniemi. 1983. *Two-level Morphology: A General Computational Model for Word-Form Recognition and Production*. Ph.D. thesis, University of Helsinki. http://www.ling.helsinki.fi/ koskenni/doc/Two-LevelMorphology.pdf.

Karlheinz Mörth and Wolfgang U. Dressler. 2014. German plural doublets with and without meaning differentiation. In Franz Rainer, Francesco Gardani, Hans Christian Luschützky, and Wolfgang U. Dressler, editors, *Morphology and Meaning*, John Benjamins, Amsterdam, Current Issues in Linguistic Theory 327, pages 249–258.

Jaak Pruulmann-Vengerfeldt. 2010. *Praktiline lõplikel automaatidel põhinev eesti keele morfoloogiakirjeldus.* Master's thesis, Tartu Ülikool. https://cyber.ee/uploads/2013/04/Pruulmann-Vengerfeldt_msc.pdf.

Maire Raadik, editor. 2013. *Eesti õigekeelsussõnaraamat.* Eesti Keele Sihtasutus, Tallinn.

Anna M. Thornton. 2012. *Reduction and maintenance of overabundance. A case study on Italian verb paradigms*, Edinburgh University Press, volume 5, pages 183–207.

# Extracting inflectional class assignment in Pite Saami
## Nouns, verbs and those pesky adjectives


Joshua Wilbur
Albert-Ludwigs-Universität Freiburg
Department of Scandinavian Studies
Freiburg Research Group in Saami Studies
joshua.wilbur@skandinavistik.uni-freiburg.de


2017-12-24


### Abstract

The main goal of this paper is to describe to what extent the three main open word classes in Pite Saami (nouns, verbs and adjectives) can be automatically assigned to inflectional classes in language technology, specifically for a Finite State Transducer. For each of these word classes, the relevant structural features necessary for determining inflectional class membership are described. In this, a clear difference between the behavior of nouns and verbs, on the one hand, and that of adjectives, on the other hand, is ascertained. While morphophonology, as seen in the paradigmatic behavior of all three word classes, is complex and features a number of types of stem alternations, nouns and verbs are predictable, while adjectives are not. With this in mind, a basic algorithm for extracting inflectional class assignment for nouns and verbs is presented for use in a LEXC framework. In contrast to this, adjectives must be assigned to inflectional classes manually. The main TWOLC rules used to trigger morphophonological alternations are also outlined. The Pite Saami lexicographic database that forms the backbone for the LEXC stem files is managed using FileMaker Pro database software, and the workflow used to extract and update LEXC files from that database is described, focussing on the differences between nouns and verbs, and adjectives. In this, light is shed on how, on the one hand, nominal and verbal inflectional patters are highly complex yet reliably systematic, while adjective morphophonology is complex and unpredictable.



### Kokkuvõte

Selle artikli peamine eesmärk on kirjeldada, mil määral saab kolme põhilist avatud sõnaklassi (substantiive, verbe ja adjektiive) pite saami keeles automaatselt flekteerida kasutades keeletehnoloogia FST-d. Artiklis kirjeldatakse iga sõnaliigi muuttüübi määramiseks vajalikke strukturaalseid omadusi ning näidatakse, et adjektiivid on substantiividest ja verbidest selgelt erinevad. Samal ajal kui kõigi kolme sõnaklassi paradigmaatilist käitumist iseloomustab kompleksne paljusid tüvevahelduse tüüpe hõlmav morfofonoloogia, saab substantiivide ja verbide muutumist ennustada, kuid adjektiivide oma mitte. Seega kirjeldatakse artiklis







*Proceedings of the 4th International Workshop for Computational Linguistics for Uralic Languages (IWCLUL 2018)*, pages 156–170,
Helsinki, Finland, January 8–9, 2018. ©2018 Association for Computational Linguistics

substantiivide ja verbide muuttüübi määramiseks kasutatavat algoritmi, mille väl-
jund on LEXC formaadis. Adjektiivide fleksiooniklass tuleb aga määrata käsitsi.
Tuuakse välja ka peamised TWOLC reeglid, mida kasutatakse morfofonoloogilise
vahelduse tekitamiseks. LEXC tüvefailide põhialuseks on pite saami keele leksi-
kograafiline andmebaas, mida hallatakse FileMaker tarkvaraga; artiklis kirjeldatakse sellest andmebaasist LEXC failide väljavõtmise ja nende uuendamise töö-
voogu, keskendudes erinevustele nimisõnade ja verbide, ning adjektiivide vahel.
Näidatakse, et substantiivide ja verbide fleksioonimustrid on küll komplekssed,
kuid väga süstemaatilised, samas kui adjektiivide morfofonoloogia on keeruline
ning raskesti ennustatav.

# 1 Introduction

Pite Saami is a critically endangered Saami language spoken in Swedish Lapland,
mainly in and around the municipality of Arjeplog.[1] No pedagogical materials have
been published for Pite Saami, although a few speakers have put together some basic
teaching resources for their own use. No digital resources exist from before the turn of
the millennium, and, until recently, no standard orthography existed either. However,
starting in 2008, a local lexicographic project and language documentation project created a foundation for digital language technology resources for Pite Saami, as outlined
below. Specifically, a group of Pite Saami language activists carried out a wordlist
project titled *Insamling av pitesamiska ord* 'Collection of Pite Saami words' (Bengtsson
et al. 2008-2012), which ultimately resulted in the publication of the first Pite Saami
dictionary (Bengtsson et al. 2016) and orthographic standard (Wilbur, 2016b), together
in a single volume (Wilbur, 2016a). As a further result of this collaboration, additional
digital linguistic resources are now available for Pite Saami. A searchable version of
the ever-growing wordlist is available on-line at http://saami.uni-freiburg.de/psdp/pite-
lex/. Language technology tools are under development for Pite Saami in cooperation
with Giellatekno at the University of Tromsø; specifically, these consist of a Finite
State Transducer (FST) and a Constraint Grammar.

In mid-2016, the project *Syntactic patterns in Pite Saami: A corpus-based explo-
ration of 130 years of variation and change*[2] began compiling a thorough corpus of
both spoken and written Pite Saami texts, the oldest of which were published in the
late 19th century in Halász (1893). Using the combination of the electronic lexicography resources and language technology tools mentioned above, corpus creation for
this syntax project is completed as automatically as possible. This idea is presented
in detail in Gerstenberger et al. (2017), but a brief overview is provided here. The
corpus consists of Pite Saami texts (in both spoken and written mode) transcribed in
current orthographic standard and collected in the ELAN format[3] and following the
common structure stipulated by projects carried out by the Freiburg Research Group
in Saami Studies.[4] A python script runs each token through the FST processor, and
then automatically creates annotations for lemma, morphological categories and part
of speech based on this. Simultaneously, an implementation of constraint grammar is
used in order to reduce the number of and, ideally, completely rule out, ambiguities

---

[1] Cf. Valijärvi and Wilbur (2011) and Wilbur (2014, 1-7) for more on the sociolinguistic situation of Pite
Saami.

[2] Cf. saami.uni-freiburg.de/psdp/syntax/.

[3] ELAN is free software used to annotate multimedia recordings; cf. https://tla.mpi.nl/tools/tla-
tools/elan/.

[4] This common ELAN structure can be found at https://github.com/langdoc/FRechdoc/wiki/ELAN-tiers.

that occur during FST processing; however, as this project is still at an early stage in describing syntactic structures in Pite Saami, the constraint grammar implementation for Pite Saami is also only in an initial stage.

The LEXC files that provide the lexical input to FST are a sort of lexicon themselves, since they present a collection of stems assigned to inflectional classes (based on their morphophonological behavior), as well as a TWOLC file providing orthographic (phonological) rules for generating and analyzing wordforms. However, the information contained in the LEXC files for stems is mainly limited to the base form, the underlying representation and an inflectional class assignment; on the other hand, the current Pite Saami lexical database contains significantly more information for each entry, including e.g. translations, gradation patterns and stem extension patterns, just to name a few categories. Because this extensive database exists and is continually being corrected and supplemented, it is clearly preferable to extract the relevant LEXC stem files from it, rather than adding these by hand on an individual basis. The Pite Saami lexical database is managed using the database software File-Maker Pro.[5] While FileMaker Pro is hardly ideal from the point of view of likely all computational linguists,[6] FileMaker Pro databases can be highly complex, and this is currently the structure the Pite Saami data is in. Although a better, open-source solution is desired in the medium-term, for the time being, this is the tool used in the project.

## 2 Pite Saami morphophonology and FST

While Pite Saami language structures may be represented in the corpus using various transcription methods, every text in the corpus is at least transcribed using the current standard orthography (as presented in Wilbur (2016b)).[7] Entries in the lexicographic database also use this standard. For this reason, this is also the transcription standard which provides the character strings used for processing with FST.

As is true for all the Saami languages, paradigmatic stem alternations can be used to define inflectional classes, and these are prevalent throughout the language's inflected words.[8] In addition to outlining the LEXC rules for the main open word classes of nouns, verbs and adjectives, the main TWOLC rules intended for dealing with the Pite Saami stem alternations in both consonants and vowels (including effects of vowel harmony) will be presented briefly.

Aside from being stored and run locally, the resources presented in the following sections are hosted by Giellatekno[9] at the University of Tromsø. The source documents (LEXC and TWOLC, among others) can be accessed at https://gtsvn.uit.no/langtech/trunk/langs/sje/. Language technology tools for analyzing and generating Pite Saami wordforms can be found online at http://giellatekno.uit.no/cgi/index.sje.eng.html.

---

<sup></sup>[5] http://www.filemaker.com.

[6] Cf. Wilbur (2017) for both a description and a critique of FileMaker Pro as a lexical database.

[7] Note that there is no officially recognized orthography for Pite Saami. By the fall of 2017, both the Norwegian and Swedish Saami parliaments indicated they intend to officially recognize a Pite Saami orthography in the near future. It remains to be seen to what extent any official Pite Saami orthography will adhere to the orthography presented in Wilbur (2016b) (and the accompanying website at saami.uni-freiburg.de/psdp/stavningsregler/).

[8] An initial approach like this is presented for nouns, verbs and adjectives in the relevant chapters in Wilbur (2014), but the present analysis goes beyond this, and is informed by continuing research that has taken place since that publication.

[9] http://giellatekno.uit.no.

| Noun class | | | | Example | | |
|---|---|---|---|---|---|---|
| | | Stem-final-C | | | | |
| Name | Syll. | NOM.SG | all others | Lemma | NOM.PL | Gloss |
| N_EVEN | 2 | | | juällge | juolge | 'leg/foot' |
| N_CONTR | 2 | ✓ | | båtsoj | buhtsu | 'reindeer' |
| N_ODD | 2 | ✓ | ✓ | árran | árrana | 'fireplace' |
| N_ODD_OPEN | 2 | | ✓ | biena | biednaga | 'dog' |
| N_EVEN4 | 3 | ✓ | ✓ | mánnodak | mánnodaga | 'Monday' |

Table 1: The main criteria for determining FST-Inflectional classes for Pite Saami nouns, including representative examples

| Case | Number | |
|---|---|---|
| | SINGULAR | PLURAL |
| NOM | juällge | juolge |
| GEN | juolge | julgij |
| ACC | juolgev | julgijd |
| ILL | juallgáj | julgijd |
| INESS | juolgen | julgijn |
| ELAT | juolgest | julgijst |
| COM | julgijn | julgij |
| ABESS | juolgedak | juolgedaga |
| ESS | juällgen | |

Table 2: An example noun paradigm, showing *juällge* 'leg/foot'.

## 2.1 LEXC inflectional classes for nouns

Noun lemmata are named using the nominative singular wordform, and thus entered in the database using this form. Example nouns and the information required to calculate the inflectional class for each class are presented in table 1, and an entire nominal inflectional paradigm for *juällge* 'leg/foot' is provided in table 2. The naming system for inflectional classes for nouns is based roughly on Saami linguistic tradition, and uses the terms *even* and *odd* (referring to the syllable count of the nominative plural form[10]) and *contr* (for 'contracted' stems). Subdividing nouns into inflectional classes is done based on the syllable count of the base form (under 'Syll.' in table 2), and the behavior of a stem final consonant, if there is one at all (under 'stem-final-C'). For lemmata with a stem final consonant, noun classes are further determined by whether the stem final consonant occurs in the nominal singular form and/or in the other paradigm slots. These features are sufficient to unambiguously assign any given noun lemma to the correct general inflectional class, and this is done using pattern recognition in the FileMaker Pro database (see § 3). In fact, further subclasses arising due to morphophonemic alternations (such as consonant gradation and umlaut) and variation within Pite Saami also exist, but this somewhat simplified version fully illustrates the main functionality of the algorithm.

Some recent loan words with three or more syllables and with principle stress on the penultimate syllable (such as *antänna* 'antenna' or *universitähtta* 'university') initially may appear to deviate from this system. However, by simply treating the

---

[10]In Pite Saami, the nominative plural form and the genitive singular forms are syncretic.

| Verb class | | | Example | | |
|---|---|---|---|---|---|
| Name | Syll. | -j-ext | Lemma | 3SG.PRS | Gloss |
| V_EVEN | 2 | | båhtet | båhtá | 'come' |
| V_CONTR | 2 | ✓ | gullit | gullija | 'fish' |
| V_ODD | 3 | | ságastit | ságasta | 'speak' |

Table 3: The main criteria for determining FST-Inflectional classes for Pite Saami verbs, including representative examples

| Tense/ Mood | Person | Number | | |
|---|---|---|---|---|
| | | SINGULAR | DUAL | PLURAL |
| IND-PRS | 1st | buoldáv | bulldin | buälldep |
| | 2nd | buoldá | buälldebehtin | buälldebehtit |
| | 3rd | bualldá | buälldeba | bulldi |
| IND-PST | 1st | bulldiv | buldijme | buldijme |
| | 2nd | bulldi | buldijden | buldijde |
| | 3rd | buldij | buldijga | bulldin |
| IMP | 2nd | buolde | buällden | bulldit |

Table 4: An example verb paradigm, showing *buälldet* 'ignite'.

penultimate and final syllables as the stem, these behave in the same fully predictable manner as native lemmata.

## 2.2  LEXC inflectional classes for verbs

Verb lemmata are named using the infinitive wordform, and thus entered in the database using this form. Example verbs and the information required to calculate the inflectional class for each class are presented in table 3, and an entire verbal inflectional paradigm for *buälldet* 'ignite' is provided in table 4. As with the noun classes, the naming system for inflectional classes for verbs is based roughly on Saami linguistic tradition, and uses the terms *even* and *odd* (referring to the syllable count of the infinitive form) and *contr* (for 'contracted' stems). Subdividing verbs into inflectional classes is done based on the syllable count of the infinitive form (under 'Syll.' in table 3), and whether a stem extension is present in finite forms.[11] These features are sufficient to unambiguously assign any given verb lemma to the correct general inflectional class, and this is done using pattern recognition in the FileMaker Pro database (see § 3).

Some recent loan words with three or more syllables and with principle stress on the penultimate syllable (such as *adopterit* 'adopt') initially may appear to deviate from this system. However, by simply treating the penultimate and final syllables as the stem, these behave in the same fully predictable manner as native lemmata. With this in mind, the only actual exceptions to the above classes are the copula verb (*årrot* in the infinitive, but with most inflectional forms based on an *l-* stem) and the negation verb (which lacks non-finite forms). As a result, the latter two verb lemmata are each in an inflectional class of their own.

---

[11]Lemmata in the V_EVEN class are further subdivided based on the vowel of the second syllable, but these supplementary details are not shown here for reasons of simplicity.

| Criterion | Attributive | Predicative | |
|---|---|---|---|
| | | SINGULAR | PLURAL |
| stem gradation | str/wk/ø | str/wk/ø | str/wk/ø |
| suffix | -s/ø | -s/ø | -s/ø |
| extension | -X/ø | -X/ø | -X/ø |

Table 5: Morphophonological criteria used to determine assignment to adjective inflectional classes.

| Adjective class Name | Attrributive | Predicative | | Gloss |
|---|---|---|---|---|
| | | SINGULAR | PLURAL | |
| A_BIVVAL | -is | ø | -a | |
| | bivvalis | bivval | bivvala | 'warm' |
| A_AMAS | wk | wk | str/-a | |
| | amas | amas | abmasa | 'foreign' |
| A_AAJDNA | ø | ø | ø | |
| | ájdna | ájdna | ájdna | 'only' |
| A_UNNE | -a | -e | -e | |
| | unna | unne | unne | 'little' |
| A_FIEROK | ø | ø | -a | |
| | fierok | fierok | fieroga | 'finished' |
| A_GALMAS | str | wk/-s | str/-sa | |
| | galbma | galmas | galbmasa | 'cold' |

Table 6: Selection of six inflectional classes for adjectives and the morphophonological features that distinguish them, including the representative examples.

## 2.3   LEXC inflectional classes for adjectives

The descriptions for noun and verb inflectional classes in the previous two sections show that assignment to inflectional classes in those cases are quite straightforward. While the morphophonology is rather complex, especially for nouns, the system is very consistent, and thus predictable. Indeed, the total number of classes is reasonable and clearly limited.

On the other hand, the morphophonological behavior of Pite Saami adjectives is quite the opposite, despite the fact that the basic adjective inflectional paradigm implemented in the current Pite Saami FST only consists of three slots: attributive, predicative singular and predicative plural (as opposed to 17 slots for nouns and at least 21 for verbs).[12] As is the case with assigning inflectional classes to nouns and verbs, the morphophonemic behavior (as reflected in the orthographic representation) of a given adjective lemma throughout a paradigm is extracted; this includes stem alternations in the initial vowel slot and the consonant center (stem gradation), stem extensions, as well as the form of any discernible suffixes present. The possible values of the relevant morphophonological criteria are presented in table 5.

Table 6 provides a few examples of differing adjective paradigms in order to provide an impression for the variation in patterning. Wilbur (2014) sets forth nine adjec-

---

[12]Whether comparative and superlative forms are types of morphological derivation or inflection, and whether case-marked adjective forms which occur in elliptical constructions should be included in the core adjectival paradigm, are theoretical discussions well beyond the scope of the current paper.

tive inflectional classes,[13] but the current analyses is well beyond that, and currently has 28 inflectional classes, with new classes added on a fairly regular basis as new adjectives are added to the database.[14]

To provide still another impression of how inconsistent adjectives are, the following figures are provided anecdotally. At the time of writing, 99 adjective paradigms have been deduced as part of ongoing analyses of the Pite Saami lexical database,[15] and, based on this set, 28 different inflectional classes have been found.[16] This number is likely to increase since more adjective entries in the database have yet to be scrutinized, but even if it does not, the ratio of adjective inflectional classes to lemmata is significantly higher than for nouns or verbs.

While historically, a -s-suffix may be posited as a marker for attributive forms (Rießler, 2016, 215-228), this is clearly not a productive rule in Pite Saami.[17] Not only are there plenty of instances for attributive forms without such a suffix, but there are examples for predicative forms with such a suffix. Any attempts to link stem mutation patterns such as umlaut or consonant gradation to marking attributive forms is also fruitless, since there are numerous counter examples.

In addition, variation in adjective wordforms is also more common and seemingly random compared to noun and verb lemmata, and this makes it even more difficult to assign adjectives to a specific inflectional class, as they often can belong to more than one class. For instance, *guhkke* 'long' is the predicative form, while two different attributive forms are found, in seemingly free variation: *guhka* and *guhkes*. Currently, not enough is known about which adjectives are subject to such variation, so it is too early to decide whether such lemmata should be considered belonging to a single inflectional class with variation in its forms, or to two different lemmata, each in its own inflectional class. For the time being, the latter analysis is preferred.

Ultimately, due to the lack of correlation between the 'basic' form of any given adjective lemma (whether this is considered the predicative singular form, as is typically the case in Saami lexicography, or the attributive form) and the inflectional class it belongs to, each adjective lemma has to be assigned to an inflectional class manually. Or, at a very minimum, the attributive form and the predicative form must be paired manually, and the inflectional class extracted from these forms. This is a significant

---

[13]Wilbur (2014) uses the phrase "correspondence patterns" (131) in a seeming attempt to avoid the term *inflectional class* for adjectives altogether. Indeed, he claims that "there is no clear or consistent morphological relationship synchronically between attributive adjectives and the corresponding predicative adjectives" (134).

[14]Note that this seeming lack of any consistency and higher frequency in variation for adjectives compared to other open word classes is nothing specific to Pite Saami, but true for other Saami languages as well; cf. e.g., the 25 inflectional classes posited for North Saami attributive adjective forms alone in Sammallahti (1998, 71-73), the 12 inflectional classes posited for North Saami attributive adjective forms in Svonni (2009, 75-76) (who also points out that "[D]en attributiva formen ... bildas (delvis) oregelmässigt" (74)), or the claim by Rießler (2016, 201) that "the system of attributive and predicative marking is highly irregular in the Saamic languages".

[15]This dataset formed the basis for the Pite Saami dictionary published as Bengtsson et al. (2016), but is continually being revised, improved and expanded. It can be accessed at http://saami.uni-freiburg.de/psdp/pite-lex/.

[16]Just as a comparison, the database contains 2437 noun lemmata in five inflectional classes, and 1642 verb lemmata in three inflectional classes.

[17]It is common in Saami linguistics to posit the predicative singular form as the base form; however, I choose not to follow this tradition because of a complete lack of any consistent evidence in the synchronic system to indicate that the attributive form can be predicted based on the predicative form. Indeed, both predicative and attributive forms should be included as lexical entries in any lexicographic data collection, as Svonni (2009, 74) points out for North Saami: "Den attributiva formen böjs alltså inte och bildas (delvis) oregelmässigt och brukar därför anges i ordböcker".

| Base V | | Resulting V |
|---|---|---|
| á | → | ä |
| a | → | i |
| ie, ä | → | e |
| å, ua/uä, uo | → | u |

Figure 1: Sets of vowel alternations triggered by vowel harmony, with the base vowel on the left, and the resulting raised vowel on the right.

difference to the noun and verb lemmata described above, which can be reliably assigned to the correct inflectional class based on the basic form and a few supplemental pieces of information, as indicated in table 1 and table 3 above. Currently, FST inflectional categories for Pite Saami adjectives are named after the predicative singular form of one of the adjectives in each class, unlike the more generic names used for noun and verb classes.

## 2.4 Morphophonological processes in TWOLC

As evidenced by the inflectional classes for nouns, verbs and adjectives described above, Pite Saami features complex morphophonology (as is typical for all Saami languages). In addition to marking certain morphological categories using suffixes, almost every wordform also features non-concatenative morphology in the form of stem alternations, both in the word-initial vowel slot and in the "consonant center" (the consonant slot between the first and second vowels of a Pite Saami foot[18]). These two main morphophonological processes occur together, but operate on the initial vowel and the consonant center independently, and are referred to here as *umlaut* and *consonant gradation*; these are described here briefly. Umlaut is seen in the paradigmatic alternation of two vowel sets. In the one set, *ua* (and its allophone *uä*) alternate with *uo*, and in the other, *ä* alternates with *ie*, with the former set of each pair limited to wordforms in grade III. Consonant gradation is a similar alternation in principle, but concerns paradigmatic alternations in the segments in the consonant center. Here, a number of patterns are evident, all of which alternate at least in quantity, and sometimes in quality as well. For instance, a geminate can alternate with a singleton (*rr~r*), a preaspirated segment can alternate with its unaspirated equivalent (*hp~b*), or a tripartite consonant cluster can alternate with a bipartite cluster, thereby losing its middle member (*jbm~jm*).[19] For more details on Pite Saami morphophonology, see Wilbur (2014, 74-79).[20]

In addition, there is one phonological feature significant enough to mention here, partly because it is reflected in orthographic forms: regressive phonological assimilation. It is referred to as *vowel harmony*, and only applies within a prosodic foot. In this, a closed back vowel (*i* or *u*) in the second vowel slot triggers raising of the initial vowel. The choice of the resulting vowel depends on the base vowel affected by the harmony; the possibilities are presented in figure 1.

To analyze and generate these morphophonological alternations and the phonological rule as represented by orthographic character strings in FST, a **Two-Level**

---

[18]Cf. Wilbur (2014, 25-30) for a description of word-level prosodic structures in Pite Saami.

[19]In the actual phonetic realization of this third type, the second member is always pronounced as an unreleased plosive homorganic with the third consonant in the cluster, e.g. [jp͡m] for <jbm>.

[20]Note however that the description of vowel harmony on pages 79–81 in Wilbur (2014) is correct in its essence, but does not accurately reflect the status of this phenomenon as being truly phonological.

| Tag | Function |
|---|---|
| ^WG | require weak grade |
| ^G3 | require grade III |
| ^UAUML | trigger *ua* diphthong |
| ^IJ | V2-*e* becomes *i* |
| ^V2O2U | V2-*o* becomes *u* |
| ^V2E2AA | V2-*e* becomes *á* |
| ^CDEL | delete stem final consonant |

Table 7: Pite Saami TWOLC morphophonological triggers and their functions.

Compiler (TWOLC) is used (Beesley and Karttunen, 2003). Triggers are defined which cause these alternations, and are assigned to morphological slots in the definition files of the various inflectional classes (the LEXC affix files). For instance, *weak grade* is represented in the input by the tag ^WG, and since specific choices for an umlaut vowel or a consonant set align with weak grade, this tag is introduced in the relevant slots in the inflectional class definitions. For example, for the nominal inflectional class N_EVEN, this means that NOM.PL, GEN, ACC, ILL.PL, INESS, ELAT, COM and ABESS slots include the tag ^WG. A list of the triggers and their functions is found in table 7. A more thorough example is provided below in § 2.5.

In summary, the Pite Saami TWOLC file contains 13 rules for implementing the various consonant gradation patters, 5 rules for umlaut, and one for vowel harmony. In addition, there are supplementary rules for deleting a final consonant, selecting the voiceless variant of a final plosive, and triggering slot-specific vowel alternations in the second vowel slot.

## 2.5  Implementation example

In this section, a selection of TWOLC and LEXC code examples are provided to illustrate how morphophonology is implemented in the Pite Saami FST. Specifically, the generation of an accusative plural form jävrijd for the noun lemma *jávvre* 'lake' is presented.

To begin with, the code presented in figure 2 is the entry in the LEXC noun stem file. This provides the upper and lower forms for the lemma,[21] the assignment to the nominal inflectional class N_EVEN, and an English translation (just as a reference).

```
jávvre:jávvre N_EVEN "lake" ;
```

Figure 2: Code snippet for an example noun stem entry in the LEXC lexicon

From here, the LEXC nominal affix file adds inflectional tags and suffixes to the upper and lower forms, respectively, as shown in the code presented in figure 3. Here, the continuation classes mark the form to be generated as being a noun (+N) in plural accusative (+Pl+Acc) with a suffix −jd (added in two steps). Furthermore, it is morphophonologically characterized by weak grade using the tag ^WG, and as subject to a raising of the second vowel slot's vowel using the tag ^IJ.

---

[21]In this example, the entry is redundant because both the upper and lower sides are identical. However, since many Pite Saami lemmata do not have identical upper and lower representations (cf. e.g. the examples in 1, 2 and 3 below), all entries contain both sides explicitly, even when redundant.

```
LEXICON N_EVEN
+N:^WG N_EVEN_WK ;

LEXICON N_EVEN_WK
:^IJ%>j N_EVEN_J ;

LEXICON N_EVEN_J
+Pl+Acc:d    ENDLEX ;
```

Figure 3: Code snippet for continuation classes adding accusative plural morphology to N_EVEN nouns in the LEXC lexicon

For this example, three morphophonological rules stored in the TWOLC file are relevant; these are presented here. The rule named "Consonant Gradation for xxy:xy" in figure 4 deals with the alternation in the stem's consonant center. Here, when

```
"Consonant Gradation for xxy:xy"
Cx:0 <=> Vow:+ Cx _ Cy Vow:+ Cns:* %^WG: ;
    where Cx in ( ŋ ŋ ŋ v v v v v v v )
          Cy in ( g k n d j k l r g s )
          matched ;
```

Figure 4: Code snippet for a consonant gradation rule for the pattern xxy:xy

matched pairs of characters for which the first character is doubled,[22] the second instance of the doubled character is deleted when preceded by a vowel as well as followed by a vowel, an optional consonant, and, crucially, a ^WG tag. In the example, the antepenultimate set is present: v and r in the lemma jávvre, so the second r is deleted, resulting in a consonant center rv.

The treatment of vowel characters requires two steps in this example. Initially, the vowel in the second vowel slot is altered from e to i[23] by the rule named "V2 E to I before j-suffixes" and presented in figure 5. This occurs when preceded by at least

```
"V2 E to I before j-suffixes"
e:i <=> Vow:+ Cns:+ _ %^IJ:0 ;
```

Figure 5: Code snippet for the raising of the second vowel triggered by certain suffixes featuring a -j-segment

one consonant and at least one vowel character, and, crucially, when followed by a ^IJ tag. As a result, the e in the example jávvre becomes i.

The resulting i in the second vowel slot then provides the input for the general vowel harmony rule, which is called "Default VH" and is presented in figure 6. For this rule to take effect, a vowel character from a subset represented by the tag VHtrig and defined in the TWOLC file to consist of [e:i | i | o:u | u ] in a word's second vowel slot must be present.[24] This then triggers an alternation in the initial vowel

---

[22]Note that the set of character pairs in this rule is in fact much longer, but for reasons of space, it has been shortened significantly in figure 4.

[23]Phonologically speaking, the vowel is raised.

[24]In the rule in figure 6, the tags # and .#. require a word or compound boundary at the left edge, thus restricting the affected slot to the initial vowel position.

```
"Default VH"
Vx:Vy <=> [#|.#.] Cns:* _ Cns:+ VHtrig Cns:* Vow:* %>:0 ;
    where Vx in ( á a ä å )
          Vy in ( ä i e u )
          matched ;
```

Figure 6: Code snippet for the vowel harmony rule (regressive vowel height assimilation in the initial vowel slot with i/u in the second vowel slot)

slot as set forth in the set of matched characters in this rule. In this example, á then becomes ä.

In summary, the LEXC stem and affix files together with the TWOLC rules can be implemented in FST to correctly generate and anaylze the form jävrijd as being a noun in accusative plural for the input lemma string jávvre. Partly with the help of LEXC tags, the consonant rule outputs rv from an initial rrv, and the two vowel rules alter the vowels in the first and second vowel slot from initially á and e to ä and i, respectively, in the inflected form jävrijd.

## 3    Determining inflectional classes with FileMaker Pro

The Pite Saami lexical database, which is the source of the LEXC files, is currently a FileMaker Pro database. While this GUI-based software is far from the ideal choice for programmers or coders, in it essence, it successfully allows one to keep complex relational data sets.[25] The program has its own powerful but cumbersome GUI-based scripting methodology, and this is used to extrapolate inflectional class assignments for nouns, verbs and adjectives. The ability to export the database into XML format makes it possible to then use XSLT to transform the data into the desired plain-text output structure, which, in this case, is a LEXC stem file.[26]

### 3.1    Automatic inflectional classes for nouns and verbs

While stem alternations in word forms within inflectional classes for nouns and verbs are complex, they are also surprisingly systematic, as indicated in § 2.1 and § 2.2 above. In almost every case, membership in a specific inflectional class can be derived exclusively from the shape of the citation form. As a result, it is possible to set up algorithms which automatically assign lemmata to the correct inflectional class.

Here, the basic process is explained. While the lexical database contains more than just citation forms,[27] only entries corresponding to the citation form of a lemma (in other words, nominative singular for nouns and infinitive for verbs) are subject to evaluation to begin with. In an initial script, nouns and verbs are identified based on the value in the part-of-speech field. The syllable count of each entry is determined automatically with a script that counts vowel grapheme and grapheme combinations.

---

[25]Cf. Wilbur (2017, 305-307) for a discussion of advantages and, crucially, disadvantages to using FileMaker Pro as a lexical database, or indeed for any data set.

[26]Note that, while an XLT stylesheet can be applied automatically during export from FileMaker Pro, it is only possible using the outdated version 1.0 of XSLT.

[27]Because the source of the majority of the entries in the database is a group of native speakers without any training in linguistics or lexicography, a not insignificant number of entries consist of inflected forms or sometimes entire phrases.

Then, lemmata are further divided into groups based on the syllable count (groups of bisyllabic and trisyllabic lemmata).

Then, for nouns, the existence of a stem-final consonant is determined, and whether this is present in the nominative singular form (the entry itself) and/or in oblique case-number paradigm slots. This is sufficient to allot the main nominal inflectional classes (as portrayed in table 1), but sub-classes for inflectional patterns reflecting more specific morphophonological alternations (such as stem final -e- alternating with stem final -á-) are assigned based on unicode string values of stem-final segments.

For verbs the process is even more straightforward. Trisyllabic verbs are assigned to class V_ODD, bisyllabic verbs with a stem extension are in class V_CONTR and all others are in V_EVEN, as illustrated in table 3. Membership in the further sub-classes can be determined unambiguously based on the vowel immediately preceding the -t infinitive suffix.

Compounds are marked by hand in the database, and the resulting inflectional classes are determined based only on the final compound element. A compound boundary is inserted which prevents phonological rules (TWOLC) from applying before it.

With the above process in mind, a noun or verb lexical entry can clearly be assigned to the correct inflectional class. Then, a few other smaller FileMaker Pro scrips extract the appropriate form for the LEXC database files in preparation for exporting. Thus a noun entry such as *biena* 'dog', which has a bisyllabic stem and lacks a stem-final consonant, is correctly identified as belonging to N_ODD. The right and left sides of the LEXC entry are thus calculated in FileMaker Pro as biena and biednag. Similarly, the verb *gullit* 'fish', which has a bisyllabic stem in the infinitive but a -j-extention for the stem in a number of paradigm slots, is assigned to the V_CONTR class. These data and the English translation are then exported from FileMaker Pro into XML. In the export process, an XSLT style sheet is applied so that the lines in (1) and (2) are included in the appropriate LEXC stem files:

```
(1)   biena:biednag N_ODD "dog" ;
```

```
(2)   gullit:gul'li V_CONTR "fish" ;
```

## 3.2  Semi-automatic inflectional classes for adjectives

As described in detail in § 2.3, the morphophonology of Pite Saami adjectives is, on a lexeme-by-lexeme basis, equally complex with that of nouns and verbs, but the assignment of adjectives to inflectional classes is significantly less transparent. This is due not only to common variation among speakers, but also to the vast number of classes, despite the fact that adjective paradigms only have three slots in their most basic form. Partly because of this variation and mainly due the lack of any consistent correspondence of morphophonological behavior across paradigms, it is not possible to automatically assign inflectional classes to adjective lemmata based on the form of the lexeme itself.[28]

Note that it is possible to separate adjectives into a (seemingly) limited set of inflectional classes (currently 28), but, crucially, membership in a specific class cannot

---

[28]As mentioned above, the question as to whether the attributive form or the predicative form should be considered representative for a given adjective lemma is in fact impossible to answer in a satisfactory way (at least synchronically) due to the lack of any consistent correspondence between the two forms; this will therefore not be further addressed here.

be derived from the representative lemma form, syllable count and another data category. While the citation form of nouns and verbs is sufficient for inflectional class assignment in those cases, both the predicative singular and the attributive forms of a given adjective have their own entry in the Pite Saami lexical database (although in cases where these forms are the same, there is only one entry, and this is marked as being valid for both paradigmatic slots). Once the assignment to a specific class is set, then other wordforms (such as the predicative plural) can be derived (in a computational sense, not morphologically) using the LEXC adjective affix file. For purely practical purposes, the predicative singular form is used as the base for calculating the entry in the LEXC adjective stem file.

To deal with the lack of derivable assignability, the current solution in the FileMaker Pro lexical database consists of two steps. First, inflectional classes are defined in a related database table. Second, attributive and predicative singular forms are assigned to the correct inflectional class on an individual basis. Once inflectional classes are assigned, then the LEXC stem file can be updated automatically by exporting to XML and applying an XSLT style sheet, just as for noun and verb lemmata. Due to the unpredictable nature of adjectives, processing them requires more manual work. But ultimately, an adjective entry such as *årås* 'new', which has an attributive form *årrå* (strong grade, without a stem-final consonant), a predicative singular form *årås* (weak grade, with a stem-final consonant) and a predicative plural form *årråsa* (strong grade, with a stem-final consonant and plural-marking -*a* suffix), is classified as belonging to A_GALMAS, even though this is done manually. The right and left sides of the LEXC entry are thus calculated in FileMaker Pro as galmas and galbma, and the result is a line in the LEXC adjective stem file, as shown in (3).

(3)    `galmas:galbma A_GALMAS "cold" ;`

While the LEXC file is created automatically, the actual assignment to the correct inflectional class is a manual process, and thus the process is semi-automatic.


## 4   Summary and implications

In this paper, I have outlined how inflectional classes can be determined for the main open word classes in Pite Saami (nouns, verbs and adjectives), and how class assignment can be computed using a FileMaker Pro lexical database. Noun and verb morphophonology is quite complex, but is easily predictable based on the representative lemma form, syllable count and stem-final consonant behavior. Adjectives, on the other hand, are equally complex, but not reliably assignable to a specific adjective inflectional class, and thus require manual assignment. Furthermore, I have covered the basic phonological rules as implemented in TWOLC for Pite Saami. Regardless of how inflectional class assignment occurs, LEXC files can be extracted on an ongoing basis from the lexical database in expanding and supplementing the potency of the Pite Saami FST generator and analyzer.

While the FST backbone is certainly nothing new, its successful implementation for Pite Saami is an important step towards not only recognition of Pite Saami as an official Saami language in Norway and Sweden, but also for other revitalization efforts that are based on language technology (such as spell checkers and pedagogical tools). The language technology infrastructure is not entirely complete at this stage; for instance, closed word class LEXC files need updating and expanding, and a constraint grammar implementation for reliably avoiding unnecessary wordform ambiguities in Pite Saami texts is only in its embryonic stages. Nonetheless, the current set of tools is already being used successfully to automatically annotate tokens in the Pite Saami corpus of both spoken and written texts by adding lemma, part of speech, morphophonological categories and English glosses. While using FileMaker Pro is hardly an ideal solution, it is clearly an effective one in this particular case. Continued improvement and refinement of the Pite Saami language technology infrastructure should prove to be useful for both the language community and linguistics research in the future.

## Abbreviations

| | |
|---|---|
| ABESS | abessive case |
| ACC | accusative case |
| COM | comitative case |
| ELAT | elative case |
| ESS | essive case |
| FST | Finite State Transducer |
| GEN | genitive case |
| ILL | illative case |
| IMP | imperative mood |
| IND | indicative mood |
| INESS | inessive case |
| -j-ext | *-j-* stem extension |
| NOM | nominative case |
| ø | no overt marker (zero morpheme) |
| PL | plural |
| PRS | present tense |
| PRT | past tense (preteritum) |
| SG | singular |
| str | strong grade |
| syll. | syllable count |
| V | vowel segment |
| wk | weak grade |

## References


Kenneth R. Beesley and Lauri Karttunen. 2003. Two-level rule compiler http://web.stanford.edu/ laurik/.book2software/twolc.pdf.

Nils-Henrik Bengtsson, Marianne Eriksson, Inger Fjällås, Eva-Karin Rosenberg, Gry Helen Sivertsen, Valborg Sjaggo, Dagny Skaile, and Peter Steggo. 2008-2012. Insamling av pitesamiska ord. (Pite Saami wordlist project, unpublished).

Nils-Henrik Bengtsson, Marianne Eriksson, Inger Fjällås, Eva-Karin Rosenberg, Gry Helen Sivertsen, Valborg Sjaggo, Dagny Skaile, Peter Steggo, and Joshua Wilbur. 2016. Pitesamisk ordbok. In Wilbur (2016a), pages 13–121.

Ciprian Gerstenberger, Niko Partanen, Michael Rießler, and Joshua Wilbur. 2017. Instant annotations. Association for Computational Linguistics, ACL Anthology, pages 25–36.

Ignácz Halász. 1893. *Népköltési gyűjtemény*, volume 5 of *Svéd-Lapp Nyelv*. Magyar tudományos akadémia. Arjeplog.

Michael Rießler. 2016. *Adjective attribution*. Number 2 in Studies in Diversity Linguistics. Language Science Press.

Pekka Sammallahti. 1998. *The Saami languages*. Davvi girji.

Mikael Svonni. 2009. *Samisk grammatik*. Universitetet i Tromsø.

Riitta-Liisa Valijärvi and Joshua Wilbur. 2011. The past, present and future of the Pite Saami language. *Nordic Journal of Linguistics* 34:295–329.

Joshua Wilbur. 2014. *A grammar of Pite Saami*. Number 5 in Studies in Diversity Linguistics. Language Science Press.

Joshua Wilbur, editor. 2016a. *Pitesamisk ordbok samt stavningsregler*. Number 2 in Samica. Albert-Ludwigs-Universität Freiburg.

Joshua Wilbur. 2016b. Stavningsregler. In Wilbur (2016a), pages 123–197.

Joshua Wilbur. 2017. The Pite Saami lexicographic backbone. ГОУ ВО КРАГСиУ, pages 299–308.

# Analysing Finnish with word lists:
# The DDI approach to morphology revisited


Atro Voutilainen
FIN-CLARIN
University of Helsinki
atro.voutilainen@helsinki.fi

Maria Palolahti
FIN-CLARIN
University of Helsinki
maria.palolahti@helsinki.fi


## Abstract


Morphological lexicons for morphologically complex languages provide good text coverage at the cost of overgeneration, difficulty of modification, and sometimes performance issues. Use of simple, manageable lexicon forms – especially lists – for morphologically complex languages may appear unviable because the number of possible word-forms in a morphologically complex language can be prohibitively high. We created and experimented with a list-based lexicon for a morphologically complex language (Finnish), and compared its coverage with that of a mature morphological analyser on new text in two experimental settings. The observed smallish difference in coverage suggests the viability of using simple and easy-to-modify list-based lexicons as an initial part of morphological analysis, to increase developer control on the vast majority of input tokens.


## Tiivistelmä


Morfologiset leksikot morfologisesti kompleksisille kielille mahdollistavat korkean kattavuuden käytettäessä morfologista analysaattoria tekstien analyysiin. Toisaalta täysimittaiset morfologiset leksikot tuottavat toivottujen analyysien lisäksi paljon semanttisesti outoja analyyseja. Lisäksi morfologisen leksikon jatkokehittäminen haluttua sovellusta varten edellyttää parhaassakin tapauksessa huolellista ja työlästä perehtymistä morfologiseen kuvaukseen ja kehitysympäristöön. Listamuotoinen leksikko olisi yksinkertainen ja helppo muokata, ja siksi periaatteessa soveltajaystävällisempi vaihtoehto morfologiselle leksikolle. Listamuotoista leksikkoa voidaan pitää kuitenkin epätodennäköisenä vaihtoehtona morfologiselle leksikolle, koska esimerkiksi suomen morfologia (runsas taivutus, johto-oppi ja yhdyssananmuodostus) mahdollistavat suomen sananmuotojen erittäin korkean määrän. Tässä artikkelissa esittelemme kokeiluja, joissa olemme luoneet listapohjaisen leksikon suomen kielelle ja vertailleet sen kattavuutta kypsän morfologisen analysaattorin kattavuuteen kahdella koejärjestelyllä. Havaittu ero kattavuudessa on melko pieni, mikä tukee oletusta listapohjaisen leksikkomuodon käyttökelpoisuudesta morfologisesti kompleksisen kielen käsittelyssä.





*Proceedings of the 4th International Workshop for Computational Linguistics for Uralic Languages (IWCLUL 2018)*, pages 171–181,
Helsinki, Finland, January 8–9, 2018. ©2018 Association for Computational Linguistics

# 1   Introduction

In NLP, a text analysis pipeline usually contains a basic component for lexical analysis: provision of a lexical analysis (or several, in case of lexical ambiguity) to tokens (word-like units). The knowledge base used by a lexical analyser can consist of a long (but simple) list of tuples (e.g. word-form, lemma, tags for POS and inflection) or of a complex morphological lexicon (lexical entries, inflectional or derivational morphemes, rules for combining these to account for correspondences between surface forms and lexical forms and rules for adding appropriate grammatical tags to the lexical analyses).

In a festschrift to a notable researcher in finite state morphology, Ken Church (2005) somewhat provocatively argues for a DDI ("don't-do-it") approach to morphology: though traditionally a practical memory-sparing necessity for morphologically complex languages, lexical analysis with rule-based morphological lexicons tends to produce, as a side effect, spurious analyses that compromise the utility of the NLP pipeline in practical applications. Church gives examples from text-to-speech synthesis, information retrieval, part-of-speech tagging and spelling correction as support for his argument for a simple list-based lexical analysis. In the absence of a list-based lexicon, the application designer may skip the use of a linguistic lexical component altogether in favour of a more simplistic technique, as Kettunen (2013) has shown in the case of an IR system.

The authors of this paper have worked with linguistic models for Finnish NLP (morphology, tagging, syntax) in the symbolic/linguistic (rather than statistical/ML) paradigm. Though we are sceptical about adopting the DDI approach as such to morphology or other levels of linguistic analysis, we accept that there is a grain of truth in Church's argument about morphology: use of a full-fledged morphological lexicon for analysing a morphologically complex language can compromise developer control over the resulting analysis. Modifying a complex morphological lexicon for satisfactory analysis from the application point of view may be unrewarding even for an experienced linguist; for those inexperienced in morphology (i.e. most of the application builders) the only options may be either using the morphological lexicon as such (with all its undesirable side effects) or looking for other solutions to replace linguistic components entirely.

Methods to increase control over lexical analysis to facilitate successful integration in practical applications should be of interest to computational linguists, too. A list-based lexicon is arguably simple and easy to manipulate without the risk of unwelcome side effects. Should a list-based lexicon work on a morphologically complex language (in this case, Finnish) with a reasonable coverage, inclusion of a list-based, easy-to-manage lexicon (e.g. as a first part of morphological analysis) might be a user-friendly option to increase usability of an NLP pipeline in an application.

We are not aware of studies on attempting to generate and evaluate extensive list-based lexicons for morphologically complex languages. In this paper, we report generation of a large list-based lexicon for Finnish, and compare its performance to that of a mature linguistic morphological analyser in the analysis of new text. We also report a part-of-speech tagging experiment with the two alternative lexical analysers to get some data on how the use of a list-based lexicon affects tagging accuracy.

Next, we review some data on Finnish morphology and lexicons and consider options to generate a list-based lexicon.

## 2  Issues with a morphological lexicon

A full-scale morphological lexicon for a morphologically complex language has the desirable property for the application developer in that it enables recognition and analysis of a high percentage of the word-forms of the language, though the language has a very large number of potential word-forms. Unfortunately, there are also some features related to morphological lexicons and their development or maintenance that make morphological lexicons less desirable for application developers.

- OVERGENERATION.  Even though a mature morphological analyser provides a correct and useful analysis to most of its input, full account for inflection, derivation and compounding in the morphological grammar also tends to result in semantically/ontologically spurious analyses, use of which is likely to compromise application performance. As an example, here is a morphological analysis for the Finnish sentence *Lisäaineisiin kuuluu niin askorbiinihappo kuin myös beetakaroteenikin.* (Additive substances include not only ascorbine acid but also beta-carotene):

```
"<Lisäaineisiin>"
        "lisäaine" N Pl Ill #2
        "lisäaineinen" A Pl Ill #2
        "lisäaineisi" N Sg Ill #3
        "lisäaineisä" N Pl Ill #3
"<kuuluu>"
        "kuulua" V Act Ind Pres Sg3 #1
        "kuuluu" Adv #1
        "kuuluu" N Sg Nom #2
"<niin>"
        "ne" Pron Dem Pl Ins #1
        "niin" Adv Dem #1
        "niin" Adv #1
        "niin" CCM #1
"<askorbiinihappo>"
        "askorbiinihappo" N Sg Nom #2
"<kuin>"
        "kui" N Pl Ins #1
        "kui" N Sg Gen #1
        "kuin" Adv #1
        "kuin" CC #1
        "kuin" CS #1
        "kuu" N Pl Ins #1
"<myös>"
        "myödä" V Act Imprt Sg2 S #1
        "myös" Adv #1
        "myös" CC #1
"<beetakaroteenikin>"
        "beetakaroteeni" N Sg Nom Kin #2
"<.>"
        "." Pun
```

Along with conventional analyses, the Omorfi analyser (Pirinen, 2015) also provides rather implausible alternatives that challenge downstream processing, such as:

- side effects of compounding: "lisäaineisi" (additive substance daddy), "lisä-aineisä" (additive substance father), "kuuluu" (moon bone)
- side effects of inflection: "ne" (by means of those), "kuu" (by means of moons).
- inclusion of non-standard Finnish in the lexicon, e.g. spoken and archaic varieties: "kui" (how), "myödä" (sell)

- COMPLEXITY. Developers of morphological lexicons usually are fully aware of the problems of overgeneration, and make efforts to keep overgeneration in control without too heavily sacrificing the recognition rates. As morphological lexicons for languages like Finnish tend to be complex in any case, fixing encountered problems in the morphological lexicon is probably not an option for the casual application developer: uninformed changes to the organisation of the lexical classes are likely to produce undesired side effects in other parts of morphological analysis.

- PERFORMANCE ISSUES. Though morphological lexicons are typically run with machines that use finite-state technology known for its efficiency, the resulting morphological analysers are not necessarily particularly competitive in terms of analysis speed. The performance cuts may result from the excessive size of the finite-state automata as well as from use of external processing to circumvent morphology-internal management limitations.

- LACK OF STANDARD. If the morphological lexicon is developed or maintained (in an open-source environment) without a strict adherence to a well-documented standard, there is also the risk that an update to the morphological lexicon contains undocumented changes to some mid- or high-frequency lexical classes or morphology that silently change subsequent processing results for the worse.

Given that there is a management/control problem with complex morphological lexicons, there is a need for a simple, manageable solution, such as the lexicon as an enumeration of word-forms with their lemmas and morphology. With improvements in computing resources, the list-form lexicon – even for a morphologically complex language – may be an option, as Church (2005) actually suggests.

How should a list-form lexicon for a language like Finnish be used? Church argues for lists as a stand-alone component for lexical analysis (no morphology is needed). Our view is less extreme: also morphological lexicons are useful and needed, e.g. to support creation of an initial (unedited) list-based lexicon, and to provide an analysis to tokens not recognised by the list lexicon.

The main question so far is, whether it is an option in the first place to generate a useful list-based lexicon for a morphologically complex language like Finnish. Koskenniemi (2013) provides some well-known statistics about Finnish:

- The inflectional system in Finnish morphology is complex. Each Finnish noun has about 2,000 inflections; each adjective, 6,000; each verb, close to 20,000.

- A rich derivational morphology as well as a fairly liberal compounding mechanism takes the complexity to much higher levels.

- Given a lexicon with a moderate number of basic lexical entries (a few hundred thousands rather than millions) and an artificial limitation to four-part compounds,[1] the number of legitimate word-forms in Finnish is already a septillion (10e24).

Technically, a list-based lexicon this long could perhaps be generated using a morphological lexicon as a word-form generator, but this is not a practical option. Our contribution is to show

- that a raw (unedited) list-based lexicon for a morphologically complex language (Finnish) focusing on actually-occurring word-forms in text corpora can be made with a mature morphological analyser

- and that the resulting list-based lexicon can be used to provide a high text coverage, if not quite as high as that available from use of a full morphological analyser.

Next, we report compilation of a list-based lexicon for Finnish by using text corpora and the Omorfi morphological analyser. We can view this automatically generated list as a "raw" list lexicon that could serve as a starting-point for modifications (addition of new information, deletion of unwanted analyses, etc.) needed for adapting lexical analysis to further uses. Then, we report comparison of the recognition rate of the resulting raw list-based lexicon with that of the Omorfi analyser itself on new text (including a comparison from a POS tagging perspective).

Finally, we discuss whether this kind of corpus-oriented list-based lexicon reaches an interesting recognition rate to serve as a basis for further work. Our aim in this paper is not to go into the kinds of modification potentially needed for adapting lexical analysis to an application or another; instead, the raw list lexicon is made publicly available with the publication of the IWCLUL proceedings in ACL Anthology.

## 3 Generation of list-based lexicon

### 3.1 Method

Freely available collections of Finnish text were downloaded from the Web; sentence extraction and tokenisation was performed; a word list was generated from the tokenised sentences (even tokens that occurred only once in the corpus were included). The word-list was analysed with the Omorfi morphological analyser; the analysed tokens were submitted to non-contextual disambiguation for pruning out analyses with more compound boundaries ("#1" for non-compounds, "#2" for two-part compounds, etc.) than an alternative analysis for the token in question has. The tokens with the compound-wise simplest analyses were converted into a list.

For example, the word-form *edustavien* is analysed by Omorfi as three-ways ambiguous (the first two are non-compounds - a participle and an adjective for "representative"; the last one is a compound noun *edus* (frontside) *tavi* (common teal):

```
edustavien
        "edustaa" V Act PcpVa Pl Gen #1
        "edustava" A Pl Gen #1
        "edustavi" N Pl Gen #2
```

---

[1] five- and six-part compounds are not very uncommon either

In this case, a spurious reading can be safely discarded with this heuristic (assuming most lexicographers would reject an entry for the Finnish equivalent of frontside common teal). The first two readings are then converted into entries for inclusion in the list lexicon, e.g:

```
edustavien~"edustaa" V Act PcpVa Pl Gen
edustavien~"edustava" A Pl Gen
```

## 3.2  Corpus data

The downloaded corpora from which the tokens were extracted were the following:

- Finnish Wikipedia (fiwiki*pages-articles.xml.bz2)

- EUBookshop corpus for Finnish, from the Opus corpus (Tiedemann, 2012)

- Europarl corpus (Koehn, 2005)

- Suomi24 corpus (unmoderated Finnish-language discussion forum, containing a large amount of informal Finnish and typos)

- FiWaC corpus (Ljubešić et al. 2016)

In all, the extracted sentences contain close to 3 billion tokens.

## 3.3  List lexicon

The resulting raw list lexicon contains 9.74 million entries for all parts of speech (file size: 443MB). Compared with the number of entries in a morphological lexicon, a list lexicon of ten million entries is very large. Compared with the estimated number of potential word-forms in Finnish (a septillion, see above) ten million is almost non-existent.

# 4  Evaluation 1: coverage of lexical analysers

## 4.1  Method

The test texts were tokenised by a tokeniser for Finnish before submitting them to the lexical analysers used in the comparison. This enables identical tokenisation and easier comparison of the lexical analysers without compromising performance of either analyser. The tokenised texts were then submitted to lexical analysis. Coverage rates (percentage of tokens analysed for each lexical analyser) were calculated. The tokens that received an analysis only from the morphological analyser (but not from the list-based analyser) were extracted, counted and classified into compounds and non-compounds (most of the tokens without analysis were compound nouns).

## 4.2  Analysers

As morphological analyser, we used the freely available Omorfi morphological lexicon (Pirinen, 2015) in connection with the HFST package (Lindén et al. 2009). Omorfi is a wide-coverage mature lexicon and morphological grammar that has been developed and refined for several years. The morphological description for Finnish closely follows the state-of-the-art descriptive grammar *Iso suomen kielioppi* (Hakulinen et al. 2004).

The list-based Finnish lexicon was run with a simple Perl program . It takes about 19 seconds for the Perl program to parse the large list-based lexicon; lexical analysis itself is reasonably fast, based on the data structure used.

### 4.3   Test data

The test data consist of news articles and columns from YLE (Finland's national public service broadcasting company) and OKM (Ministry of education and culture). In all, the test data contain 25,503 tokens. The data were shuffled at the sentence level for copyright reasons.

### 4.4   Results from evaluation 1

- RECOGNITION RATES. The Omorfi analyser gave an analysis to 98.8% of the tokens (25,193 tokens out of 25,503). The list-based analyser gave an analysis to 97.1% of the tokens (24,772 tokens out of 25,503).

- DIFFERENCES. There were 421 tokens in the test data that received an analysis from Omorfi but not from the list-based analyser. Of these 421 tokens, 359 (85.3%) are compounds (compound nouns for the most part). As a point of comparison, only 4.5% (1150) of the tokens in the whole test corpus were compounds. The compounding mechanism seems to be the most important source of gaps in the coverage of the list-based lexicon, relative to the morphological lexicon.

- SPEED OF LEXICAL ANALYSIS on a HP Elitebook laptop (Intel Core i5-4300U CPU @ 1.90GHz × 4, with 15.3 GiB of memory) with Ubuntu Linux. Omorfi: about three thousand tokens per second. List analyser: about 1.5 million tokens per second.

## 5   Evaluation 2: morphological disambiguation with lexical analysers

In this second evaluation, we looked at how the use of a list-based lexicon affects performance of a linguistics-based constraint tagger on the test text used in the previous evaluation.

### 5.1   Grammars

The grammars run on the morphologically analysed sentences were written by Maria Palolahti as a part of an ongoing project, the documentation and results of which will be published later. The grammars are based on the Constraint Grammar framework (Karlsson et al. 1995); the parsing software used is vislcg3 (Bick and Didriksen, 2015).

Before ambiguity resolution proper, a local heuristic CG was applied for adding morphological analyses to tokens not analysed by the lexical analyser. In the CG

available at `http://scripta.kotus.fi/visk/etusivu.php`
available at `http://visl.sdu.dk/~eckhard/analyzer.pl`

formalism, a typical APPEND rule adds a lemma and a morphological analysis to a token based on the form of the token itself and/or its local syntactic context. For instance, a token with an apparent genitive ending that is followed by a postposition may be analysed as a noun in the genitive. Specific APPEND rules are followed by default APPEND rules to ensure that all tokens get an analysis before disambiguation starts.

Morphological disambiguation is based on constraints that operate on a combination of lexical and morphological information. Constraints are grouped as subgrammars ordered on the basis of the linguistic phenomenon to be resolved and on the basis of their reliability. A mature CG typically contains a few thousand constraint rules that resolve a large majority of the ambiguity in the input with a low error rate, to make further levels of analysis and use feasible. The grammars used in the present experiment contain several thousand constraints.

## 5.2   Method

The two CGs were run in sequence on the outputs of the two lexical analysers. The disambiguated text versions were compared to each other using the Linux "sdiff" program. The differences were examined one by one by the first author. Those cases where only one of the systems produced a correct analysis were marked to indicate, which pipeline produced the correct analysis. The symbol "O|" indicates the pipeline with the Omorfi morphological analyser produced the correct analysis; "L|" indicates that the correct analysis was produced by the pipeline with the list-based lexical analyser.

```
List-based analyser                   Morphological analyser (Omorfi)
Kaipaan         V_Act_Ind_Pres_Sg1 Kaipaan         V_Act_Ind_Pres_Sg1
valoa           N_Sg_Par              valoa           N_Sg_Par
,               Pun                   ,               Pun
kevyitä         A_Pl_Par              kevyitä         A_Pl_Par
vaatteita       N_Pl_Par              vaatteita       N_Pl_Par
,               Pun                   ,               Pun
torikahveja     N_Sg_Nom           O| torikahveja    N_Pl_Par
ja              CC                    ja              CC
pehmeiden       A_Pl_Gen              pehmeiden       A_Pl_Gen
iltojen         N_Pl_Gen              iltojen         N_Pl_Gen
vaivattomuutta N_Sg_Par               vaivattomuutta N_Sg_Par
.               Pun                   .               Pun
```

For instance, in the above example sentence *Kaipaan valoa, kevyitä vaatteita, torikahveja ja pehmeiden iltojen vaivattomuutta* (I miss light, light clothes, coffee in the market place and the ease of soft evenings) the compound *torikahveja* (market coffees) was analysed differently by the two pipelines. The analysis by the Omorfi pipeline (Noun Plural Partitive) was marked as correct with the "O|" tag. The differences were then counted and analysed.

## 5.3   Results from evaluation 2

In the 25,503 tokens in the test data, there were 254 tokens that received a correct analysis from one tagging pipeline but not from the other. As can be expected, the differences were unequally divided:

- Of the differences, 220 were such that the pipeline with the Omorfi morphological analyser has the correct reading and the other pipeline with the list-based lexicon has not (i.e. the local CG that adds new lemmas and analyses to out-of-vocabulary words made a misprediction).

- Of the differences, 34 were such that the pipeline with the list-based analyser has the correct reading and the other pipeline with the Omorfi analyser has not.

In terms of analysis correctness, the pipeline with the Omorfi analyser thus has 186 (220 minus 34) fewer misanalyses than does the pipeline with the list-based lexical analyser (difference between the two pipelines: 0.7%).

The majority of the misanalyses resulted from an incorrect analysis by the local heuristic grammar. To a much smaller extent, there were also at least two other types of error:

- DOMINO EFFECT: a token analysed correctly by both lexical analysers was disambiguated incorrectly due to misanalysis of a word in the context by the heuristic APPEND grammar

- RULE ORDER: the two lexical analysers sometimes provide the alternative analyses to a token in a different order, which can affect the application order of CG disambiguation rules and result in different analyses (especially when there is a mispredicting disambiguation rule in the grammar).

## 6   Discussion and future work

We have shown that a simple operable list-based lexicon with a text coverage nearly equal to that of a morphological lexicon can be generated with a mature morphological analyser by focusing on actual tokens found in large text corpora (instead of attempting to enumerate all possible word-forms in the language). Given that modification of a morphological lexicon can be prohibitively difficult for an application developer, access to a list-based lexical component may provide substantial additional control over lexical analysis (and downstream NLP) to the application developer. We also observed a substantial analysis speed improvement when using the list-based lexicon.

Heuristic grammar-based analysis of word-forms in a morphologically complex language is a difficult task, which suggests that a morphological lexicon should be used on forms not represented in the list-based lexicon. In any case, generation of a high-quality list-based lexicon without a solid morphological lexicon and analyser would probably require a prohibitive amount of manual work. Bypassing linguistic morphology altogether (the DDI approach) does not seem justified by our experiments.

We have not addressed the question, what kinds of modifications could be made to a raw list-based lexicon to enable successful integration of a NLP pipeline in an application. Release of the raw list-based lexicon itself hopefully facilitates future experimentation.

## Acknowledgements

We are grateful to two anonymous IWCLUL referees for useful comments on an earlier version of this paper. We are also grateful to IWCLUL participants for a lively post-talk discussion, and in particular to Kimmo Koskenniemi for his solemn promise to make still another morphological lexicon for Finnish.

## References

Eckhard Bick and Tino Didriksen, 2015. CG-3 — Beyond Classical Constraint Grammar. *Proc. NODALIDA 2015*.

Kenneth Church, 2005. The DDI Approach to Morphology. In Antti Arppe et al. (Eds.), *Inquiries into Words, Constraints and Contexts. Festschrift in the Honour of Kimmo Koskenniemi on his 60th Birthday*. Gummerus.

Auli Hakulinen, Maria Vilkuna, Riitta Korhonen, Vesa Koivisto, Tarja Riitta Heinonen and Irja Alho, 2004. *Iso suomen kielioppi* [Big Finnish Grammar]. http://scripta.-kotus.fi/visk/etusivu.php. URN:ISBN:978-952-5446-35-7.

Fred Karlsson, Atro Voutilainen, Juha Heikkilä, Arto Anttila (Eds.), 1995. *Constraint Grammar: a language-independent system for parsing unrestricted text*. Walter de Gruyter.

Kimmo Kettunen, 2013. Managing word form variation of text retrieval in practice – why language technology is not the only cure for better IR performance. *Proc. Trends in Information Management 2013*.

Philipp Koehn, 2005. Europarl: A Parallel Corpus for Statistical Machine Translation. *Proc. MT Summit 2005*.

Kimmo Koskenniemi, 2013. *Johdatus kieliteknologiaan, sen merkitykseen ja sovelluksiin* [Introduction to Language Technology, its significance and applications]. URL: http://hdl.handle.net/10138/38503. ISBN 978-952-10-8677-9.

Krister Lindén, Miikka Silfverberg and Tommi Pirinen, 2009. HFST tools for morphology - an efficient open-source package for construction of morphological analyzers. *International Workshop on Systems and Frameworks for Computational Morphology*.

Ljubešić, Nikola; Pirinen, Tommi and Toral, Antonio, 2016, *Finnish web corpus fiWaC 1.0*, Slovenian language resource repository CLARIN.SI, http://hdl.handle.net/-11356/1074.

Tommi Pirinen, 2015. Omorfi - Free and open source morphological lexical database for Finnish. *Proc. NODALIDA 2015*.

Jörg Tiedemann, 2012. Parallel Data, Tools and Interfaces in OPUS. *Proc. LREC 2012*.

# Author Index